Peace and Justice
Shall Embrace

Peace and Justice
Shall Embrace

Power and Theopolitics in the Bible

Essays in honor of Millard Lind

Edited by

Ted Grimsrud
and Loren L. Johns

Foreword by Paul Keim

Pandora Press U.S.
Telford, Pennsylvania

Co-published with Herald Press
Scottdale, Pennsylvania

Pandora Press U.S. orders, information, reprint permissions:
pandoraus@netreach.net
1-215-723-9125
126 Klingerman Road, Telford PA 18969
www.netreach.net/~pandoraus/

The paper used in this publication is recycled and meets the
minimum requirements of American National Standard for Information
Sciences--Permanence of Paper for Printed Library Materials, ANSI Z39.48-1984.

All Bible quotations are used by permission, all rights reserved and except when
otherwise indicated are from the *New Revised Standard Version Bible,* copyright
1989, by the Division of Christian Education of the National Council of the
Churches of Christ in the USA; RSV from the *Revised Standard Version of the Bible,*
copyright 1946, 1952, 1971 by the Division of Christian Education of the National
Council of the Churches of Christ in the USA.

Library of Congress Cataloguing-in-Publication Data
Peace and justice shall embrace : power and theopolitics in the Bible :
essays in honor of Millard Lind / edited by Ted Grimsrud and Loren
L. Johns ; foreword by Paul Keim.
p.   cm.
Includes bibliographical references and indexes.
ISBN 0-9665021-1-6 (trade paper : alk. paper)
1. Peace--Biblical teaching. 2. Justice--Biblical teaching. 3. Bible. O.T.--
Criticism, interpretation, etc. I. Lind, Millard, 1918- . II. Grimsrud,
Ted, 1954- . III. Johns, Loren L.
BS1199.P4P43 2000
261.7-dc21   99-41416
                                                         CIP

10 09 08 07 06 05 04 03 02 01 00 99   10 9 8 7 6 5 4 3 2 1

For Millard C. Lind,
scholar, teacher, friend

Contents

Contributors 9

Millard Lind: A Faithful Teacher in the Church 11
    Paul Keim

1. WHAT KIND OF POLITICAL POWER? THE UPSIDE-DOWN KINGDOM
    IN MILLARD LIND'S READING OF THE HEBREW BIBLE 17
    Daniel Liechty

2. MAKING YAHWEH'S RULE VISIBLE 34
    J. Denny Weaver

3. PROPHETS IN CONFLICT: NEGOTIATING TRUTH IN SCRIPTURE 49
    James E. Brenneman

4. HEALING JUSTICE: THE PROPHET AMOS AND A "NEW" THEOLOGY
    OF JUSTICE 64
    Ted Grimsrud

5. DENOUNCING LIES, MODELING TRUTH: LENT AND EASTER RE-
    FLECTIONS ON JEREMIAH AND JESUS 86
    Arthur Paul Boers

6. EZEKIEL ON FANON'S COUCH: A POSTCOLONIALIST DIALOGUE
WITH DAVID HALPERIN'S *SEEKING EZEKIEL* 108
Daniel L. Smith-Christopher

7. POWER IN WISDOM: THE SUFFERING SERVANT OF
ECCLESIASTES 4 145
Douglas B. Miller

8. POWER, LOVE, AND CREATION: THE MERCY OF THE DIVINE
WARRIOR IN THE WISDOM OF SOLOMON 174
Tom Yoder Neufeld

9. REIMAGING POWER: TOWARD A THEOLOGY OF NONVIOLENCE .. 192
Ray C. Gingerich

Millard C. Lind: A Biographical Sketch 217
Paul Keim

Publications by Millard Lind 219
Sarah Lind

Scripture Index 233

Author Index 242

Subject Index 247

The Editors 251

Contributors

Arthur Paul Boers, Oblate O.S.B., Bloomingdale, Ontario. Pastor, Bloomingdale Mennonite Church, Kitchener, Ontario. M.A., Associated Men-nonite Biblical Seminary; M.Div., McCormick Theological Seminary; M.Th., Waterloo Lutheran Seminary.

James E. Brenneman, Pasadena, California. Pastor, Pasadena Mennonite Church, Pasadena, California; Professor of Old Testament, The Episcopal Theological School at Claremont, Claremont, Cal. M.Div., Fuller Theological Seminary; M.A./Ph.D., Claremont Graduate University.

Ray C. Gingerich, Harrisonburg, Virginia. Professor of Theology and Ethics, Eastern Mennonite University. M.Div., Associated Mennonite Biblical Seminary; Ph.D., Vanderbilt University.

Ted Grimsrud, Harrisonburg, Virginia. Assistant Professor of Theology and Peace Studies, Eastern Mennonite University. M.A., Associated Mennonite Biblical Seminary; Ph.D., Graduate Theological Union.

Loren L. Johns, Bluffton, Ohio. Associate Professor of Religion, Bluffton College. M.Div., Associated Mennonite Biblical Seminary; Ph.D., Princeton Theological Seminary.

Paul Keim, Goshen, Indiana. Academic Dean, Goshen College. M.Div., Associated Mennonite Biblical Seminary; Ph.D., Harvard University.

Daniel Liechty, Bloomington, Illinois. Formerly Psychosocial Coordinator of the Montgomery Hospital Hospice Program. Now Assistant Professor, School of Social Work, Illinois State University. M.A., Associated Mennonite Biblical Seminary; Ph.D., University of Vienna; M.S.W., Bryn Mawr School of Social Work; D.Min., Graduate Theological Foundation.

Sarah Lind, Madison, Wisconsin. Translation Researcher, United Bible Societies. M.A., University of Wisconsin.

Douglas B. Miller, Hillsboro, Kansas. Associate Professor of Biblical and Religious Studies, Tabor College. M.Div., Associated Mennonite Biblical Seminary; Ph.D., Princeton Theological Seminary.

Daniel L. Smith-Christopher, Los Angeles, California. Professor of Theology, Loyola-Marymount University. M.Div., Associated Mennonite Biblical Seminary; Ph.D., Oxford University.

J. Denny Weaver, Bluffton, Ohio. Professor of Religion, Bluffton College. M.Div., Associated Mennonite Biblical Seminary; Ph.D., Duke University.

Tom Yoder Neufeld, Waterloo, Ontario. Associate Professor of Religious Studies and Peace and Conflict Studies, Conrad Grebel College. M.Div., Harvard Divinity School; Th.D., Harvard Divinity School.

Millard Lind
A Faithful Teacher in the Church

PAUL KEIM

In the eighty-first year of his life, the following essays are offered by students of Millard Lind as an expression of our affection and regard for his teaching. We hope what we learned from him will be clear through these studies—be it Hebrew language and culture, Old Testament book studies, prophetic theology and ethics, or expositions of Old Testament and ancient Near Eastern law.

We understand ourselves not merely as imitators of Millard's ideas and insights, but as those who have been liberated and equipped to apply his insights on our own. Millard's style was not one of revealing *the* truth to us, but of inspiring us to recognize the texts of the Old Testament as more than an object to be studied. Millard inspired us to listen to these texts as dynamic conversation partners around which we gathered, with him as our guide.

In his classes, Millard helped us understand that continuities of the human experience bind us to the dilemmas of biblical stories and wisdom. Above all, he helped us to see political aspects of these texts within their own contexts. This aspect of Scripture had remained largely unappreciated in our tradition, despite the traditional Mennonite emphasis on peacemaking and the radicalization that emphasis represented for our relationship with state authorities in the various places Mennonites have settled over the years.

Millard helped us learn to appreciate the political, economic, and social aspects of these texts without undermining the religious

11

and meditative features of Scripture and of Bible study. Indeed for many of us, the dynamics of discovering this political aspect of biblical texts deepened our appreciation for its religious aspects and led to a deeper understanding of what faith means in living communities.

Millard's style was humble and inviting rather than heavy-handed or draconian. Without exhibiting much outward emotional engagement, he would dispassionately present texts in such a way that we became animated and were enabled to understand the implications of what he was saying for our own situations. Millard's exposition of Scripture convinced us that the Bible continues to speak meaningfully. He helped us to understand that our own lives and communities must continue to be brought under the scrutiny of Scripture's teachings—not only in terms of piety, but even more in terms of justice and righteousness.

Millard spoke with authority against a kind of antinomianism to which Mennonites, like other Christians, have been particularly susceptible. He spoke out against any facile equation of a Christian "grace" set over against a Jewish "law." He recognized that such an attitude was theologically suspect: it not only deprecates the Hebrew Bible as an organic whole, but it also undermines the power of the two-testament Christian Bible as an organic whole by robbing the messianic gospel of its interpretive frame.

Though Millard's work was more directly exegetical than theological, he nonetheless taught us much about the theology of the Hebrew Bible and of the Christian Bible. He showed how the economic implications of the Jubilee had real political force in the faith and life of ancient Israel, regardless of historical judgments about its actual implementation in Israel in the period of the monarchy. It becomes part of the messianic vision of late-biblical religion and thus informs the development of Christian theology.

Millard helped us understand Israel's law as part of God's healing mercy, with revolutionary implications for the ordering of human societies—both in the ancient Near East and for the people of faith today. The message of the Old Testament prophets, beginning with Moses, coheres closely with the message of Jesus—and continues to provide normative guidance for modern Christians.

The essays in this volume exhibit many of the themes implicit and explicit in Millard Lind's work. At the heart of Millard's program was a recognition of and appreciation for the dynamics of international and domestic politics in the texts of the Hebrew Bible.

This recognition provides a background against which the politics of Jesus can more fully be recognized and understood. These understandings contribute in turn to a fuller appreciation of intertextual and intertestamental unity. Like other sectarian/perfectionist/utopian groups with histories of political quietism, conservatism, and naïveté in matters of policy and politics, contemporary North American Mennonites have especially needed to hear this message.

Millard Lind's teaching opened doors for his students—points of entry into a portion of the tradition that had remained closed for a long time, or had been visible only through the lens of a narrow hermeneutical grid. This was possible in part because he had been trained in the languages and cultures of the ancient Near East himself. He came to understand the importance of that cultural background for an adequate understanding of the biblical traditions. His pedagogical strategy was to illuminate familiar and unfamiliar biblical texts with texts from the ancient Near East that were relevant and germane.

Millard also played a pioneering role in introducing the so-called "higher-critical" methods of biblical interpretation to Mennonite students. His commitment to pursue truth zealously certainly caused some tensions for Millard. However, his commitment to the text and to the church has never been questioned. The critical methods were never destructive tools in his hands, nor were they an excuse for abstraction. Rather, they were always used to probe more deeply into the texts themselves. In many respects, Millard used historical-critical tools as an extension of the inductive method of Bible study he had learned. One must read and understand the text first of all. One must understand the text in its own context as much as possible. And one was then free to apply the text to the life of the church.

In the essays that follow, we can see a bit of the fruit of Millard's influence on several generations of Mennonite biblical scholars, theologians, ethicists, and pastors. These essays share in common the "Lindian" passion for the integration of faith and practice, drawing on the church's Scripture as the model and inspiration for that integration.

In "What Kind of Political Power? The Upside-Down Kingdom in Millard Lind's Reading of the Hebrew Bible," Daniel Liechty traces the impact of one of his formative professors on his worldview. Liechty, as theologian, historian, social worker, therapist, and professor, credits Lind for opening up to him an explicitly political reading of the literature of the ancient Near East that provides the framework for the sorts of ethical commitments that subvert power politics.

Theologian J. Denny Weaver salutes Lind in "Making Yahweh's Rule Visible" for his help in crystallizing for Weaver the conviction that peacemaking and biblical interpretation must be mutually reinforcing practices. Weaver reflects on this connection in light of his experience of nonviolent resistance to oppression in Haiti.

James E. Brenneman's essay, "Prophets in Conflict: Negotiating Truth in Scripture," seeks to extend Lind's prophetic hermeneutic by applying it to questions of tensions *within* the biblical text. Brenneman, a pastor and biblical scholar, argues for a trajectory within the Old Testament that points to the way of peace by critiquing earlier perspectives within the canon.

In "Healing Justice: The Prophet Amos and a 'New' Theology of Justice," theologian and ethicist Ted Grimsrud draws on the book of Amos in reflecting further on biblical understandings of justice. Inspired and guided by Lind's pioneering work toward constructing a consistently pacifist understanding of justice, Grimsrud argues that the biblical perspective offers a clear alternative to modern, Western, coercive, and impersonal notions of justice.

Pastor Arthur Paul Boers honors the enormous impact Lind has had on several generations of Mennonite preachers in "Denouncing Lies, Modeling Truth: Lent and Easter Reflections on Jeremiah and Jesus." In this essay, Boers offers a set of meditations emphasizing prophetic justice and its application for our contemporary setting. Boers insists that biblical faith has major political consequences.

In "Ezekiel on Fanon's Couch: A Postcolonialist Dialogue with David Halperin's Seeking Ezekiel," biblical scholar Daniel L. Smith-Christopher fulfills well Lind's strong desire that his students model his creativity in thinking new thoughts and questioning old assumptions. In a highly original interdisciplinary discussion, Smith-Christopher suggests that the writing of the prophet Ezekiel reflects a context similar to what we today call post-traumatic stress. Understanding Ezekiel's text in light of the post-traumatic stress suffered in the Exile enables the modern reader to appreciate his message in a new way, without resorting to dehistoricized theories about Ezekiel's psychological pathologies.

In "Power in Wisdom: The Suffering Servant of Ecclesiastes 4," biblical scholar Douglas B. Miller provides insightful reflections on the relationship between power and justice, drawing on a biblical text not traditionally associated with such themes. In so doing, Miller follows in the tradition of his teacher, who time after time enlightened students to the ethical implications of texts rarely mined for such material.

Like Miller, biblical scholar Tom Yoder-Neufeld also draws upon wisdom writings as a helpful source for ethical reflection in "Power, Love, and Creation: The Mercy of the Divine Warrior in the Wisdom of Solomon." Yoder-Neufeld extends Lind's concerns with the figure of the divine warrior to literature from a later period.

Our final essay is by theologian and ethicist Ray Gingerich: "Reimaging Power: Toward a Theology of Nonviolence." In this essay, Gingerich draws inspiration from Lind's work in challenging scholars interested in doing peace theology to take up the task of thoroughly rethinking the meaning of power. Gingerich proposes a sketch for such rethinking, arguing that genuine power is not power as expressed in the violence of kings and warriors, but as expressed in the active nonviolence of prophets.

To complete the volume, biblical scholar Sarah Lind, Millard's daughter, has provided a comprehensive bibliography of her father's writings.

Millard was not, so far as I am aware, familiar with Parker Palmer's terminology regarding the "heart" of our disciplines. Nevertheless, when I read Palmer's book, *The Courage to Teach,* years after being in Millard's classroom, I immediately thought of him. In those classes, Old Testament law, the worlds of the ancient Near East, the politics of prophetic texts, and the radicalness of biblical teaching became the "great things" that informed and invigorated us.

Along with his other students, I continue to be grateful to Millard for this gift. I am delighted to be able to commend these essays to those interested in understanding and following our peaceable and just God.

— Paul Keim
Goshen, Indiana

1

What Kind of Political Power?

The Upside-Down Kingdom in Millard Lind's Reading of the Hebrew Bible

DANIEL LIECHTY

During my first year of theological seminary, Millard Lind introduced me to an explicitly political hermeneutic for studying the literature of the ancient Near East. While a portion of the enthusiasm I felt with this new method was certainly time-bound — during the mid-1970s every cultural tea leaf was given a "political" reading — I continue to feel some of that excitement twenty years later.

THE LEGITIMATION OF POLITICAL AUTHORITY

The roots of this political hermeneutic as taught to me are found especially in the writings of Henri Frankfort, Thorkild Jacobsen, and Alexander Heidel. As these scholars looked at the religious myths of ancient Egypt and Mesopotamia, they saw that a recurring and central concern in these narratives was to establish a theology of the state. These stories provided answers to doubts about the legitimate authority of the state. Providing such legitimating stories was even more important than giving an account of the origins of the natural order. Heidel, for example, wrote of the *Enuma Elish*, the Babylonian story of creation:

> The story of the creation of the universe was added not so much for the sake of giving an account of how all things

17

came into being, but chiefly because it served to further enhance the glory of Marduk and helped to justify his claim to sovereignty over all things visible and invisible.... [The *Enuma Elish*] is not only a religious treatise but also a political one.[1]

The Egyptian and Mesopotamian states differed in their historical genesis, which was reflected in the creation myths each culture produced. The Egyptian state grew out of the strong chieftain system that developed among the tribes in the Southern region. Through conquest and voluntary unification, these tribes came together into the people of Egypt.

When a consciousness of themselves as a distinct people and nation emerged, it was as a people united under the Pharaoh. This consciousness was then reflected in their stories of creation, with a pantheon of gods united from the beginning under *Horus*, the Great God, whose symbol (the falcon) was the symbol of the Pharaoh. The system of Pharaoh's rule was presented as an integral piece of creation itself, and the Pharaoh himself was pictured as a divine being. Ruling in the strictest sense by divine right, the Pharaoh was charged with the task of keeping peace between the human and the divine realms. As Frankfort comments,

> The Egyptian State was not a man-made alternative to other forms of political organization. It was God-given, established when the world was created; and it continued to form part of the world order. In the person of the Pharaoh a superhuman being had taken charge of the affairs of man. And this great blessing, which ensured the well-being of the nation, was not due to a fortunate accident but had been foreseen in the divine plan. The monarchy was as old as the world, for the creator himself had assumed kingly office on the day of creation.... [The Pharaoh's authority] was founded not in the social order, but in the cosmic

---

[1] Alexander Heidel, *The Babylonian Genesis* (Chicago: University of Chicago Press, 1942), 11.

order. Kingship, in Egypt, was as old as the world. It dated
from the first day of creation.[2]

In the Egyptian creation stories,[3] the institution of the monarchy was presented as an essential component of creation itself.
There was no memory of a pre-kingship period, and this was
reflected in these stories, which pictured the monarchy as being in
existence from the beginning. As a divine being, the king partici-
pated in both the divine and human realms and kept peace
between these realms. It would have been unthinkable within this
ideology to imagine a civilized society in which the hierarchies of
executive power represented by the kingship system were not the
center of the social order. Divine executive power and royal executive power were not related by analogy. They were one and the
same.

The process by which kingship as an institution emerged in
Mesopotamia differed from the Egyptian process in that a trace
memory of the pre-kingship period continued. According to the
Jacobsen thesis,[4] the oldest political institution among the Mesopotamians was the loose confederation of tribes. Whatever executive
power existed, remained relatively decentralized within this loose
confederacy.

In response to specific circumstances, such as a threat of
invasion by outside armies, this loose confederacy could unite
under a single leader. However, this was done by consent, which

---

[2] Henri Frankfort, *Ancient Egyptian Religion* (New York: Columbia
University Press, 1961), 30, 50.

[3] Versions of these myths can be found in several locations. Under
Millard Lind's tutelage, we almost exclusively used the unabridged ver-
sion of J. B. Pritchard, *Ancient Near Eastern Texts*, 3d ed. (Princeton:
Princeton University Press, 1969), referred to simply as *ANET*. While
many abridged versions are available, my references here are to David
Adams Leeming, *The World of Myth: An Anthology* (New York: Oxford
University Press, 1990). The Egyptian and Babylonian creation myths are
found there in the first chapter.

[4] Thorkild Jacobsen, "Primitive Democracy in Ancient Mesopotamia," *Journal of Near Eastern Studies* 2 (1943): 159–72.

could be withdrawn. The power of the central leader was limited in scope and duration to what was required for response to a given specific circumstance. Eventually, a leader was able to consolidate his power among the tribes and establish a ruling institution that did not dissolve at the end of a crisis. This later evolved into a full-blown centralized monarchy no less absolute than was found among the Egyptians. Because that trace memory of a pre-kingship phase could not simply be erased, the Mesopotamian creation stories therefore extended into two phases of creation.

The first phase of creation dealt with the physical world, which began in a sexual union of *Apsu* (fresh water) and *Ti'amat* (saltwater). The second phase dealt with the creation of the political order. In response to the overwhelming threat of the angry *Ti'amat*, the pantheon of lesser gods surrendered supreme authority to one of their own number, *Marduk*, as their protector. *Marduk* defeated *Ti'amat* and established the city of Babylon. There he set up his own throne and temple.

The differences between the Mesopotamian and Egyptian stories are important. In the Egyptian stories, the monarchy was perceived as an integral part of the process of creation itself. In the Mesopotamian stories, kingship was part of a second phase of creation. The establishment of the monarchy was a political response to an earlier situation of disorder and confusion. In the Egyptian stories, the king was himself a divine being and carried the power of divine being in his person. In Babylon, the king was not viewed as a divine being himself. Rather, the king was seen as a successor, servant, and agent of the divine *Marduk*. Divinity was associated with the *office* rather than the *person* of the king. Any human being occupying that office had to be invested with divine power.

The similarities between these stories are also instructive. Both traditions of stories led to the conclusion that a world without centralized executive authority could be nothing other than confused and chaotic—fearful and macabre. Both proclaimed the necessity of centralized executive power focused in a human monarch. Both proclaimed religious support for this centralized executive authority as the bulwark of the divine order against the forces of disorder, chaos, dread, and evil.

A political reading of these creation stories demonstrates that these religious myths lent religious support for identifying the power of the monarch with the power of the divine. This in itself would not have been exciting for me. After all, as an undergraduate at Eastern Mennonite College, I had already digested Samuel Horst's course in the history of political philosophy. There I had learned that the mustering of religious support for the power of the state was the normal course for human society. One can trace this ideology from Hegel's ideology of the state as "the Divine Idea as it exists on earth," through Calvin's theocracy, to the medieval doctrine of the divine right of Kings and on back to the claims of divinity for the Caesars in Rome. That this ideology extended even further back to the ancient Egyptians and Babylonians was interesting but it was not surprising.

However, a shocking realization energized this young student of theology as much as anything ever has since. It came when, in a course on Jeremiah during my first semester at the seminary, I watched as Millard Lind led our class in applying these same principles of political interpretation to the biblical literature of the ancient Hebrews. Though I had soaked up twenty years of good, solid Mennonite preaching on the prophets, here for the first time I began to experience the depths of the struggle going on among the Hebrew people. It was not just a struggle between a faithful remnant and idolaters (read: *us* versus *them*); it was a struggle over the nature and meaning of political power and legitimacy themselves. While there certainly was in the Hebrew Bible a tradition that pointed toward the confluence of the monarchy and divine authority, Millard Lind's teaching and writings opened my eyes to another tradition in the text: that of an anti-kingship tradition.[5]

According to Millard's interpretation,[6] the formative event for the Hebrew political consciousness, an experience of crisis and deliverance from which grew their root concept of executive power, was the event that happened at the Sea of Reeds. According to the stories of the tradition, under the leadership of Moses, the fleeing Hebrew slaves were cornered between the waters and the armies of the Egyptian Pharaoh. Their deliverance came in the form of a nature miracle, which allowed the fleeing slaves to escape through the water. This miracle of deliverance the Hebrews attributed to divine intervention through their leader Moses.

---

[5] The best single source is Frank Crüsemann, *Der Widerstand gegen das Königtum: Die antiköniglichen Texte des Alten Testaments und der Kampf um den frühen israelitischen Staat* (Neukirchen: Kreuzverlag, 1978).

[6] Lind's major writings have been published in two volumes. The first is based on his Ph.D. thesis, *Yahweh Is a Warrior: The Theology of Warfare in Ancient Israel* (Scottdale, Pa.: Herald Press, 1980). The second volume is *Monotheism, Power and Justice: Collected Old Testament Essays* (Elkhart, Ind.: Institute of Mennonite Studies, 1990). The most important of the essays collected in that volume for this subject are "The Anomaly of the Prophet," 109–19; "The Concept of Political Power in the Old Testament," 135–54; "Paradigm of Holy War in the Old Testament," 182–96; "Power and Powerlessness in the Old Testament," 203–10; and "A Political Alternative: An Examination of Ezekiel's Recognition Statements," 260–74).

In trying to convey the excitement generated by this material in me and among my fellow students, it is important to remember that at that time almost every one of these essays were circulated among us in unpublished, typescript versions. Numerous such unpublished essays by other professors—especially John Howard Yoder and Clarence Bauman—also circulated among the students. Reading these essays in their nascent form carried with it the feeling of something new, underground, anti-establishmentarian—perhaps even risky or forbidden. The closest analogy might be to the *Samizdat* material that circulated among university students in communist countries.

It matters little whether one pictures this event with the drama of Cecil B. de Mille or with the more mundane imagination of the scholarly demythologizer. Recent sociological criticism suggests that only some of the tribes experienced it directly. Nevertheless, at least some of the tribes in Palestine accepted it as foundational, along with other elements of Mosaic tradition.[7]

Some readers today take the text at face value, holding that all the Hebrew tribes experienced this miracle of deliverance. Others follow the recent sociological criticism. In either case, the formative experience of crisis and deliverance at the Exodus did not take place under a warrior-leader armed with instruments of violence. It took place under a prophet-leader armed with the moral authority of God's charismatic election. *The divine legitimation for wielding political power and authority that was conferred in this foundational event was not upon a warrior carrying a sword, but upon a prophet carrying a staff.* Kingship remained associated with God alone. And God chose to reveal God's will to the nation through the election of charismatic leaders selected on the basis of God's choice alone. The selection was not made on the basis of military ability, personal strength, or other characteristics associated with a warrior-king.

This shift from warrior-king to prophet-leader as the focus for authoritative divine intervention had a profound effect on the Hebrews' understanding of what constitutes legitimate executive authority and power. It led to policies that in a conventional sense can only be seen as bizarre. For example, in some cases the army was purposely *weakened* before entering into battle, as recorded in Judges 7.[8]

---

[7] For example, Norman K. Gottwald, *The Tribes of Yahweh: A Sociology of the Religion of Liberated Israel, 1250–1050 BCE* (Maryknoll, N.Y.: Orbis Books, 1979).

[8] In the context of ancient Near Eastern literature, speculation about whether reports of such policies are historically accurate or are the result of later pious editing is less interesting than the bold fact that such an anti-militaristic tradition of piety existed at all.

As in Mesopotamia, the liberated Hebrews developed a form of national government based on a loose confederacy of tribes. This tribal confederacy also could unite under a single military leader in times of crisis. The same factors that functioned as a *counter* to centralization among the Mesopotamians (the need for consensus, the ad hoc nature of the investment of authority, which limited it in scope and duration) functioned in the Hebrew confederacy as well.

In Mesopotamia this confederacy had evolved into centralized kingship at a relatively early stage in the people's national history. Among the Hebrews, however, the tradition of the kingship of God was mediated through the charismatic prophet and judges. This undoubtedly lengthened the generations during which the tribal confederacy functioned. This tradition undoubtedly worked to make it more difficult to achieve the consensus needed for united action under one military leader. It shortened the time during which such consensus would hold once it was achieved. And it produced tribal leaders eager to guard the decentralized structure of the confederacy against the perceived abuses of power that would occur under a centralized monarch. In the context of the history of political thought and institutions in the ancient Near East, this was certainly something new.[9]

---

[9] During my seminary years, the influence of the Biblical Theology movement was quite strong. One of the privileged methods of interpretation we employed was contrasting "Hebrew" thought with ancient Near Eastern thought for the Jewish Bible and with "Greek" thought for the Christian Bible. God's revelation would be located in the perceived differences. This approach rescued from Fundamentalism a working concept of divine revelation, but it also usually led to progressive conclusions. For example, we saw that God's revelation (which, following Karl Barth, we knew was first and foremost a revelation of Godself) was not in the divine command to perform ritual sacrifice, since such commands were common to the general ancient Near Eastern environment. God's revelation was found in the prohibition of human sacrifice. Later, it was found in Amos, where we see the eventual devaluation of sacrifice entirely in

Among the Hebrews, the congealing of a national identity and consciousness, the institution of the religious cult, the formation of a civil law, and other pivotal political events—these all took place in the period before there was a human king. This made it impossible to disseminate an ideology of kingship as the foundation and sine qua non of the political life of the people.

For Israel's neighbors, conceptions of legitimate political authority were reflected in their creation stories. We would expect to see the same thing in the creation stories of the Hebrews. And indeed, we do see a marked contrast to the stories of creation found among Israel's neighbors. In Israel's accounts, no warfare was involved in bringing order from chaos (the void). Creation took place not as a result of executive force analogous to military violence, but simply by the power of God's own speech-act. The first human beings were not created under the power of a political hierarchy, but rather were pictured as self-governing in a garden paradise. This picture is significantly different from the pictures we get in the creation stories of Israel's neighbors.

The drama of creation did not, in the biblical versions, center on a narrative of the forces of order defeating the forces of chaos.

---

favor of the command to do justice, which was unique in the general environment.

Even apart from the fact that such a hermeneutic assumes a simplistic and stereotyped view of complex cultural phenomena, this method sparked its own "fundamentalisms." I remember, for example, at least one student-lounge debate about whether God's revelation was most perfectly embodied in the occupation of the farmer, the shepherd, or the fisherman. I cannot remember who defended which position, but I can say with certainty that none of the debaters actually followed those occupations.

My point here is only that while I do see some environmentally new and even unique things occurring in the political history of Israel, I am no longer inclined to invest any of these with the added authority of divine revelation. Similarly, I would not see the value of the anti-kingship tradition lessened in any way if further research were to show that anti-kingship was an undercurrent in all of the societies in the ancient Near East.

Rather, it was located in the human freedom to accept and obey the divine counsel or to reject this counsel in favor of "finding out for themselves." The establishment of centralized political institutions, such as Cain's city and the Tower of Babel, was presented more as a consequence of human pride and disobedience to the divine counsel than as gifts of God and of divine origin. From the collection of Hebrew creation stories in Genesis 1–11, one cannot conclude that kingship or any other centralized political institution of power was divinely established, integral to the natural order, or in any other way religiously supported. The absence of this divine legitimization of centralized political institutions is remarkable.

One can conclude only that, as with Israel's neighbors, their historical experience of the political drama of crisis and deliverance was reflected in their creation stories. For the Hebrews, their formative experience of kingship was that of being oppressed by it. Kings had oppressed them as slaves in Egypt and as rural peasants and conscripted soldiers in rebellion against the feudal domination of various Palestinian city-states. This anti-kingship tradition is expressed nowhere more strongly that in the Hebrew people's own texts recounting the end of their 400-year tribal confederacy and the establishment of human kingship among them.[10]

DYSFUNCTIONAL WARFARE

Judges 7 recounts a rather bizarre military policy. Gideon intentionally weakened his army before taking them into battle against the Midianites. Nevertheless, he was successful in the battle. The success of Gideon in defeating the Midianites caused the people to call for Gideon to become their king and to establish a dynasty. Gideon rejected this, reminding the people that they already had a king, none other than the Lord (Judg. 8:22-23)!

---

[10] Again, one may wonder whether the "anti-kingship" texts render an unadulterated account of how human kingship came about among the Hebrews or whether they reflect the shaping of a later tradition of pious editing. This issue is less interesting than the fact that the anti-kingship tradition developed at all.

Gideon used this cry of the people for a human king to reinforce the ideology of the unmediated kingship of God. After Gideon died, however, there was support for his son to become king.

Immediately following this text is the Fable of Jotham, in which various trees are approached about becoming king (Judg. 9:8-15). The splendid and useful trees—the olive tree, the fig tree, and the grapevine—disdained the office, since they were already doing much more productive work. Only the thorn bush (NRSV: "bramble") was willing to become king. Kingship was pictured as a parasite on society, and it served no useful purpose. The intention of this fable was quite clear, as John Bright saw: "Only a worthless bramble of a man, who has no useful employment, would aspire to be king."[11]

In 1 Samuel 8:5-22 the anti-kingship tradition is forcefully presented in a way that reflected the actual Hebrew experience of the centralized, despotic political authority of the oriental monarch. In this text, the people again cried out for a human king. They knew quite well that in doing so, they were expressing a desire to be like the other nations. The texts stated explicitly that kingship was not a divine institution but was actually a rejection of God. The people's rejection of God's kingship in favor of a human king was presented as another step in a long history of incremental rejections of divine authority. The rejection paralleled, it appears, the incremental rejections of divine counsel "in the beginning," which led to the great Flood.

Samuel the prophet outlined clearly what the people could expect from having a monarchy: military conscription, high war taxes, and high taxes generally. Their young women would be forced into service in the court, a privileged aristocratic class would arise, and the people would experience forced labor and slavery. Yet the people wanted a human king. So Samuel finally anointed Saul as king (an act symbolizing that even in a monarchy, the prophetic office took a position superior to that of the royal office).

---

[11] John Bright, *The Kingdom of God* (Nashville: Abingdon, 1968), 32.

The Hebrew people desired a human king "like the other nations." This warrior-king would mediate the divine will and establish that natural connection between human executive force and divine power on which glorious empires are built. However, what they got was something quite different. God's favor did not rest on their human king either because of his person or his office. God's favor remained with the king only so long as the king ruled with justice for the weak, the widows, the orphans, and the foreigners in the land.

These were the very considerations that acted as a powerful counterforce to empire building! Furthermore, during the period of the kings, the office of the prophet did not wither and die. It was actually strengthened. The more the various kings tried to act as though they were the mediators of the divine will on earth, the more the prophets would bravely confront them with public accusations of wickedness and unfaithfulness. The Hebrew historians' later judgment of a given king was based exactly on whether, at that point of being so confronted, a king persisted in his ways, or whether he humbled himself before the prophet and repented.

In leading us through these texts, Professor Lind repeatedly emphasized a point that lit a fire in the heart of this young student from a theologically conservative, evangelical-leaning Mennonite upbringing. In these texts—the calling of the prophet, the poetic praise for God's military deliverance, the prophetic discourses against the nations—the authors intentionally used language that was explicitly political. These people intentionally placed the calling of the prophet on the same plane of history as did other nations in the calling of their monarchs. The justice demanded by the prophets was a public justice with a political policy and a political program. There was no legitimate reading of these texts as being a dialectic of "spiritual" versus "political" power. The only dialectic here concerned *what kind of political power* would prevail.

My immediate response to Millard's reading of these texts was that they had direct application in the present! Irresistible historical forces may have moved the Anabaptists from their socially provocative beginnings to becoming the "quiet, rural people of the land." Yet there was certainly no biblical justification for remaining apolitical in our current North American circumstances. These prophets were a call to action!

THE PHILOSOPHERS' STONE

When I arrived at the seminary, I was already well acquainted with the basics of Marxist thought. I was especially impressed with the Marxist criticism of institutional religion and the role it plays in preserving the social hierarchy. This "negative" criticism of religion was a key piece of my personal belief system. On the positive side, my personal beliefs were shaped by a mix of Harold S. Bender's *The Anabaptist Vision;* Jürgen Moltmann's *The Crucified God;* and John Howard Yoder's now-classic volume *The Politics of Jesus.*

In retrospect, the common thread in these books is their focus on servant-discipleship as defining true religious life. Each of these books points in its own way to a nonviolent political ethic of "revolutionary subordination" (Yoder's term). I soon added Millard Lind's political interpretation of the Hebrew Bible to this theological mix. It felt like the pieces fit perfectly.

Human history suddenly made sense. Human history was an ongoing struggle over the question of what kind of politics we would have. Would the "highest good" in human life be defined by the strong, those able to muster on their side the most violent executive force (the majority view)? Or would it be defined by the needs of the weak, those who cannot or will not resort to violence (the minority view)? This was the dialectic of human history. Tiny blades of grass will eventually break through even the thickest concrete. Likewise, each time the pro-violent people thought they had finally stamped out the dissenting view for good, they would discover that it was still present!

There it was, in the Hebrew and early Christian refusal to honor any human monarch or emperor as divine; in the admonition to become as servants, that the last shall be first, that the poor in spirit are blessed. There it was, in that long line of evangelical brethren (the Ludwig Keller thesis) who stood against the symbiosis of religious and state power symbolized by Constantine; in the Anabaptist rejection of military service and loyalty oaths (the exceptions to which only proved the rule). There it was in the history of the Jewish Diaspora, a history of the people who consistently chose suffering over surrender and yet could never be conquered, even by the demonic Nazi regime. There it was in Rousseau's doctrine of the social contract, insisting that legitimate authority came from below, not from above, and remained legitimate only so long as leadership serves the people. There it was in Marx's criticism of the state, insisting that the state is nothing other than the organized violence of the ruling class for purpose of maintaining its usurpation of privilege. There it was in Joe Hill, standing up to the sheriff's armed thugs and helping exploited miners to organize. There it was in Gandhi's movement in South Africa and India, and in Martin Luther King's movement in North America.

Truth is always related to Truth. As I saw it, Truth happens in human history when the weak are empowered by the strong. God's truth happens when the motivation for this shift in power is the conscious seeking of justice. And Gospel Truth happens when the methods employed in the creation of this shift are those of conscientious nonviolence.

By the time I left seminary, I felt I had grasped the philosophers' stone.

Deconstruction and Reconstruction

Has my mind changed since then? Certainly it has changed in form if not in substance. I see now that I was too apt to focus on the state itself as the embodiment of the negative side of this human dialectic. I was certainly influenced in this, as noted above, by Marx's criticism of the state as, by its very nature, the organized violence of the ruling class. I was also influenced in this by a conservative Mennonite view of "nonresistance," which taught that coercive violence was integral to the core of all states, regardless of the particular form (monarchical, democratic, totalitarian, etc.) of the state. I see with hindsight, however, that I was also deeply influenced by a general distrust of the United States government, which many felt in the wake of events surrounding Vietnam, Watergate, Argentina, the continuing arms race, and other clear abuses of power.

In retrospect, I was too quick to lump together all of the collective programs pursued through the mechanisms of the state and to view them equally as inherently tainted morally. At that time my vision was that collective programs for welfare, education, and other such agenda would be carried out by an interlocking network of voluntary associations. This network would completely bypass the mechanisms of the state, ignoring the state as irrelevant to the most basic and important human communal concerns.

In my M.A. thesis, which I wrote during my senior year at seminary (1978), I argued that if we were to outline a Christian political theology, it would not resemble the Marxism of liberation theologians, the realism of the Niebuhrians, the liberalism of mainline Protestants, or the conservative Republicanism of the evangelical Protestants. A truly Christian political theology would lie firmly in the camp of anarchy, and it would occupy the particular field within that camp called "nonviolent/peaceful anarchism" by the political theorists.[12]

Within a few years this view was put forth independently by other writers, first by Vernard Eller and then by Jacques Ellul.[13]

---

[12] With only cosmetic changes from the original 1978 version, I published that thesis as "Christian Freedom and Political Freedom," *Conrad Grebel Review* 4/2 (1986): 101–23.

[13] Vernard Eller, *Christian Anarchy* (Grand Rapids: Eerdmans, 1987); Jacques Ellul, *Anarchy and Christianity* (Grand Rapids: Eerdmans, 1991). It would feel like hubris to claim priority for my formulations over those of Eller and Ellul, even though my specific work on Christian anarchy preceded their books by a number of years. I had devoured Ellul's trilogy on technique and propaganda during college, and a number of Ellul's theological works were main sources for my thesis. Furthermore, while writing the thesis, I was taking part in Marlin Miller's seminar on Ellul. Eller had been a guest lecturer in my undergraduate department, and I

Yet I now see it as imbalanced, and my thesis has been largely ignored by Mennonite theologians.[14] As I write this essay, I am a hospice social worker. My solidly middle-class existence is nearly 100 percent supported by Medicare and Medicaid funding. If nothing else, economic expediency has brought me to soften my views on at least some state programs and policies.

Interaction with various social and intellectual influences has broadened my thinking considerably since seminary. Immediately after seminary, the Mennonite Central Committee sent me to Eastern Europe. As a twenty-four-year-old, I had never lived in an environment in which the people I rubbed shoulders with on a daily basis were not predominantly Mennonite. During the past twenty years, I have lived mainly in Budapest, Vienna, New York City, and Philadelphia. Sometimes weeks pass without face-to-face interaction with another Mennonite. This alone must have had some influence on my style of critical reflection. My personal beliefs have been deconstructed and reconstructed several times in the course of doctoral training in both theology and psychotherapy.

Yet a positive core remains. My search for a philosophers' stone — that single idea that can successfully explain the totality of human history — has surely atrophied. Yet I am committed in the

---

was well acquainted with his work on the social philosophy of Kierkegaard. Let us say simply that in my formulation of Christian anarchy, I demonstrated that I had read accurately and applied appropriately an implication in the work of these men that others had not noticed.

[14] My academic and thesis adviser, Professor John H. Yoder, did try repeatedly to point out to me that there were problems in my focus on the state itself in my thesis. He suggested that I consider more carefully the moral differences between the programs of a democratic state, with its opportunities for genuine citizen input into the policies, and those of a totalitarian state, in which there is no opportunity for citizen input. At the time that was difficult for me to hear. It sounded too much like special pleading for American democracy. Had I heeded Yoder's advice, I would have written a more balanced thesis, which would perhaps have produced more interest.

deepest part of my being to nonviolence, to pacifism in the broadest sense. I do not assume that violent conflict is inevitable and therefore do not prepare in advance for violent conflict. If violent conflict does occur, I seek reconciliation rather than revenge or punishment.

I retain a strong sense of suspicion when, in society or in the church, the majority group with power assumes the right to set policy "for the good of everyone," especially when this moves against the convictions of a less-powerful minority. I think John Rawls is on the right track in suggesting that public policy benefiting primarily the bottom of the social hierarchy better approximates an ideal of "justice" than does a public policy benefiting primarily those higher up in the social hierarchy. I continue to hold that the essence of true religion is found in voluntarily assuming the role of a servant-disciple, and in living according to the principles of nonviolent, revolutionary subordination.

A few years ago I outlined what I see as the three most basic themes of early Anabaptist spirituality: (1) the immediacy of the human relationship with God; (2) a life of discipleship; and (3) the corporate nature of the Christian life.[15] These three points suggest a thorough transvaluation of values in the American sociopolitical context. They express my core beliefs as well as any other statements.

My personal confession of faith is in the hidden authenticity of a truly upside-down kingdom. Though we can neither understand nor explain it, the power of love will persuade and succeed over the power of violence. Millard Lind, in his teaching and writings as well as by his personal example as professor, elder Christian, and human being, played a significant and continuing role in instilling in this student that core of positive faith.

---

[15] Daniel Liechty, ed., *Early Anabaptist Spirituality: Selected Writings* (New York: Paulist, 1994), 8–14.

2

Making Yahweh's Rule Visible

J. DENNY WEAVER

It took several moments before the labored English words from the quiet, elderly voice began to sink in. He said only, "When I hear you praying, I have hope." But as the words penetrated my consciousness, I sensed the presence of God. I have never felt closer to God than at that moment.

An important element of preparation for that moment was the study of the Old Testament, in particular the study of the Prophets that I did some thirty years ago with Millard Lind. In this essay, I will sketch the relationship between my experience with the elderly gentleman and the understanding of the Bible and what it means to be one of God's people that I began to develop in those courses.

The weighty moment came at the culmination of my first trip to Haiti with Christian Peacemaker Teams[1] (CPT) in December 1992. When the elderly gentleman addressed us, our team was in the heart of Port-au-Prince. We had formed an uneven circle around a statue that served as a symbol of Haitian freedom. In full view two or three hundred meters away were the two buildings that housed the government powers of Haiti—the capitol building and the army headquarters.

---

[1] Christian Peacemaker Teams is an initiative among Mennonite, Church of the Brethren, and Quaker congregations that supports violence-reductive efforts and nonviolent peace activism around the world.

Haiti was experiencing government by the military junta that had deposed the democratically elected President Jean-Bertrand Aristide in a coup. Army rule was repressive. Haitians were forbidden to meet in groups of more than four persons without an army permit. It was government policy to obliterate Lavalas, the movement that had brought Aristide to the office of President. People who mentioned the name of Lavalas or of Aristide in public were subject to arrest. Sometimes they just disappeared in the night. More than once our little group of North Americans was cautioned not to mention those names when walking in the street, lest we bring suspicion on the Haitians walking with us.

Of Haiti's total population of six million, an estimated 250,000 Aristide supporters were living in the underground rather than risk death at the hands of the army. Many had left their homes precipitously, slipping out a back way when friends or family came to warn them of army personnel approaching their houses. Most of those in the underground had come to the attention of the army, either because they had worked publicly for Lavalas or had worked in social programs organized by Lavalas to address such needs as literacy or the fair sale of crops.

Prior to our action at the statue, our CPT delegation spent the previous week talking with people in the underground, attempting to hear their stories and to give them a voice. A part of our public gathering around the statue in the heart of Port-au-Prince was to speak for these suppressed and oppressed people. Earlier we had read aloud for Haitian TV cameras a statement from an underground Haitian. As foreigners, we could stay things Haitian nationals could not. Thus protected by our status, a member of our team read an eloquent and poetic call from the underground for Haitians and foreigners alike to continue to struggle nonviolently for justice in Haiti. I took great satisfaction from participating in a group that enabled public expression of these suppressed Haitian voices. But it remained for the elderly gentleman's comment to open my eyes to the full significance of the experience.

Our group around the statue recited a liturgy, sang songs, and prayed together. The elderly gentleman's expression of hope in our worship revealed to me in a new way the significance of our action. Of course it was important to witness against injustice and oppression and to give voice to oppressed Haitians! But we were doing it as *Christians*, as God's people. At that moment I realized that both symbolically and actually we were the shalom community of God's people, making visible and present God's peace, in contrast to the oppressive powers resident in the capitol building and army headquarters in full view across the avenues. The elderly man had felt that peace, and in his words I experienced it too.

Those of us gathered in that circle were there because we were Christians committed to nonviolence. Our gathered CPT circle expressed our solidarity with suffering people. Our gathering witnessed to another way—to the peaceable kingdom of God. Though the vision is not yet fully realized, we acted out the peaceable kingdom of Isaiah 11 for a brief moment as we stood in that circle. We protested the violence and injustice on the doorsteps of those who perpetrated violence and injustice. Although the cleansing was not complete, it seemed a bit like Jesus' cleansing of the temple. For a few minutes, our circle was more than a symbol: in the hope expressed by the elderly Haitian man, the reign of God was present.

This gathering was what the church should be: a witness to the reign of God in the world, an institution to point out injustice and to speak on behalf of justice, and a community where peace, justice, and reconciliation are visible and real. Haitians as Haitians are not the church, nor is their oppression necessarily suffering for the cause of Christ. But their oppression is real, and the church *is* the church when it exposes that injustice and gives a visible witness to peace and justice as experienced under the rule of God.

Clearly our actions around that statue were symbolic. A mere thirty people, we did not bring obvious change to Haiti on that Wednesday morning. But we did make a visible, symbolic enactment of peace and justice, ... and for a brief moment the reign of God was present. Around that statue in downtown Port-au-Prince, with the elderly gentleman murmuring in my ear, I was living in the Old Testament narrative I first learned from Millard

Lind, in particular the story of Jeremiah's battle of the yokes with Hananiah.

A prophet of the Southern Kingdom, Jeremiah's public career covered the forty years of that kingdom just before its fall in 587 (627–587 BCE). In 597, Nebuchadnezzar, king of Babylon, had invaded Jerusalem. Judah's King Jehoiachin (also called Jeconiah and Coniah), who had reigned only three months, was carried into Exile, along with the royal family, their retinue, other leading citizens, and a significant portion of the temple vessels. Nebuchadnezzar installed an uncle of Jehoiachin on the throne as a vassal. He reigned under the name of Zedekiah.[2]

Opinions varied concerning the exiles and whether Nebuchadnezzar's rule should be accepted. The majority no doubt considered the deportation a brief interlude that would soon be reversed. After all, it did not seem possible that Jerusalem, Yahweh's city, would come under foreign domination. Those who interpreted Zion theology to proclaim the invincibility of the city (Pss. 46; 48; 76) believed that Yahweh would soon act again to save the city, as he had done previously.[3] Those who held this view considered Jehoiachin the real king of Judah, and they expected his return in the near future, along with the temple vessels and treasure. One faction of those who retained faith in the near return of King Jehoiachin maintained hope that assistance against Babylon would come from Egypt or through an alliance with Egypt.

Jeremiah supported none of these views. He considered Jehoiachin unfit to rule (Jer. 22:24-30). He opposed any alliance with Egypt. He expected a long Exile, and he advocated full submission to the rule of Nebuchadnezzar. Jeremiah 27 and 28 narrate

---

[2] J. Maxwell Miller and John H. Hayes, *A History of Ancient Israel and Judah* (Philadelphia: Westminster, 1986), 408.

[3] Miller and Hayes, *History*, 409. Ben Ollenburger has demonstrated that the security of Zion provided by Yahweh "is made conditional on the posture of the community," which is expressed in terms of "faith and trust" in Yahweh. See *Zion, the City of the Great King: A Theological Symbol of the Jerusalem Cult*, Journal for the Study of the Old Testament Supplement Series, no. 41 (Sheffield, England: JSOT, 1987), 148.

the prophet's public, symbolic, and confrontational means to convey that message. Using wood and straps, he constructed the kind of yoke oxen might use to pull a load. Apparently Jeremiah wore the yoke daily to symbolize the message that he had from Yahweh, that Israel should submit to the yoke of the king of Babylon and abandon thoughts of a near return of the exiles.

Jeremiah propagated his message widely. Jeremiah 27:3-11 recounts delivery of the message to the various kings who sent emissaries to negotiate with Zedekiah. The kings were to know that it was Yahweh who appointed rulers, and that Yahweh had given the lands into the hands of Nebuchadnezzar, king of Babylon. Jeremiah's message implied that their alliances, whether with each other or with King Zedekiah, were useless. Yahweh's word, as symbolized by the yoke Jeremiah wore, is that the nations should put their necks under the yoke of the king of Babylon and serve him.

For those who refuse to submit, said Yahweh, "I will punish that nation with the sword, with famine, and with pestilence … until I have completed its destruction" (27:8). Prophets, diviners, and any advisers who say differently "are prophesying a lie," and the king who listens to such a lie will be "removed far from [his] land" (27:10). On the other hand, those who submit to the yoke of the king of Babylon, "I will leave on [the] land, says the LORD, to till it and live there" (27:11).

Jeremiah took that same message to King Zedekiah. Zedekiah seemed beholden to the people around him. A series of court prophets had visions of independence from Babylon and pushed Zedekiah to resist Nebuchadnezzar. Jeremiah counseled the contrary. "Bring your necks under the yoke of the king of Babylon," Jeremiah said to Zedekiah, "and serve him and his people, and live. Why should you and your people die by the sword, by famine, and by pestilence, as the LORD has spoken concerning any nation that will not serve the king of Babylon?" The prophets who say otherwise "are prophesying falsely" in the name of Yahweh (27:12-15).

Finally, Jeremiah proclaimed the same message to the priests and the citizens of Judah generally. "They are prophesying a lie" who say that the vessels will soon be brought back from Babylon. "Do not listen to them; serve the king of Babylon and live. Why should this city become a desolation?" (27:16-17).

Chapter 27 shows Jeremiah engaged in a symbolic action that likely witnessed against the majority opinion. He spoke a word of Lord to the reigning powers that opposed what they wanted to hear. Our action around the statue in Port-au-Prince could claim Jeremiah's act as something of a model. We spoke and acted out a word that we believed came from Yahweh. Without identifying Haitians as the church, Christians were speaking out to name an oppressive situation and to call for the liberation of suffering and oppressed people. The powers we addressed resided in the buildings in plain sight across the boulevard: in the army headquarters and the capitol building.

Jeremiah's act pointed to a reality different from that of his hearers. They saw a near return. Jeremiah believed that seeking a near return would lead to devastation, while submission to the conqueror would preserve the city and lead eventually to the return of the exiles and the temple treasure. Our action around the statue also pointed to a different reality. By joining hands and uniting our hearts and voices in prayer and song, we became the new reality of the people of God. We made visible the reign of God as an alternative to the oppressive powers that faced us. Like Jeremiah, we called people to forsake the current path and to experience the rule of Yahweh. The elderly gentleman murmuring in my ear sensed that and made me sense it.

Jeremiah's symbolic action did not go unchallenged. The response was both public and symbolic. The prophet Hananiah accosted Jeremiah in the temple, in the presence of the priests and the general populace. Like Jeremiah, Hananiah also claimed to speak the word of Yahweh. But he contradicted Jeremiah. Rather than counseling submission to Nebuchadnezzar, Hananiah said,

> Thus says the LORD of hosts, the God of Israel: I have broken the yoke of the king of Babylon. Within two years I will

bring back to this place all the vessels of the LORD's house, which King Nebuchadnezzar of Babylon took away from this place and carried to Babylon. I will also bring back to this place King Jeconiah son of Jehoiakim of Judah, and all the exiles from Judah who went to Babylon, says the LORD, for I will break the yoke of the king of Babylon. (28:2-4)

Like Jeremiah, Hananiah also engaged in symbolic action. He grabbed Jeremiah's yoke and broke it, saying, "Thus says the LORD: This is how I will break the yoke of King Nebuchadnezzar of Babylon from the neck of all the nations within two years" (28:11). And with that demonstration, Jeremiah left the scene (28:11).

Like Jeremiah's dramatic act, our act around the statue also met a kind of challenge. Our group had planned how to respond to a direct confrontation from the military, but we left the statue before any materialized. However, we did receive a direct challenge of another kind.

On our first night in Port-au-Prince, the men in our group stayed in a guesthouse run by evangelical missionaries from the United States. Around the dinner table that evening, we discussed the activities we were planning for the week, including our public demonstration, which was still in the planning stage. The next morning at breakfast, our hosts informed us that their guest rooms were no longer available for us to sleep in. They wanted nothing to do with people who would engage in "political" action against the government.

These missionaries opposed in the name of God what we planned to do in the name of God. To our team, seemed a parallel to the opposition to Yahweh's word that Jeremiah experienced from Hananiah and the other court prophets. We packed our belongings and carried them on foot several blocks to the convent, where the (Catholic) sisters, who were already hosting the women in our delegation, allowed the men to stay, crowded several to a room.

Jeremiah's account also reveals a great deal of ambiguity concerning the understanding or the conclusions his audience might draw from his action. Jeremiah and Hananiah used identical words to introduce their message: "Thus says the LORD." In terms of empowered claims or appeals to authority, they were equal. Each engaged in a symbolic act that made his message visible—Jeremiah constructed and wore a yoke; Hananiah seized it and broke it. And the first round of acts ended there. After Hananiah had snatched and broken the yoke, Jeremiah withdrew, silently acknowledging the problem of whom to believe when prophet contradicted prophet and each claimed to speak for Yahweh.[4]

Jeremiah did suggest one criterion for identifying the true prophet. Preceding prophets had prophesied war, famine, and pestilence, Jeremiah said. The greater burden of proof would now reside on the one who prophesied peace. "When the word of that prophet comes true, then it will be known that the LORD has truly sent the prophet" (28:9). In the final analysis, however, how the events turned out would be the final arbiter of which prophet—Jeremiah or Hananiah—truly spoke for Yahweh.

Like Jeremiah's action and response, our action in Port-au-Prince lacked an obvious outcome that would validate our action as Yahweh's word. Jeremiah counseled submission to Nebuchadnezzar in expectation of a return from Exile some seventy years in the future (25:11), a person's normal life span. This was hardly more attractive than Hananiah's promise of return within two years! We had no expectations that our witness to the word of Yahweh would bring a change of government anytime soon in Port-au-Prince.

Sometime after the initial face-off with Hananiah, Jeremiah returned to the fray, now apparently wearing an iron yoke. Jeremiah told Hananiah,

> You have broken wooden bars only to forge iron bars in place of them! For thus says the LORD of hosts, the God of Israel: I have put an iron yoke on the neck of all these nations so that they may serve King Nebuchadnezzar of

---

[4] John Bright, *Jeremiah*, The Anchor Bible (Garden City, N.Y.: Doubleday, 1965), 202–3.

> Babylon, and they shall indeed serve him; I have even given him the wild animals. (28:13-14)

This word from Yahweh also included a personal message for Hananiah, with an ironic twist. Because he had not previously been sent by Yahweh, now Yahweh would send him right off the face of the earth.

> Listen, Hananiah, the LORD has not sent you, and you made this people trust in a lie. Therefore thus says the LORD: I am going to send you off the face of the earth. Within this year you will be dead. (28:15-16)

And he died that same year (28:17).

Alongside his work with the yokes, Jeremiah engaged in a number of other symbolic acts. While they may have lacked the confrontational style demonstrated in the yoke, these acts proclaimed the same message. He buried and ruined a new loincloth as the basis for prophecy about the Exile (13:1-11). He slammed wine jars together, breaking them (13:12-14) as a sign of coming destruction. He remained single and childless to dramatize the coming desolation of the land of Judah (16:1-13), and he smashed a pot as a symbol of what Yahweh would do to Jerusalem (19:1-15).

The Babylonian army besieged Jerusalem. As Jeremiah was facing imprisonment in the court of the palace guard, he bought a plot of ground (Jer. 32). Enacted in the face of the imminent fall of the city, the purchase expressed faith in the promise of Yahweh that at a future time, the people would return and normal life would resume in the land.

Other prophets also engaged in symbolic activity. Isaiah, a prophet active in the Southern Kingdom whose career (742–701 BCE) spanned the fall of Samaria in 722, gave his son a name that foreshadowed the fall of Samaria (Isa. 8:1-4). When Judah had an opportunity to join an alliance with Egypt and Ethiopia in a revolt against Assyria, Isaiah strongly opposed such a coalition. For three years he walked around Jerusalem "naked and barefoot," to illustrate the shame of Egyptians and Ethiopians and as a symbol of their future Exile and of Israel's folly in trusting foreign powers (Isa. 20).

Ezekiel was among those deported to Babylon in 597.[5] Some of Ezekiel's actions do not appear completely normal. In some sort of ecstatic state, he remained speechless until given an oracle by God (Ezek. 3:27).[6] He drew the city of Jerusalem on a brick. Then he ate siege rations and lay bound on his side for a total of 430 days, the traditional number of years Israel was in Egypt.[7] In doing so, Ezekiel was acting out the siege of the city and the captivity of Northern and Southern Kingdoms. In his body he bore the punishment Yahweh was laying upon the people (Ezek. 4). In another pantomime, Ezekiel shaved his head and burned portions of the hair, with only a small portion saved, to picture the coming destruction of Judah (Ezek. 5).

Such actions in the prophetic traditions of Israel show that Jesus' own acts stood fully within that prophetic tradition. When Jesus healed on the Sabbath, the action had a deliberately confrontational element. Before he revived the withered hand, he called the man to come and stand with him in a prominent location, so that those who objected to such Sabbath activity would be sure to notice. Then Jesus looked "around at all of them," made eye contact with them, and told the man with the crippled arm, "Stretch our your hand" (Luke 6:6-11). Other reports of healing on the Sabbath make equally clear that these acts of Jesus were not only controversial, but also intentionally confrontational (Luke 13:10-17; 14:1-6). These acts had elements of both symbol and actualization. By healing on the Sabbath, Jesus engaged in an act demonstrating that the regulations propagated by the religious leadership were subverting and distorting the purpose of the Sabbath under the reign of God. But it was also more than a symbol. In the act of healing, the reign of God was made present and visible.

---

5 Ezekiel's career is often dated 593–570 BCE

6 Millard C. Lind, *Ezekiel*, Believers Church Bible Commentary (Scottdale, Pa.: Herald Press, 1996), 44.

7 Lind, *Ezekiel*, 54.

In his encounter with the Samaritan woman (John 4:1-38), Jesus confronted prevailing standards in another way. He had already violated the strict purity expectations by traveling through Samaria, rather than around it. Then he surprised the woman at the well by his willingness, as a Jew, to accept a drink from her, a Samaritan. The purity code forbade his contact with a menstruating woman. Since one could never be certain that a woman was not in the unclean state, the practice was to assume that she was unclean, a condition also extending to any vessel she touched.[8]

At their return, the disciples were surprised that he was speaking to a woman (John 4:27). Recent literature has frequently pointed out that Jesus' interactions with women raised their standing and broke the conventions of a patriarchal society. For example, Walter Wink states, "We can see that in every single encounter with women in the four Gospels, Jesus violated the mores of his time."[9]

Jesus' cleansing of the temple constitutes a third vignette that both symbolizes and effects a new reality. Jesus found the temple desecrated. The debate about the exact nature of that desecration need not concern us here. Of import is that Jesus engaged in a "cleansing" action to reclaim the temple for the rule of God (Luke 19:45-48; Matt. 21:12-13). Since it confronted the prevailing structures of the social order, this action, along with the Sabbath-day healings, is akin to modern acts of civil disobedience.

As we stood around the statue and the elderly Haitian gentlemen finally made his words clear to me, I came to believe we were engaging in activities that stood in the tradition of Isaiah, Jeremiah, Ezekiel, and Jesus. Like them, we used symbols and gestures to make God's rule visible. Stationed in front of the oppressive structures of government and the military, I could even believe that our little circle resembled a temple cleansing. In the

---

[8] C. K. Barrett, *The Gospel According to St. John: An Introduction with Commentary and Notes on the Greek Text* (New York: Macmillan, 1962), 194.

[9] Walter Wink, *Engaging the Powers: Discernment and Resistance in a World of Domination* (Minneapolis: Fortress, 1992), 129.

space within our circle, into which the elderly gentlemen stepped, the oppressive forces were momentarily expelled and God's peace reigned.

However, the relationship between the actions around the statue in Port-au-Prince and what I began to learn from Millard Lind goes beyond the acquisition of biblical models of symbolic or activist behavior. If models of activity are the only gain, then the models and their modern counterparts would have little meaning in and of themselves. One can develop symbolic acts in support of any cause. As isolated moments, the acts of Jeremiah walking around with an ox yoke or Ezekiel curling around his brick or Isaiah strolling naked around Jerusalem or CPT folks singing in a circle—none of these actions points to a significant truth or carries significant meaning when isolated from the believing community. Only the wider context or frame of reference endows such acts with their meaning.

The foundation for symbolic activity or acts of civil disobedience appears in the call of Yahweh to Abraham:

> Go from your country and your kindred and your father's house to the land that I will show you. I will make of you a great nation, and I will bless you, and make your name great, so that you will be a blessing. I will bless those who bless you, and the one who curses you I will curse; and in you all the families of the earth shall be blessed.
>
> (Gen. 12:1-3)

Yahweh's people have a mission in the world: to live as Yahweh's people. When they fulfill that mission, when they live up to the calling of Yahweh, then that people will be visible in the world. And when Yahweh's people live up their calling, other peoples are blessed.

The foundational activity of confronting the world happens when Yahweh's people live in the world as God's people in response to the call to Abraham. When God's people fulfill their mission, they may confront—and pose a clear alternative to—the segments of the world that do not profess loyalty to Yahweh or acknowledge the rule of Yahweh. The symbolic acts that have ultimate significance are those that reflect God's people and make visible God's people in the world.

When Isaiah or Jeremiah or Ezekiel spoke or acted, it was in response to the effective word of God: "Thus says the LORD." Their proclamations and their acts witnessed to the rule of Yahweh and to what was expected of God's people. Thus identity with God's rule (or God's will) gives meaning to the symbolic actions of Isaiah, Jeremiah, and Ezekiel.

In the long perspective, the people of God claim their identity from the life, death, and resurrection of Jesus Christ. Jesus' symbolic actions, such as healing on the Sabbath, accepting service from a woman and a Samaritan, and cleansing the temple, have meaning as actions that make visible the rule of God. These actions demonstrate what the reign of God looks like for those who live it and live within it. As the one whose person and whose life is most fully identified with the rule of God, Jesus' actions make the preeminent statement of what the rule of God looks like in the world. This larger framework of the reign of God, made visible and present in the prophetic acts and in the life and teaching of Jesus, provides the meaning of CPT actions in Haiti.

Our action around the statue had meaning if and when it was shaped by or reflected the reign of God. And the presence of the reign of God was initiated with the call to Abraham. It was continued through the children of Israel and in the prophets who critiqued them, and revealed most fully in the life and teaching of Jesus Christ. Actions around a statue in Port-au-Prince by CPT ultimately are valid not merely because they point out injustice or protest Haitian government actions, or because they are staged in front of Haitian power structures. If and when these actions acquire validity, they do so when the actions show what it means to be the people of God in continuity with the biblical people of God, who began with Abraham, continued in the tradition of Israel and her prophets, and then in Jesus.

Locating symbolic actions within the framework of the people of God also makes a significant negative point, making clear what symbolic action is *not*. In the case of Port-au-Prince, we were tempted to identify the victims of oppression as God's people and to include in the reign of God all those entities that served to alleviate oppression. In September 1994 the United States launched an invasion of Haiti with the stated purpose of restoring President Aristide to power. Even some peace-church folks supported those acts by the military because the military seemed for a time to lessen oppression and secure greater freedom in Haiti.

My experience on another trip to Haiti posed the temptation strongly to include the military within God's rule. Our delegation had a meeting with the Directrice Générale of the Ministry of Women's Affairs. Her office was located in the former army headquarters, on whose balcony we had seen soldiers standing when we had the vigil at the statue on my first trip. During a tour of the building, I stood in what was once the office of the coup leader who had deposed President Aristide. Now this building was being remodeled and the Ministry for Women's Affairs had taken over a segment of it. It seemed like the temple had been cleansed.

That Jesus' actions in the prophetic tradition provided a ready context for our actions made the demonstration *feel* like a temple cleansing—but that it could not be. While we could rejoice in the conversion of the building to more wholesome purposes, the governmental agencies that produced the change—whether the United States army or the Haitian government—are not representatives of the people of God, even though God may use them for God's purposes. After all, Jeremiah himself had said that Yahweh was using Nebuchadnezzar to punish rebellious Israel.

God's people are a faith community, not a political entity defined by geographical space. They represent the reign of God. Theologically, the actions of armies and governments do not represent the reign of God, even when they produce a momentary lessening of oppression.

If being the people of God as a witness to the world provides the wider framework for our actions, then we are living within the biblical story. In the Bible we find the story of God's people—a story that began with Abraham and continued through Israel to

Jesus. The story that identifies us as God's children and as followers of Jesus comes from the Bible. When we act in ways that make visible the people of God, we are living within a story shaped by the Bible. Our actions around that statue in the heart of Port-au-Prince were an incarnation and continuation of the Bible's story. I know now that these actions of CPT in Port-au-Prince were a continuation of what it means to be the people of God and to live within the story of the Bible.

3

Prophets in Conflict
Negotiating Truth in Scripture

JAMES E. BRENNEMAN

THE JUXTAPOSITION OF BIBLICAL THEOLOGIES

The task of Old Testament (biblical) theology in an age of pluralism and skepticism is one of the more important undertakings to which serious Bible readers can set their minds and hearts. That task, though claimed by some to be "bankrupt,"[1] remains critical to all "people of the Book," especially to those who claim the Bible as our source of truth. The task of biblical theology is complicated by the many conflicting theologies within the sacred corpus we call Scripture — our guide to faith and practice.

The problem is illustrated whenever two or more biblical prophets, each legitimately representing God's divine revelation, are juxtaposed in the canon of Scripture. Their different historical journeys from text to Scripture land them side-by-side in a compressed history, arguing against each other. What is a serious reader of Scripture to do?

The answer to the question of how to negotiate texts, true and false prophecy, right and wrong readings, will determine how we live our lives under the guidance of God's word to us. So the task is crucial and formidable. Yet we have no alternative Scripture that has been untrammeled by prophetic disputes and blatant

---

[1] Walter Wink, *The Bible in Human Transformation: Toward a New Paradigm for Biblical Study* (Philadelphia: Fortress, 1973), 1.

advocacy for one point of view over another.[2] Dispute and advocacy are in the very nature of worthy confession. Certainly, Scripture is worth such vigorous engagement.

I propose in this brief encounter between two opposing prophetic traditions to suggest several possibilities for negotiating an understanding that is enhanced by the Bible's own internal disagreements. It may be that a bible that said absolutely the same thing consistently from cover to cover would have long ago been relegated to the dustbins of history. As a book of controversy, the Bible mirrors reality. Like so many shoppers in a grocery line peeking through the tabloids, we're lured back, if for no other reason than by the scandals within. The Bible may be many things, but it is not boring.

HERMENEUTICS AND METACOMMENTARY

Millard Lind was well aware of these conflicts within Scripture, not least of which is the Bible's ambivalent views on violence and warfare. Millard spent the better part of his life research attempting to negotiate a particular historical-critical reading from the controversial "texts of terror." He came down on the side of Yahweh's exclusive prerogative for war in his book *Yahweh Is a Warrior*, thus hoping to limit human involvement to the gallery of pacifist spectator. In the context of the historical-critical debates of the last century in biblical studies, Lind's work is a critical counterpoint to those readers who saw in Scripture either unequivocal support for their own warring instincts or, in the case of the "Yahweh as warrior" motif, simply a pious mythical retrojection into the past.

It is not the place of this essay to take up that debate, especially since, from a historical-critical point of view, I am persuaded by Lind's conclusions. However, a difficulty not addressed by Lind's research, or by historical-critical readings in general, is the fact that most Bible readers do not read the Bible with such a

---

[2] Walter Brueggemann, *Theology of the Old Testament: Testimony, Dispute, Advocacy* (Minneapolis: Fortress, 1997).

finely tuned historical-scientific approach. Most readers read the Bible as Scripture, as canonical literature—a literature that juxtaposes conflicting theologies in such a way that they compete for our allegiance. Even if it were possible to educate biblical readers in the necessary work of historical-critical exegesis—a task I fully appreciate—a hundred years of such readings have shown them to be every bit as contradictory as the conflicting texts they sought to adjudicate in the first place.

Lind's remarkable legacy would be supplemented if one were to develop a method of negotiation that finds its validity less in the historical-critical orthodoxy of the past than in a self-conscious confessional reading that stands or falls on explicit criteria established by the readers in public debate. Such an endeavor would place all historical reconstructions—even good ones, like Lind's—in the category of hermeneutics and metacommentary,[3] letting the chips fall to the most persuasive argument, as encouraged by the form-critical genre of the "better sayings" in the book of Proverbs (12:9; 15:16, 17; 16:8; 17:12).

For our purposes here, and in honor of Professor Lind, I will compare two prophetic traditions in mortal conflict. He has commented on both in his own works,[4] though not specifically in the direction established here. The true prophet Hosea under the command of Yahweh (1:4-5) critically challenges the biblical account of Jehu's massacre, which was also commanded by Yahweh through true prophets Elijah and Elisha (2 Kings 9–10).

---

[3] Frederick Jameson, "Metacommentary," in *The Ideologies of Theory I: Situations of Theory, Essays 1971–1986* (London: Routledge and Kegan Paul, 1988), 3–16.

[4] Millard C. Lind, "Elijah: Man of Two Mountains" (Elkhart, Ind.: unpublished ms., Chapel Address, Associated Mennonite Biblical Seminary, Sept. 1976), and "Exasperated Love: An Exposition of Hosea 5:8–6:6," *Interpretation* 38/4 (Oct. 1984): 398–403.

HOSEA ON JEHU'S MASSACRE

And Yahweh said to Hosea,

> Call his name Jezreel; for yet a little while and I will punish the house of Jehu for the blood of Jezreel, and I will put an end to the kingdom of the house of Israel. And on that day I will break the bow of Israel in the valley of Jezreel.
>
> (Hos. 1:4-5, RSV)

Here Hosea was told in direct speech by Yahweh to name his firstborn child "Jezreel" (1:4). Of all the names Gomer and Hosea might have chosen for their new little one, *Jezreel* would not likely have been found in any baby-naming scrolls offering suggestions to new parents. In the days of Hosea, naming a child "Jezreel" would be like naming a child "Hiroshima" or "Auschwitz" today.[5] But Yahweh commanded Hosea to do just that!

The politics of naming their son "Jezreel" was not lost on Hosea's audience. Memories would immediately have surfaced of Yahweh's prophet Elijah confronting Baal's prophets on Mount Carmel, which overlooked the Jezreel plain (1 Kings 18:20-40). Memories would also have been evoked of Elijah's damning Baal's Queen Jezebel and the whole house of Ahab to the dogs. It was, after all, Jezebel's judicial murder of Naboth that gained her custody of some prime agricultural real estate in the Valley of Jezreel (1 Kings 21:17-24). Jezreel was also the name of a town in that valley, the winter capital of Israel's king Omri and his royal lineage, which included Ahab and his sons.

The name *Jezreel* means "God sows" — a perfect name for the rich farm country lying between Mount Carmel and Mount Tabor in Northern Galilee. The name conjures up the Baal myth of Mother Earth, spread-eagle in the valley between two kneecapped mountains, impregnated by Baal's raining sperm, reenacted in ritual ceremonies of orgiastic delight. Not a bad context for the effec-

---

[5] Hans Walter Wolff, *Confrontations with Prophets* (Philadelphia: Fortress, 1983), 25.

tive use by Hosea of the promiscuous wife motif so controversial in his prophecy![6]

Most importantly, in view of Yahweh's command to Hosea about Jezreel, it was in Jezreel that Jehu, the commander of the Israelite army, carried out a merciless, bloodthirsty rampage in a coup d'état that makes Saddam Hussein look rather grandfatherly (2 Kings 9–10). Still, Yahweh commanded Hosea to name his son "Jezreel."

The primary reasons given for Yahweh's interest in naming Hosea and Gomer's babies is clear enough. They were named as prophetic speech-acts that certified Yahweh's intentions. Daughter LoRuhamah was so named to describe Yahweh's loss of pity for Israel (1:6). Their third child, LoAmmi, was named this to show the extent of Yahweh's rejection of Israel as God's people (1:9). And their firstborn son, Jezreel, was so named to declare Yahweh's intent to "put an end to the kingdom of ... Israel" altogether (1:4, RSV). Even more exacting, the name *Jezreel* proclaims Yahweh's intent "to punish the house of Jehu for the blood of Jezreel" (1:4, RSV).[7]

THE DEUTERONOMISTIC HISTORIAN ON JEHU'S MASSACRE

Here then is the biblical rub, where the controversy erupts. Years earlier, according to the Deuteronomistic History (DH) in the book of Kings, Yahweh had praised Jehu for faithfully fulfilling Elijah's prophecy to annihilate the dynasty of Ahab:

> And the LORD said to Jehu: "Because you have done well in carrying out what is right in my eyes, and have done to the house of Ahab according to all that was in my heart, your sons of the fourth generation shall sit on the throne of Israel." (2 Kings 10:30, RSV)

---

[6] Hans Walter Wolff, *Hosea*, Hermeneia Commentaries (Philadelphia: Fortress, 1973), 14; and Wolff, *Confrontations with Prophets*, 25.

[7] Herbert G. May, "An Interpretation of the Names of Hosea's Children," *Journal of Biblical Literature* 55 (1986): 288–89.

Second Kings 9–10 indicates that Yahweh had blessed what Jehu did, and Elijah and Elisha had sanctioned it. With each bloody episode at the hand of Jehu, a proclamation declared the event to be the fulfillment of the word of Yahweh given to Elijah and Elisha. Elisha sent one of his disciples to the battlefront to anoint Jehu as the new king of Israel. The disciple expanded Yahweh's command, given by Elisha (9:3), to include the annihilation of the whole house of Ahab, including Jezebel (9:6-10). The story unfolds with poetic justice. Joram of Israel (son of Ahab and uncle to Ahaziah of Judah) and Ahaziah (grandson of Ahab) come to meet Jehu in the vineyard of Naboth, the Jezreelite. Joram is killed there while Ahaziah flees, only to be mortally wounded down the road.

The text asserts without reservation that these political murders were the beginning of the fulfillment of the "word of the LORD" as spoken through Elijah (9:36; cf. 1 Kings 21:23-24). Shortly thereafter, Jehu continued his extermination of all possible political rivals. He asked for the heads of all Joram's sons (Ahab's grandsons)—seventy in all—to be delivered to him, dumped at the city gates of Jezreel for all to see (2 Kings 10:6). Jehu reasoned that those who carried out his order were justified so that "there shall fall to the earth nothing of the word of the LORD which the LORD spoke concerning the house of Ahab; for the LORD has done what he said by his servant Elijah" (10:10, RSV).

Yahweh was further implicated in the purge after Jehu "showed off" his "zeal for Yahweh" by wiping out all the rest of Ahab's family in the capital city of Samaria "according to the word of Yahweh that he spoke through Elijah" (10:17). Then Jehu undertook one final slaughter of Baal worshipers after pretending that he himself had converted to Baalism as a ruse to get them to come to their deaths in worship with him. One is reminded of the eerie similarities between Jehu's ruthlessness and the massacre of Bishop Oscar Romero during worship in El Salvador by certain government-sponsored terrorists. Though most of the world decried the massacre in San Salvador, Yahweh praised Jehu for nearly the same cowardly tactics, declaring his deed a fulfillment of "all that was in my [Yahweh's] heart" (10:30).

As the texts of Kings and Hosea stand, each appeals to conflicting Yahweh speeches for their authority in assessing Jehu's massacres—to very different effect. In Kings, Jehu is a hero; in Hosea, he is a villain. There is no concern whatsoever in the Kings account for "the blood of Jezreel" (Hosea's term). Far from it! Yahweh explicitly endorses the bloodthirstiness of Jehu.

Indeed, Hosea could easily have borrowed the Jehu account in Kings as told to back up his own condemnation of Israel's apostasy years later. Hosea might have effectively argued that just as Yahweh's word came to pass in the case of Jehu's utter destruction of the house of Ahab, so too, would God now destroy the house of Jeroboam II and carry it into Exile. The name Jezreel could have been used by Hosea in support of the bloody Assyrian conquest of Israel: like Jehu, like Shalmaneser.

But Hosea didn't do that. Instead, he used as one of his arguments for Israel's demise the very bloodthirstiness that might have been his better argument. As the texts stand, Hosea is criticizing an earlier interpretation that had as its authoritative base repeated reference to Yahweh speeches affirming Jehu's violent campaign. The true prophet Hosea speaks against the true prophecies of Elijah and Elisha and their interpretative history (DH).

Intertextual "Dialogue" as Theological Critique

What is a biblical reader to do? Was Jehu to become fodder for condemnation by Yahweh (Hosea 1:4) ... for doing the very thing for which Yahweh had once celebrated him (2 Kings 9-10)? Was the house of Jehu to be punished on par with Ahab because—oddly enough—he had faithfully obeyed the commands of Yahweh through Elijah and Elisha? Is Hosea's assessment of Yahwistic history the correct reading? What are the implications for readers of these texts today who find in Scripture clearly articulated Yahweh speeches that conflict? How does one decide such questions when to decide one way or the other can make a difference between life and death for many?

This intertextual dialogue has led to a fractured debate among commentators. Some have argued for a whole new level of analysis called metacommentary, which comments on the commentator's point of view in making this or that critical assessment.[8] In general, the consensus among commentators is clearly to side with Hosea, though rarely does the commentator reveal explicitly the criteria for arriving at that view. A common "feeling" emerges that leans in favor of Hosea as taking the higher and morally more sensitive approach than the Elijah and Elisha cycle. But here we arrive at interpretive judgments being made between two true prophets based on criteria other than form-critical or historical arguments. Since both stories are bound up in straightforward Yahweh speeches, the traditional form-critical arguments that depend on such speeches as signals of truth are of little help here.

If one attempts to use traditional historical-critical criteria to determine the historicity of the events in question, the web of contradiction becomes even more difficult to untangle. On one hand, one might argue that "earlier is better," as Lind does of Yahweh's exclusive prerogative in warfare as depicted in Exodus 15. For Lind, all later narratives that include human participation in warfare are sullied when compared with the earliest historical standard (Exod. 15) as reconstructed by him. On the other hand, one might argue on historical-critical terms that "later is better," a progressive revelation of sorts. Anabaptists have long used just such an argument in defending Christ's teachings as normative over all other biblical instruction. A later-is-better concept of progressive revelation would tilt the interpretive scale toward Hosea. To complicate matters for historical-critical interpreters, does the fact that the final redaction of the Deuteronomistic History (Kings account) is later than Hosea's prophecy give it the upper hand in the argument—the last word, so to speak?

With good biblical precedent, the temptation is strong to use another historical criterion—that of fulfillment (Deut. 18:21-22)—as the deciding factor in debates between conflicting prophets, such as the one we have here between Elijah and Elisha on one hand and Hosea on the other. But did not the claims of both Elijah-

---

[8] See Jameson, "Metacommentary."

Elisha and Hosea come to pass? Are both true and therefore equally valid for patterning after them our lives? For the most part, commentators are buffaloed in answering that question.

Some make the spiritual argument. Jehu's sin was one of the "heart" and "attitude."[9] From this perspective, Hosea's complaint of Jehu was that Jehu's actions were grossly and purely political. It was Jehu's lack of piety that brought him censure. This is usually the argument of last resort for dealing with the violent bloody texts of Scripture. How many sermons have we heard that read the conquest of Canaan in just such spiritual terms? They are read as accounts of overcoming spiritual malaise, praying through to spiritual victory. Such readings, though acceptable in a narrow personal devotional context, are largely unacknowledged attempts to avoid the very critical sociopolitical judgments modeled for us by Hosea! Do we really believe that if the Elijah-Elisha tradition had shown Jehu to have spent more time praying and less time driving wildly in his chariot (2 Kings 9:20), his murderous spree might then have warmed Hosea's heart?

Another assessment of Hosea's criticism of the Elijah-Elisha tradition is that he simply didn't know he was contradicting that tradition because he didn't know it.[10] His was a new and independent word with no connection to the ninth-century traditions of Elijah and Elisha. One has to wonder, however, whether it would be possible for such an independent tradition of Hiroshima-like magnitude about Jehu to come down to Hosea without Hosea also knowing of the ministry of Elisha and Elijah. Besides, that doesn't help readers here and now, who have both traditions side-by-side in the book we call Scripture. Hosea may not have known, but we do, and we must decide how to understand these conflicting interpretations.

---

[9] Jacques Ellul, *The Politics of God and the Politics of Man* (Grand Rapids: Eerdmans, 1972).

[10] Wolff, *Hosea*, 18.

Still another point of view draws on the standard multiple-hands argument of the historical-critical school.[11] Hosea's critique of Jehu is a doom oracle from an earlier Hosea, a "first Hosea," who was a contemporary of Jehu. Its distance from the "authentic" Hosea can then diminish this early oracle. One might say that the real Hosea did not judge Jehu's ethics at all. The real Hosea did not use that judgment as a criterion for Israel's eventual demise. From a canonical reading, such historical arguments are too often a means of avoiding the real debate going on between conflicting prophets in Scripture. Or worse, such an approach may disguise choices already made by the interpreter in the name of historical-critical reconstruction.

Finally, a more nuanced discussion suggests Hosea simply believed Jehu overstepped his mandate.[12] The difference between Hosea and his debate partners, Elijah and Elisha (DH), was one of degree, not substance. Yet nuance in the end does not help these interpreters all that much in deciding the question for or against these conflicting prophetic utterances under consideration. Their many subtleties notwithstanding, Andersen and Freedman move straight to the telling conclusion: "Paradoxically, the carrying out of Yahweh's will also violated it."[13] We haven't gained much ground in actual guidance by such a claim. It certainly offers scant praise to Yahweh: Yahweh gets us coming and going. "Damnation if you do, damnation if you don't."

THE SPOKEN WORD OF YAHWEH AS POLITICAL ACT

A review of the commentators suggests how reluctant each seems about making a straightforward choice for one canonical prophet over the other. It is still not entirely clear why commentators avoid reading these texts as critical counterpoints that

---

[11] Yehezekel Kaufmann, *The Religion of Israel* (New York: Schocken Books, 1972), 369–70.

[12] Frances I. Andersen and David Noel Freedman, *Hosea*, Anchor Bible Commentary (New York: Doubleday, 1980).

[13] Andersen and Freedman, *Hosea*, 180.

demand a choice. Commitment to a uniform, noncontradictory notion of Scripture, whether or not confessionally held, may be one explanation. Such a hermeneutic may finally prove harder to maintain logically as an ever-wider audience begins to read Scripture as literature, if not as a source for meaning and truth.

In the very juxtaposition of these canonical prophets, Scripture is modeling reading strategies crucial for negotiating the ethical minefields between the lines of conflicting biblical texts. Scripture models for us, through just such internal debates, a call to commitment and advocacy, even at the risk of being wrong (or accused by other readers and prophets as misreading God's will).

Hosea certainly stands strong in his commitments against the sacred tradition of Elijah and Elisha on the question of Jehu's brutal victory. For Hosea, the word of God was sharper than any two-edged sword of Jehu. As Millard Lind has so carefully shown, Hosea saw himself standing in the prophetic lineage of Moses (6:5; 12:14; cf. Deut. 18:18). Like Moses, Hosea is the bearer of the word of God, a word that has power to stand against kings and priests. Hosea's positive assessment of the prophet's role contrasts to his negative take on the role of kings (7:3, 7; 8:4; 9:15; 13:9-11). Hosea strongly believed that the word of Yahweh could once again bring down kings.[14]

Like the writers of the book of Kings, who recorded the Elijah and Elisha traditions, Hosea viewed the efficacy and fulfillment of God's word as important criteria for defending Yahweh's truth-yielding power. It mattered that Yahweh's word be shown to be fulfilled. Commitment to fulfillment as the final arbiter of truthfulness by both prophetic traditions underscores the claim here that Hosea cared about the *way* Yahweh's word was fulfilled as much as the *fact* of its fulfillment. Even though Andersen and Freedman were reluctant to side fully with Hosea in making the means of fulfillment as important as the ends, they were right about needing to choose one true prophet over the other. In their paradoxical conclusion, they chose ethical ambiguity over form-

---

[14] Lind, "Exasperated Love," 401-2.

critical clarity. Like so many commentators, they lacked the courage to make the same judgment that Hosea himself was willing to make in the face of counter-Yahweh speech.

In an odd sense, the spoken word of Yahweh (the Yahweh speech) was, for Hosea, a political act as potent as Jehu's sword. Speech was action and could be trusted to do its job actively in the world, as speech. Yahweh's word was the means to the end of its fulfillment—without the need to defend it through bloody, violent coercion. Yahweh was the only true king and was able to "strike by the prophets" and to "slay them by the words of my [Yahweh's] mouth" (6:5). Unlike the Near Eastern function of power politics, Yahweh had brought defenseless Israel out of Egypt with his own strong arm, humbling the great Pharaoh by his word.[15] Hosea lived as if the prophets were once again effective instruments through whom God could deal a decisive blow.[16] Kingship, even if allowed by Hosea, had its roots in rebellion against the rule of Yahweh, whose rule was communicated through the prophets, not the king.[17] Insofar as Yahweh's speeches to Jehu conflicted with Hosea's uncompromising hermeneutic, Hosea judged them to be wrong. Apparently Hosea saw what Lind would also come to see and argue for: Yahweh's exclusive prerogative in matters of warfare and defense. The question is whether we agree with Hosea over Elijah and Elisha on this question. It matters.

From the point of view of Hosea, the Elijah and Elisha tradition was mistaken. Hosea circumscribes the earlier Jehu traditions—especially those would-be Yahwistic claims advocating power politics that too soon turn violent and bloody in the name of God.

---

[15] Lind, "Exasperated Love," 401–2.

[16] Wolff, *Confrontations with Prophets*, 22.

[17] Millard C. Lind, "Reflections on Biblical Hermeneutics," in *Kingdom, Cross, and Community*, ed. J. R. Burkholder and Calvin W. Redekop (Scottdale, Pa.: Herald Press, 1976), 97.

A HERMENEUTIC OF COMMITMENT

Our study brings us to several broader conclusions about doing biblical theology in a pluralistic world. Could it be that "the true shape of the Bible as canon consists of its unrecorded hermeneutics which lie between the lines of most of its literature"?[18] Could it be that what is truly canonical for the reader has as much to do with how a text or tradition is read by another biblical tradition as what is said by either? The Bible models for us the interpretive principles of dispute and advocacy, dialogue and commitment.

First, the Bible models for us the principle of dialogue, even dispute. As such, we need not fear the Bible's own internal controversies, but see them as part of healthy discernment. In epistemological terms, the Bible's contradictions aid in its truth-bearing revelation. The Bible in all its canonical heterogeneity models for us its own self-correcting dialogue. Such intrabiblical conversations acknowledge that every minority and majority tradition in the Bible is in a sense "sectarian" and has a canonical right to be heard.

The Bible includes multiple voices, some in harmony, but others in serious conflict. Both Hosea and Elijah and Elisha are represented around the literary table of the biblical canon. The Bible affirms that just as a reader-prophet within the pages of Scripture is bound in some sense by his or her context, so also it is true for us. The shape of truth or falsehood is effected by the truth or falsehood of our particular understanding of a specific impression of God's will for a given historical hour. In short, Scripture affirms and even insists on dialogue between disagreeing others as a positive scriptural norm.

Second, though a canonical reading of Scripture has shown that every reader must give each tradition its due in open debate, we are also challenged by Scripture to take a decisive hermeneutic stance: commitment and advocacy. Hosea did not hesitate to pass

---

[18] James A. Sanders, *Canon and Community* (Philadelphia: Fortress, 1984), 46.

critical judgment upon an earlier tradition. He risked the challenge of his own ambiguous reality to declare against an earlier authoritative tradition what he believed to be true. As such, the Bible as canon models for us a hermeneutics of commitment, insisting that we courageously choose and advocate now this or that biblical tradition in keeping with counsel of the Spirit as understood in our interpretative communities.

The hermeneutics of commitment functioned long before canonical shape took its final form and was a necessary process in constructing the final content of sacred Scripture. And the hermeneutics of commitment continue on even after the canon of Scripture has been closed. In effect, canonical function is and has always been an open-ended process by believing communities as modeled by Scripture, even as the shape and content of the Bible reached its closure. Readers of Scripture still hold the responsibility to act with canonical authority as modeled by Hosea and others within Scripture when discerning and judging between conflicting biblical traditions and texts. Thus, believing communities are still canon-making communities in function, if no longer so in deciding the extent of the Bible's shape and content. Such commitment and advocacy remain a sobering honor for all readers of Holy Writ, no less so than for those who wrote, compiled, and judged what traditions were worthy of the name Scripture in the first place.

Finally, if it is true that intrabiblical prophetic conflicts serve as a model for doing theology between disagreeing believers, then the ethics of reading and practice—also negotiated between communities of interpretation—must come to play a crucial role in deciding between conflicting prophetic utterances within and beyond Holy Writ. Given the bloody human record of defending one's own "truth-claim" against another's apparent "falsehood," it is imperative to insist on a hermeneutic of nonviolence as a first principle in negotiating our differences. Can we not insist with Hosea that God's word alone (for us in all its glorious ambiguity) has more potency than a thousand swords of Jehu? In short, do we believe that God's word as understood by fallible humans can stand on its own in debate, without need for violent, coercive acts to ensure its fulfillment?

Hosea took a prophetic stance against the Elijah and Elisha narratives and refused to endorse Jehu's bloody fulfillment of God's word as commanded by Yahweh. Thus he models a commitment closer to that other great prophet of the Word made flesh, and so has my vote. Is such a stance truer than other biblical and reader-oriented claims to the contrary? If we are true to Scripture, the answer to that question must continue to be negotiated. "Whoever is wise, let him [or her] understand these things" (Hos. 14:9, RSV).

4

Healing Justice

The Prophet Amos and a
"New" Theology of Justice

TED GRIMSRUD

INTRODUCTION

When I was a doctoral student in the mid–1980s, I had the privilege of taking a yearlong seminar on justice from Professor Karen Lebacqz of Pacific School of Religion. At the time, Lebacqz was in the process of writing a two-volume theological study on justice.[1] As we read and discussed works such as John Rawls's classic *A Theory of Justice*,[2] and Robert Nozick's critique and alternative *Anarchy, State, and Utopia*,[3] I found myself increasingly disenchanted with these modern philosophical theories.

I was uneasy with Rawls's and Nozick's points of view, and I saw them having many problems in common — problems particularly troubling to me in light of my own faith commitments. Both reflect problematic assumptions (or faith commitments). I will mention a few, in general terms, not so much in an attempt to criticize them significantly, but rather to see if an alternative might be constructed.

---

[1] Karen Lebacqz, *Six Theories of Justice: Perspectives from Philosophical and Theological Ethics* (Minneapolis: Augsburg, 1986), and *Justice in an Unjust World: Foundations for a Christian Approach to Justice* (Minneapolis: Augsburg, 1987).

[2] Cambridge: Harvard University Press, 1971.

[3] New York: Basic Books, 1974.

Briefly, these assumptions (sometimes more true of one than the other, but largely applicable to both) include the following:

1. A fundamental rationalism, an assumption that we can come up with a notion of justice that all "reasonable" people can accept;
2. an emphasis on self-interest, a kind of faith that a balance of self-interest will lead to the common good for society;
3. individualism, an identification of the autonomous individual as the basic unit of moral discernment;
4. an emphasis on what seem to be quite abstract principles, such as "equality," "fairness," "liberty," and "entitlement";
5. a utopianism (in the sense that utopia means "nowhere") that is ahistorical and uninterested in historical developments regarding concrete justices and injustices;
6. a bracketing of any discussion of religious and faith and a rejection of any notion of "particularism"; and
7. a focus on Western consumption of goods and notions of liberty as if these are the ultimate human values.

Because of my unease with this general approach to justice, I decided to look at the Bible to see if something there that might provide help in formulating an alternative approach. I wrote a letter to my Old Testament professor, Millard Lind of the Associated Mennonite Biblical Seminary, asking if he had any help to offer. Professor Lind kindly sent me several papers, including a most-helpful essay, then unpublished, "Transformation of Justice: From Moses to Jesus."[4]

---

[4] "Transformation of Justice" was first published in 1986 as part of the Mennonite Central Committee's series of Occasional Papers of the MCC Canada Offender Ministries Program and the MCC U.S. Office of Criminal Justice. It was also included in Lind's book *Monotheism, Power, Justice: Collected Old Testament Essays* (Elkhart, Ind.: Institute of Mennonite Studies, 1990), 82–97. My references here will be to the latter version. Millard's graciousness in responding to my inquiry was typical of his approach to his students. I offer this essay in gratitude to his scholarship and his personal kindness.

Lind is one of the few pacifist theologians and biblical scholars I know who has accepted the challenge of trying to rethink justice. A pacifist theory of justice that could serve as an alternative to
the problematic approaches mentioned above continues to be an
urgent need.[5]

This essay is one more fragmentary attempt to point toward
a thoroughgoing Christian pacifist approach to justice. I strongly
believe, following Lind, that the Old Testament is a crucial
resource for such a resource. In fact, if we can get beyond what
Canadian social theorist George Grant called "English-speaking
justice"[6] (in other words, beyond the Western philosophical tradition represented in recent years by Rawls and Nozick) and look at
the biblical materials on justice (including the Old Testament) on
their own terms, we will find that they are a tremendous resource
for a pacifist approach to justice.

---

[5] Other attempts to address this need include the following: C. Norman Kraus, "Toward a Biblical Perspective on Justice" (unpublished
paper presented to Mennonite Central Committee Peace Theology Collo-
quium, Elkhart, Ind., Nov. 1978); Ted Grimsrud, "Peace Theology and the
Justice of God in the Book of Revelation," in *Essays in Peace Theology and
Witness*, ed. Willard M. Swartley, (Elkhart, Ind.: Institute of Mennonite
Studies, 1988), 135–53; Harry Huebner, "Justice and the Biblical Imagination," in Harry Huebner and David Schroeder, *Church as Parable: Whatever
Happened to Ethics?* (Winnipeg: CMBC Publications, 1993), 120–46; Glen
H. Stassen, "Narrative Justice as Reiteration," in *Theology Without Foundations: Religious Practice and the Future of Theological Truth*, eds. Stanley
Hauerwas, Nancey Murphy, and Mark Nation (Nashville: Abingdon,
1994), 201–25; Perry B. Yoder, *Shalom: The Bible's Word for Salvation, Justice, and Peace* (Newton, Kans.: Faith & Life Press, 1987). Howard Zehr,
not a professional theologian, is one of the grandfathers of the restorative
justice movement in the criminal justice field and has written an insightful study *Changing Lenses: A New Focus for Crime and Justice* (Scottdale, Pa.:
Herald Press, 1990). Karen Lebacqz's two books mentioned above are
also important resources but were not written from an explicitly pacifist
point of view.

[6] George P. Grant, *English-Speaking Justice* (Sackville, N.B.: Mount
Allison University Press, 1974).

In this paper, I will focus on one Old Testament text that speaks of justice in particular, the book of Amos. My assumption, which I cannot do more than assert here, is that Amos is a *representative* text. What we find in Amos concerning justice we also find elsewhere in the Bible.

HISTORICAL SETTING

The oracles in the book of Amos were addressed to the ruling elite of the ancient Jewish kingdom of Israel. Israel, the Northern Kingdom, had split off from Judea. Amos especially challenged the ruling elite in Samaria, which was the capital and primary center of urban power of mid-eighth century Israel (BCE).[7]

Israel knew peace and prosperity in the mid-eighth century. The main superpower of the day, Assyria, was not much of a factor internationally (at least temporarily, it turned out), due to its internal problems, nor was anyone else. Given this lack of outside interference, Israel reached its largest geographical size during the reign of King Jeroboam II in 786–746 BCE. The book of Amos gives glimpses of the people's enthusiastic self-confidence (6:1; 8:3) and their popular religiosity, which held that the nation's prosperity was the inevitable result of its faithfulness to God.

However, all was *not* well—which is why Amos came from Tekoa in the south to prophesy. Israel had a tradition of egalitarianism as a society and was near the end of a social transformation. Some scholars attribute this egalitarianism to the "conquest" of Canaan following the Hebrews' liberation from Egypt, holding that this so-called conquest was really a peasant revolt followed by wide-ranging land reform.[8] The law and the social practices of Israel institutionalized a concern for marginalized, vulnerable people (such as widows and orphans), and a commitment to minimiz-

---

[7] Robert C. Coote, *Amos Among the Prophets: Composition and Theology* (Philadelphia: Fortress, 1981), 16.

[8] Coote, *Amos*, 28; cf. also Norman Gottwald, *The Tribes of Yahweh: A Sociology of the Religion of Liberated Israel, 1250–1050* (Maryknoll, N.Y.: Orbis, 1979).

ing the social stratification between a few wealthy and powerful elite and a mass of poor—even landless—peasants.[9]

A key aspect of this land reform was the inheritance system. It served not as a means of keeping control in the hands of a rich elite, but as a means whereby the peasantry could continue to control their own resources. Foundational to this system was the belief that Yahweh was ultimately the Lord of the land and holder of eminent domain.[10] The land was Yahweh's gift for the good of everyone, not for the sake or the profit of a few.

Closely connected with the inheritance system was a decentralized legal system—the court in the gates of the villages (the area that served essentially as the village's town square). One of the main concerns of this decentralized legal system was to help the weaker members of the society who otherwise were without power and influence. Without the justice of the court, they would not be able to maintain themselves in the social order.[11]

The Israelites' view of the covenant they had with God provided the "ideological" basis for this social ordering. God had established their nation in gracious love and desired the people to live in communion with God and with one another. The covenant community was accountable to God: if it did not maintain its faithfulness, it was liable to be judged.

Amos came onto the scene to announce that the threatened judgment was indeed about to be carried out. The social transformation of Israel was a decisive move *away from* covenant faithfulness.

Poverty and distress were widespread among the people at the bottom of the socioeconomic ladder. The inheritance system had faded away. Control of the land was shifting increasingly to

---

[9] Lind, "Transformation," 85.

[10] Coote, *Amos*, 28.

[11] James Luther Mays, *Amos: A Commentary* (Philadelphia: Westminster, 1969), 92.

the hands of a few centralized owners. These owners exploited the peasants for their own gain.[12]

The origins of this transformation dated back at least to the reign of Solomon. Walter Brueggemann summarizes Solomon's main "accomplishments" thus: (1) an economics of affluence; (2) a politics of oppression; and (3) the establishment of a controlled, static religion.[13] Several generations after Solomon, Israel's King Ahab epitomized this "royal consciousness" in the well-known case of his murderous expropriation of Naboth's vineyard—in blatant disregard of the inheritance laws (1 Kings 21). By the time of Amos, the situation had only worsened.

This realignment of land ownership cut to the heart of the community's commitment to "covenant loyalty" (Heb.: חֶסֶד; as in Exod. 20:6, "steadfast love"), which had led them to pay special attention to those on the bottom of society in living response to their liberator God. This God had cared for the Israelites when they were impoverished and enslaved in Egypt and had saved them so that they might take responsibility to show the nations what a community based on God's justice looks like.

AMOS'S GENERAL MESSAGE

In chapters one and two, Amos begins by prophesying against Israel's neighboring nations. This sets his listeners up for the punch line, which begins in 2:6. In speaking against the nations, Amos gains the sympathy of his listeners, who all agree that the nations are, of course, terrible and unjust.

However, beginning in 2:6, Amos charges *Israel* with crimes deserving the same decisive judgment. In these verses he focuses particularly on transgressions against the harmonious ordering of Israelite communal life: (1) selling into debt slavery the innocent

---

[12] Coote, *Amos*, 26–27.

[13] Walter Brueggemann, *The Prophetic Imagination* (Philadelphia: Fortress, 1978), 31.

and needy; (2) oppressing the poor; (3) abusing poor women; and (4) exploiting debtors.[14]

These transgressions, according to Amos, profane God's holy name (2:7). That is, "*every moral* infringement is an act of profanation of God's name. Every contempt and abuse of the weak and defenseless is ultimately a contempt of Yahweh himself."[15]

In 3:2, Amos turns Israel's complacent view of its place as God's chosen, covenant people *on its head*. He insists that privilege entails responsibility and that the unfaithful Israelites have been irresponsible. Therefore, they are even worse than the despised pagans who never knew God.[16]

Due to Israel's moral failure, the nation's salvation history will become judgment history in its near experience. Amos preaches a transcendent ethic. God is not identified with Israel as such; God is identified with *justice and righteousness*. When Israel itself is unjust, it also is judged.[17]

Because of its past history as the recipient of God's gracious acts, Israel knows that the cause of the needy is the cause of God.[18] Because the powers-that-be in Israel have forgotten God's justice, the society will be destroyed. The whole book of Amos contains impressive imagery that drives home this world-shattering thought.

The problem in Israel was not that the people did not intellectually know the precepts of the law or their concern for the needy. Rather, the leaders and judges simply refused to administer the law fairly. This refusal led to disregard for justice. And

---

[14] Hans-Walter Wolff, *Joel and Amos* (Philadelphia: Fortress, 1977), 165–67.

[15] Shalom M. Paul, *Amos: A Commentary on the Book of Amos* (Minneapolis: Fortress, 1991), 83 (emphasis original).

[16] John Barton, *Amos's Oracles Against the Nations: A Study of Amos 1:3–2:5* (New York: Cambridge University Press, 1980), 36; Paul, *Amos*, 101–2.

[17] Mays, *Amos*, 8.

[18] Wolff, *Joel*, 173.

worse, injustice ran rampant in the midst of thriving religiosity.[19] People flocked to the shrines but totally disregarded God's call for them to show justice to the needy. Amos's message is essentially that religion was making things *worse* for Israel. Their ritualistic faithfulness is masking ethical unfaithfulness.

Because of Israel's unfaithfulness, Amos proclaims, judgment is coming. The context for this judgment was Israel's history as God's covenant people. God had delivered them from Egypt and had given them the law to order their common life, and land on which to live out God's will. However, Israel was now rejecting God's ways of justice and goodness. In by doing so, they were breaking their side of the covenant. Destruction—actually, *self-destruction*—inevitably followed.

In Israel, a veneer of peace and prosperity covered a corrupt reality. Rather than being a sign of God's favor, this surface reality (even with its apparent peace and prosperity) and the process that created it, were about to be judged and destroyed by God. But this veneer could not forever hide the fact that so many people were poor while a few were rich and insensitive:

> [4]Alas for those who lie on beds of ivory,
>   and lounge on their couches,
> and eat lambs from the flock,
>   and calves from the stall;
> [5]who sing idle songs to the sound of the harp,
>   and like David improvise on instruments of music;
> [6]who drink wine from bowls,
>   and anoint themselves with the finest oils,
>   but are not grieved over the ruin of Joseph!
> [7]Therefore they shall now be the first to go into exile,
>   and the revelry of the loungers shall pass away.
>
> (Amos 6:4-7)

---

[19] Ronald E. Clements, *Prophecy and Covenant* (London: SCM, 1965), 76–77; Paul, *Amos*, 138–39.

Even worse, the rich *were contributing* to the problems of the poor. Even the court system—the one refuge of the poor—had been corrupted and turned on its head to serve the rich instead of the poor.

Amos gives an example in 2:6. "Thus says the LORD: For three transgressions of Israel, and for four, I will not revoke the punishment; because they sell the righteous for silver, and the needy for a pair of sandals." For rich creditors, money has more value than the people. The people who are needy become victims for insignificant reasons. In effect, Amos here is saying that the needy are sold "because they can not pay back the small sum they owe for a pair of sandals."[20]

This covenant disloyalty will result in judgment. In 4:6-11, Amos's narrative of disasters freely synthesizes traditional curses and depends on the general tradition that God acts in typical ways to judge those who are disloyal to the covenant.[21]

The book as a whole elaborates on this theme. "Morality was … the decisive factor in determining the ultimate destiny of the nation."[22] Amos 7:8 speaks of a moral plumb line, showing that the Israelites are like a leaning wall. Its misalignment is a metaphor for injustice. The Israelites have distorted God's intention for them (indeed, God's intentions for the nations, as well).

Amos says that despite choosing Israel for a special relationship, God *judges* Israel because of its injustice—especially the sort of injustice that injures people at the bottom of the socioeconomic scale, when people are systematically and purposefully deprived of their rightful status as full members of the covenant community.

Amos's condemnation is thoroughgoing. Unlike previous social critics, he does not say that the Israelites need only minor adjustments. He says, rather, that Israel has reached the end. Nevertheless, the canonical Amos does issue a few calls to turn back—

---

[20] Jan DeWaard and William Smalley, *A Translator's Handbook on the Book of Amos* (New York: United Bible Societies, 1979), 47.

[21] Mays, *Amos*, 80.

[22] Paul, *Amos*, 3.

implying that at least a remnant could still reconnect with God.[23] The book closes with a somewhat incongruous vision of hope in 9:11-15, a vision of redemption for a remnant. This is a kind of new exodus, a liberation from forced servitude and oppressive exploitation by the ruling elite.[24]

The book's final verses add a sense of God's ultimately *redemptive* purpose. As a whole, the book makes the point that God's people need to *live* according to God's justice. Those who do not will be judged (and self-destruct); those who do are given hope for the future. Without judgment, the poor would have no hope, since their oppressors would never be called to account. God's judgment is therefore born of God's love for the people of Israel.[25]

AMOS'S VIEW OF JUSTICE

The themes of justice and injustice pervade the book of Amos. The four texts that specifically use the term *mishpat* (מִשְׁפָּט) — usually translated "justice" — will illumine what Amos has in mind with this theme.

> [6] Seek the LORD and live,
>> or he will break out against the house of Joseph like fire,
>> and it will devour Bethel, with no one to quench it.
> [7] Ah, you that turn justice to wormwood,
>> and bring righteousness to the ground!   (5:6-7)

Justice and righteousness are clearly associated here with the presence of God as the life-bestowing force.

---

[23] For a survey of the discussion about whether the historical Amos held out any hope for the future and whether he uttered the oracles of salvation in Amos 9:11-15, see Gerhard F. Hasel, *Understanding the Book of Amos: Basic Issues in Current Interpretations* (Grand Rapids: Baker Books, 1991), 116-20.

[24] Coote, *Amos*, 123.

[25] Isaiah and Hosea, Amos's near contemporaries, also spoke of God's chastisement for the sake of God's people; cf. Isa. 19:22 and esp. Hos. 6:1, "Come, let us return to the LORD; for it is he who has torn, and he will heal us."

The people were calling evil good. The so-called "justice" at the gate had become injustice, and people were gaining wealth at the expense of the poor and weak. And they called the good evil (cf. Isa. 5:20). They abhorred the one who spoke the truth (Amos 5:10). In this manner, the Israelites were transforming what was sweet (justice) into something bitter (wormwood).

> [14] Seek good and not evil,
> that you may live;
> and so the LORD, the God of hosts, will be with you,
> just as you have said.
> [15] Hate evil and love good,
> and establish justice in the gate;
> it may be that the LORD, the God of hosts,
> will be gracious to the remnant of Joseph.   (5:14-15)

When Amos speaks of hating the advocate of the right and abhorring those who speak "the whole truth" (5:10), he apparently is referring to personal opposition to the essence of the court-justice system. Such opposition is, in God's eyes, an embrace of death.[26] True life in Israel can flourish only when God's concern for the weak is expressed in its social life. One key way this happens is when the justice at the gate is truly justice, when it is truly corrective of wrongs done. Israel is to "seek" good with a total dedication and wholeheartedness — and that "good" is clearly moral good in the social realm.[27]

Concern for this goes back to the legal code itself:

> You shall not pervert the justice due to your poor in their lawsuits. Keep far from a false charge and do not kill the innocent and those in the right, for I will not acquit the guilty. You shall take no bribe, for a bribe blinds the officials and subverts the cause of those who are in the right.
> (Exod. 23:6-8)

---

[26] Mays, *Amos*, 93; Paul, *Amos*, 170.
[27] Paul, *Amos*, 126.

The key to experiencing the presence of God, according to Amos, is not religiosity, but the exercise of justice between and among humans. The following passage emphasizes this point.

> [21] I hate, I despise your festivals,
>   and I take no delight in your solemn assemblies.
> [22] Even though you offer me your burnt offerings and grain offerings,
>   I will not accept them;
> and the offerings of well-being of your fatted animals
>   I will not look upon.
> [23] Take away from me the noise of your songs;
>   I will not listen to the melody of your harps.
> [24] But let justice roll down like waters,
>   and righteousness like an ever-flowing stream. (5:21-24)

Again, justice is connected here with *life*. Water is key to the sustaining of life in the desert. The community exists by doing justice. God finds Israel's worship unacceptable because Israel does not live as the community of God. Thus it is without life. "Ritual per se, with all its paraphernalia and panoply, simply cannot substitute for the basic moral and ethic actions of humans."[28]

For there to be life, justice and righteousness must roll down like floods after the winter rains *and* persist like those few streams that do not fail in the dry summer.

> Do horses run on rocks?
>   Does one plow the sea with oxen?
> But you have turned justice into poison
>   and the fruit of righteousness into wormwood.   (6:12)

The first part of this verse asks if the impossible could happen. The second part says that indeed the impossible can happen, that it is happening, and (implicitly) that the leaders of Israel are doing it.[29]

---

[28] Paul, *Amos*, 192.
[29] DeWaard and Smalley, *Handbook*, 137.

It is *incredible* to Amos that the rich can be content in their luxury and grieve not over the ruin of "Joseph," the destruction of the covenant community (6:6)—and that a place of justice (the court at the gate) can become unjust, poison. This staggers the mind, and he can only compare it with some incredible perversion of the natural order of things.[30]

KEY POINTS REGARDING JUSTICE IN AMOS

This leads us to observe several key points regarding justice in Amos. First, and most foundationally, Amos presents justice as inextricably tied up with life. Do justice and live, Amos asserts. Do injustice and die. Justice is not an abstract principle but rather a life force. An unjust society will die; it cannot help but collapse from its own weight. The goal of justice is life.

Second and more particularly, the goal justice seeks is life for *everyone* in the community. Because life is for everyone, justice pays particular attention to the people being denied life. Justice provides for access by *all* to the communal "good life." None can justly prosper at the expense of others, or even in the light of the poverty and need of others.

Third, Amos sees justice as part of the created order.[31] It is *unnatural* to be unjust, like a wall that is leaning, or an ox that is trying to plow the sea. To be unjust is inherently self-destructive. Injustice is the poison that kills its practitioners.

Fourth, Amos 1–2 shows that God's justice is intended for even the nations. The covenant people have special *responsibility,* due to their special awareness of God's justice. They are not punished more than the other nations; those too were destroyed, and Israel is the only one with a remnant. However, according to Amos, Israel's failure to practice justice destroys the hope of the nations. Israel's faithfulness is *for the sake of the nations,* that they might thus see the light of God's justice and love (cf. 9:7-12). When Israel is unfaithful, there is no light to be seen.

---

[30] Mays, *Amos,* 121; Paul, *Amos,* 219.
[31] Paul, *Amos,* 219.

Fifth, Amos sees justice as something to *do*: it establishes relationships, it meets needs, it corrects wrongs. Justice, in Amos, has nothing to do with meaningless religious rituals. Justice is concrete, practical, and historical. It is tied to specific acts and people. It is neither abstract nor ahistorical.

Sixth, the ultimate goal of God's justice is redemption (cf. 9:11-15). Even the judgment God metes out on Israel is for that end. It is intended to correct Israel's self-destructive injustice. The threats, warnings, and judgment of God are not for the sake of punishment as an end in itself. They are not a matter of retribution, of repaying rebellious Israel an "eye for an eye." Rather, the threats and warnings offer hope of salvation, of transformation. But if Israel does not respond, God will respect Israel's free will enough to allow its collapse as a nation-state. As we well know, this is precisely what happened: Israel played power politics to the end and succumbed to the much-superior power of Assyria.

THOUGHTS ON BIBLICAL JUSTICE IN GENERAL

Life as the Goal of Justice

In conclusion, we see in Amos's teaching—and elsewhere in the Bible—that *justice is for the sake of life*. God's justice in the Old Testament is not primarily a matter of retribution but of salvation—not primarily punitive but corrective.[32] The justice of God is power that saves God's fidelity to the role as the Lord of the covenant. Hosea 2:19 makes this point clearly: "I will take you for my wife forever; I will take you for my wife in righteousness and in justice, in steadfast love, and in mercy."[33]

The Hebrew Scriptures picture God as the one who created the earth and its inhabitants for harmonious relationships and who continually acts, even in the midst of human rebellion, to effect those relationships.

---

[32] Zehr, *Changing Lenses*, 139.

[33] Among other texts, see also Ezek. 34:16; Ps. 25:9; Isa. 1:27; and Jer. 9:24.

The Jewish and early Christian understanding of God's justice put the primary emphasis on the divine initiative, on God's readiness to do for his human creatures what they could not do for themselves, on God's readiness to "go the second mile" and more.[34]

In the Old Testament, justice is not primarily a legal concept; rather, it merges with concepts such as "steadfast love," "compassion," "kindness," and "salvation."[35] Justice has ultimately to do with how a loving Creator has made the world. To be just means living according to the Creator's will, in harmony with God, with fellow human beings, and with the rest of creation — *and* not resting until this justice has become a reality for everyone else too.

Justice as Part of the Created Order

As a second general point about the biblical perspective, we see that *justice is part of the created order.* The Old Testament connects justice and life as part of its creation theology. Old Testament theology confessed "creation" to be an act of the covenant-making God of Israel.[36] Therefore, the basic character of *creation* stands in harmony with the values of the *covenant* that sustain and nourish life — with love, justice, peace, and compassion. The Old Testament allows for no disjunction between the Creator God and the covenant-making God. Creation was, in fact, God's first covenant-making act. Thus, covenant values are part of the very fabric of creation.

This means that human life has meaning, purpose, and destiny. Human life originated as an expression of God's covenant-love. So all human action that is in harmony with God's covenant love has meaning and is part of the basic meaning of creation ... and is thereby "just."

---

34 James D. G. Dunn, *The Justice of God: A Fresh Look at the Old Doctrine of Justification by Faith* (Grand Rapids: Eerdmans, 1993), 35.

35 Eliezer Berkovits, *Man and God: Studies in Biblical Theology* (Detroit: Wayne State University Press, 1969), 331.

36 Lind, "Transformation," 95.

The creation of humans in the image of this God means that all people need relationships, with each other and with God. The purpose of human activity is to facilitate these relationships. Since all people, simply by virtue of being people, are in the image God and thus have dignity and value, discrimination and disregard of any human life can never be justified. Injustice severs relationships. Justice establishes and/or restores relationships.

God's will has to do with *all* parts of creation. Nothing is autonomous from that will. The Old Testament challenges people of faith to carry out the Creator's will in all spheres of human existence.

Ultimately, the Old Testament makes no distinction between the order of creation and the order of redemption. The Creator God and the Redeemer God are one and the same. Faithfulness to the "creation mandate" means living lives of love and justice.

Justice as the Destruction of Evil

Third, *justice is not soft on evil but rather seeks to destroy evil.* This is an expression of God's justice. However, such justice is rooted in God's love for all humans. God's love for enemies means that God hates what evil does to humankind, and God works to heal its effects. Evil ends only when the cycle of evil-fighting-evil is broken. The Old Testament model for this is the suffering servant in Isaiah — for Christians the precursor to Jesus — who did not retaliate but accepted all that the powers of evil could do and conquered them. This is the ultimate model for biblical justice.[37]

God destroys evil, ultimately not through coercive force but through suffering love. This biblical theme comes to its completion in the book of Revelation, where the Lamb, Jesus Christ, wins the final battle with the powers of evil through his cross and resurrection (cf. Rev. 19:11-21).[38]

God's love works to set right that which has been corrupted. This is *justice*. One way of characterizing justice, therefore, is to say

---

[37] Lind, "Transformation," 89–90.
[38] Grimsrud, "Peace Theology," 144–46.

that justice is how love is expressed in the face of evil. Love expressed in the face of evil acts to stop the evil and to heal its effects. That is, it is redemptive and salvific.

God's justice creates life and acts to sustain and restore life. Human justice, in the Old Testament sense, is truly justice only when it acts to sustain and restore life. As Howard Zehr writes,

> Since biblical justice seeks to make things better, justice is not designed to maintain the status quo. Indeed, its intent is to shake up the status quo, to improve, to move toward shalom.[39]

Justice as Normative for the Nations

Fourth, the Old Testament people believed that *God's justice is normative for the nations as well as for Israel*. When Amos condemns the nations for their injustices, no one would have questioned whether it was legitimate for him to do so. God's will was for *all* people, and all people were to be held accountable to how they responded to that will. Justice is imbedded in creation, which is why injustice is as unnatural as an ox plowing the sea or a wall that is leaning.

The belief that the nations are accountable to God led to primarily negative conclusions (such as those Amos expresses) about their actual practice of justice. The Israelites widely accepted that God would judge the nations for being unjust. But there are scattered examples of just people outside Israel (e.g., Ruth; Rahab the harlot; the repentant people of Nineveh in Jonah; perhaps Cyrus, the Persian). Ezekiel even uses three non-Israelites—Noah, Daniel, and Job—as prime models of righteousness.[40] These examples indicate that God's justice is knowable and doable by anyone—by virtue of being human.

---

[39] Zehr, *Changing Lenses*, 140.

[40] Ezek. 14:14; cf. Millard Lind, *Ezekiel,* Believers Church Bible Commentary (Scottdale, Pa.: Herald Press, 1996), 120; cf. also *Harper's Bible Commentary,* ed. James Luther Mays (San Francisco: Harper & Row, 1988), 672.

In general, of course, the Old Testament portrays the nations as not *in fact* living according to God's will for justice, even if theoretically they could have been able to understand it and even follow it. Thus God's revelation to Israel was intended to show God's justice even more clearly than that seen in (now fallen) creation— and to provide a better means of empowerment for living it via the elected covenant-community.

The foundation of Israel's nationhood was God's judgment against the unjust Egyptians and the liberation of the Hebrews from oppression. The conquest and gaining of a homeland was couched in terms of God's judgment against the land's previous inhabitants for their injustice. When Israel itself became oppressive, Yahweh waged war *against Israel* (cf. Jer. 6; Amos 5; Ezek. 17; Isa. 31). God's utmost concern is with justice, and God's intervention is aimed at that goal, even when that means judging God's own specially called people.[41]

In Amos 1–2, the prophet speaks in general terms of blatant injustices among the nations. From 2:6 on he speaks more specifically to Israel. This is not primarily because the nations were in principle incapable of perceiving the need to be just in the ways Israelites were taught. Rather, it reflects the idea that Israel's calling entailed a closer relationship with God. More was expected of Israel—for the sake of the nations. The nations would perceive true justice when they indeed saw it in Israel (without the aid of "special revelation") and, according to Isaiah's vision, flock to Mt. Zion to share in it (Isa. 2:1-4).

Justice as Concern for the Vulnerable

A fifth general point is that *God's justice is especially concerned with the most vulnerable members of society.*[42] The biblical teaching

---

[41] José Porfirio Miranda, *Marx and the Bible: A Critique of the Philosophy of Oppression* (Maryknoll, N.Y.: Orbis Books, 1974), 6.

[42] Zehr, *Changing Lenses*, 139–40. See also, Perry B. Yoder, *Shalom*, 24–38; and Nicholas Wolterstorff, *Until Justice and Peace Embrace* (Grand Rapids: Eerdmans, 1983), 69–72.

ends up emphasizing the poor and needy so much because in their oppression they were being excluded from community life and from the *shalom* God wills for everyone. This destroys community and eventually lessens the well-being of each person in the community.

Jeremiah identifies doing justice to the weak with "knowing" God (22:13-16). Those who "understand and know me" are those who recognize that "I am LORD; I act with steadfast love, justice, and righteousness in the earth, for in these things I delight" (Jer. 9:24). This is true for God; it is likewise God's expectation for people. Expressing love toward one's fellow human being is the inescapable condition for having communion with God. "Sow for yourselves righteousness [or justice], reap steadfast love, ... for it is time to seek the LORD" (Hos. 10:12). This becomes a call to conversion: "Return to your God, hold fast to love and justice, and wait continually for your God" (Hos. 12:6).

Such communal justice was not to be for the Israelites' own sake alone. The purpose of justice within Israel was ultimately for worldwide justice. Even in the story of Israel's initial election in Genesis 18, a major reason given for it is to bring about "justice and right" for all humankind.[43]

IMPLICATIONS

The Bible helps us understand justice. Biblical teaching redefines justice in ways that help us *do* justice in a largely unjust world. As Lind writes, "Biblical justice speaks to the world's problems of justice, and it speaks so radically (to the 'root' of the matter) that it changes the definition of justice."[44]

The Bible emphatically identifies love with justice. This inextricable connection guards us against rationalizing the treatment of some people as objects instead of as human beings—all in the name of "justice." Such "justice" becomes a dehumanizing power

---

[43] Millard C. Lind, "Law in the Old Testament," in *Monotheism, Power, Justice*, 73.

[44] Lind, "Transformation," 95.

struggle with winners and losers. And because losers are so seldom content with being losers, the battle never ends.

Holding love and justice together also guards against thinking of justice as an abstraction, separate from its function as a relationship-building, life-sustaining force. The concern for justice is *people*, much more than "fairness," "liberty," or "entitlements." "Biblical justice focuses on right relationships, not right rules."[45]

In this way of thinking, justice is primarily corrective or restorative justice.[46] Justice seeks *reconciliation*. Injustice must be opposed and resisted, but only in ways that hold open the possibility of reconciliation. What happens to the oppressors matters, too, if justice is the goal. And corrective justice rules out death-dealing acts as tools of justice, such as war and capital punishment.

In this way of thinking, *self-interest* in the narrow, individualistic way it is used by modern philosophers cannot serve as a motivating force for true justice. Biblical teachings on creation and Providence support the idea that considering God's will and the good of the community above one's own narrow, individualistic self-interest is, in the long run, the best for one's own good as well.

Biblical justice actually has many parallels with other indigenous viewpoints on justice.[47] We see this illustrated in the novels of Tony Hillerman. In a series of mystery stories, set among the Navajo in Arizona and New Mexico, Hillerman explores the tensions between indigenous views of life and justice and "English-speaking" views.

In the novel *Sacred Clowns*,[48] Hillerman brings these tensions out into the open. One of the main characters is Jim Chee, a tradi-

---

[45] Zehr, *Changing Lenses*, 153.

[46] Cf. Zehr's chapter "A Restorative Lens," in *Changing Lenses*, 177–214.

[47] For an accessible and insightful discussion of indigenous understandings of justice, see Rupert Ross, *Returning to the Teachings: Exploring Aboriginal Justice* (Toronto: Penguin Books, 1996).

[48] Tony Hillerman, *Sacred Clowns* (New York: HarperCollins, 1993), 269–273.

tional Navajo who is an officer with the Navajo tribal police. Chee becomes close friends with Janet Pete, a lawyer who is part Navajo but who grew up and was educated in white society. Chee's relationship with Pete is a subplot over a series of novels. The differences between their respective worldviews ultimately torpedo their relationship. In *Sacred Clowns*, Hillerman presents an explicit interchange that brings to the surface how indigenous justice differs from English-speaking justice.

Chee and Pete discuss the case of a hit-and-run driver. The alleged violator is basically a good person. He's a widower who is a conscientious worker and rarely drinks. However, on his birthday some friends take him to a bar and he gets drunk. On his way home, he hits a pedestrian, but when he stops, in his unfamiliar drunken haze he does not see anything so he continues on home. Chee, as a police officer, is given the task of finding this offender. He asks Pete what he should do.

She responds from the perspective of English-speaking justice. Maybe it is not that nice, she says, but the answer is clear. The reason we have laws is to punish misbehavior of this sort. Actions such as drunk driving and leaving the scene of an accident hurt people. When such things happen, the job of police officers is to find the offender, arrest him or her, present the evidence in court, and make sure the offender pays the consequences. In a case like this, when the offender is not a habitual offender, the punishment might be fairly light, a year or so in prison and several more on probation.

Chee then makes the case more complicated. He sees the guy as having important responsibilities for his grandson. The grandson was abandoned by his parents and is disabled. In other words, he is dependent upon the offender, who treats the child with love and respect.

Pete insists this doesn't change anything. These circumstances are basically irrelevant in the face of "justice." "Justice" means objectively following the laws society passes. If the laws are violated, there must be retribution. "Justice" must be served.

Here we come to the crux of the differences. Chee reflects on the meaning of justice. As a religious Navajo who honors his people's traditions, he has been taught a different concept of justice. It was not until he was an adult that he learned about "making the punishment fit the crime" or "an eye for an eye, a tooth for a tooth." As a child, he was taught that when harm is done, the response is to try to find ways to bring about restoration of harmony. If you do something wrong, you try to find ways to bring restitution for the damage. If a person continues to cause harm out of meanness, then you understand that person to be out of harmony. The response the community makes to a person who is out of harmony — in sharp contrast to English-speaking justice — is not to seek to punish, but to seek to cure, to bring *healing* to the offender. "You aren't taught he should be punished. He should be cured. Gotten back in a balance with what's around him. Made beautiful again."[49]

So, even though he works for an agency patterned on English-speaking justice, Chee himself places no value on punishment. What he values is healing, making whole, restoring a person like the hit-and-run driver to harmony with the community and to beauty within himself. In the end, Chee chooses not to arrest the hit-and-run driver, but to take help facilitate the man's healing.

Biblical justice has more in common with Navajo justice than it does with English-speaking justice. A pacifist approach to justice would do well to incorporate central motifs from the biblical view. Justice is, above all, about *healing*, about bringing wholeness and restoring beauty and harmony. Such interests are more central than retribution, impersonal fairness, the balancing of self-interests, or simply the equal distribution of consumer goods and services.

---

[49] Hillerman, *Sacred Clowns*, 272.

5

Denouncing Lies, Modeling Truth
Lent and Easter Reflections on Jeremiah and Jesus

ARTHUR PAUL BOERS

The fifty-two-chapter book of Jeremiah is generally not given serious attention on Sundays. It is seldom cited in the three-year Revised Common Lectionary, even though it is particularly appropriate for Lent and Easter. Selecting Jeremiah passages does pose dangers. One might choose what conveniently fits, using texts to reinforce the Christian Scriptures, which is how the lectionary often treats the Hebrew Scriptures. Even so, Matthew gives precedent for connecting Jeremiah to Lent and Easter. And the passages considered here do reflect major themes in Jeremiah and are thus among the most studied by Jeremiah scholars.

Through Jeremiah's lens, we will reflect on Ash Wednesday, Palm Sunday, Passion Week, and Easter Sunday. We will present the passages and their reflections in two sets. In the first two, Jesus and Jeremiah denounce lies, temptations, and false securities.[1] In the second set, Jesus and Jeremiah proclaim and model new realities.

---

[1]*Sheqer* (שֶׁקֶר) is a significant term in Jeremiah. It is "commonly translated 'lie, falsehood, deception.' While this noun is ... frequent within the Old Testament ... (111 occurrences), there is such a sudden burst of occurrences in ... Jeremiah that one immediately suspects that the concept of falsehood had a special significance in the message of that prophet." Thomas W. Overholt, *The Threat of Falsehood* (London: SCM, 1970), 1.

May our reflections bring us into a closer relationship with and obedience to God.

> Do not let the wise boast in their wisdom, do not let the mighty boast in their might, do not let the wealthy boast in their wealth; but let those who boast boast in this, that they understand and know me, that I am the LORD; I act with steadfast love, justice, and righteousness in the earth, for in these things I delight, says the LORD. (Jer. 9:23-24)[2]

ASH WEDNESDAY
AMEND YOUR WAYS AND YOUR DOINGS
Matthew 6:1-18; Jeremiah 7:1-12

In these texts, Jesus and Jeremiah called into question important religious institutions. All that they attacked, fellow believers held sacred. Both criticized mechanical, magical notions of devotion. They showed that God is not manipulated by almsgiving, multiplying prayerful words, fasting, or even worshiping in the holy temple.

Jeremiah 7:1-12 parallels chapter 26. Jeremiah went to Judah's central religious institution, the temple, to preach repentance. His challenge was so radical that he was threatened with death (26:8-11) and later barred from the temple (36:5).

The temple was crucial to Judah's faith. Even during turmoil and threat, people did not worry about defeat: "This is the temple of the LORD, the temple of the LORD, the temple of the LORD" (7:4), they used to say. They meant, in effect, "God lives in this building; we are secure and need not fear." This confidence in God's protection of the temple was a prophetic tradition. A hundred years earlier, Isaiah had "staked his reputation … on the inviolability of the city of Jerusalem: read Isaiah 31:4-5 or 37:33-35."[3] When Isaiah's prediction was fulfilled, people concluded that the previous pro-

---

[2] References to chapter and verse without citation of a biblical book are to Jeremiah unless the context shows otherwise.

[3] William Holladay, *Jeremiah: Spokesman Out of Time* (New York: Pilgrim Press, 1974), 64.

mise in the presence of a particular threat (Sennacherib) was an eternal, unconditional promise. There may also have been reinforced self-confidence resulting from Josiah's reform.[4]

We still hear such attitudes. Some believe that the U.S. is God's chosen nation and has nothing to fear. (They forget the exiles and persecutions of God's "chosen nation" Israel.) In recent memory, U.S. leaders—political *and* religious!—defined the Cold War as good America versus the Evil Empire, Christ versus antichrist, Christianity versus Communism. During the Persian Gulf War, similar claims were couched in Christian terms as political and religious establishments rushed into an unholy alliance.

We in the church often believe we have a mandate over God. In 1980, I spent an intense week of discussion with William Stringfellow and a group of pastors. The pastors were most provoked when he asked, "Has God abandoned the church?"

> If the question sounds strange in our ears, it is because American Christendom is so complacent concerning ... God. We suppose that God is indefinitely patient. And we construe this as a license for infidelity to the Word of God. Then we succumb to the temptation to so identify the Church with God that we act as if the Church *is* God. *That* idolatry of the church is the most incongruous and absurd form of apostasy.[5]

Jeremiah and Jesus did not criticize these rituals as intrinsically wrong, nor did they worry about right rituals performed with the wrong attitude. Rather, they were concerned about God's freedom from manipulation. Some believed that certain ceremonies and institutions *guaranteed* security, access to Yahweh, and defense against enemies. Jesus addressed and criticized such illusions in the Ash Wednesday Gospel text (Matt. 6:7-8). He rebuked "the mechanical, magical form of prayer used by people who think

---

[4] Holladay, *Jeremiah*, 65.

[5] William Stringfellow, *A Simplicity of Faith* (Nashville: Abingdon, 1982), 105.

that they can reach God by multiplying words or simply repeating certain formulas."[6]

Jeremiah urged people to abandon false security. People were evil but expected that the temple would protect them (7:8-11). Yahweh's name was slandered by such religion.

> You don't take the name of the Lord in vain with your lips. You take it in vain with your life. It isn't the people outside the church who take God's name in vain. They've never taken it so they can't take it in vain. It's the people on the inside ... whose lives are totally unchanged by the grace of God. They're the ones who take the name in vain.[7]

Jeremiah denounced the sort of faith that assumed that God could be worshiped by manipulation or that worship was permitted in any context. The people were *not* secure: the temple would be destroyed like that other famous sanctuary, Shiloh.

The church often perpetuates injustice and evil. Once Clarence Jordan went with an African-American to a white church. After being violently evicted, Jordan wryly noted: "Well, everything is integrated now, except the churches and jails — and I have hope for the jails."[8]

Church people are not the only ones who see our hypocrisy. When I ministered in Chicago's inner city, our afflicted neighborhood still reeled under injustices perpetuated by the infamous government of Mayor Daley. Mike Royko, in a stinging indictment of Chicago's "Boss," noted that Daley faithfully attended daily mass: "Regardless of what he may do in the afternoon and to whom, he will always pray in the morning."[9]

Jeremiah and Jesus maintained that worship conducted amid injustice is not true worship. Jeremiah asked people to amend their

---

[6] Jon Sobrino, *Christology at the Crossroads*, trans. John Drury (Maryknoll, N.Y.: Orbis Books, 1978), 148.

[7] Clarence Jordan, *The Substance of Faith*, ed. Dallas Lee (New York: Association Press, 1972), 135.

[8] Jordan, *Substance of Faith*, 124.

[9] Mike Royko, *Boss* (New York: Signet Books, 1971), 13.

"ways" and their "doings." He demanded that they execute justice, and not oppress powerless people; that they refrain from shedding innocent blood, and not pursue false gods (7:3, 5). Yahweh made a spectacular promise. If the people will do these things, Yahweh promised, "then I will dwell with you in this place, in the land that I gave of old to your ancestors forever and ever" (7:7). José Miranda puts this in a larger context, noting that Isaiah 1:12-17; Hosea 5:1, 2, 6; 6:6; 8:13; Amos 4:4-5; Micah 6:6-8; Jeremiah 6:18-21; and Isaiah 43:23-24; 58:2, 6-10 can all be summarized, "*I do not want cultus but interhuman justice.*"[10]

Jesus also was clear that obedience and justice are more important than religious observance. "*The question is not whether someone is seeking God or not, but whether [one] is seeking [God] where God ... said that [God] is.*"[11] Jesus reserved the harshest criticisms for pious hypocrites "who took pride in the fulfillment of religious trivialities but ignored 'the weightier matters of the law—justice, mercy, good faith!'" (Matt. 23:23).[12]

Thus Jesus, like Jeremiah, violated the sanctity of the temple. He valued human welfare over religious observance and broke the Sabbath to feed disciples (Matt. 12:1-8) and to heal (Matt. 12:9-14). "I desire mercy and not sacrifice" (Matt. 12:7; cf. Matt. 9:13; Hos. 6:6).

Rituals are acceptable only in the context of justice. God is exalted and worshiped in justice.[13] According to the prophets, the "meaning of 'to know Yahweh' is ... to have compassion for the needy and to do justice for them."[14] When Jeremiah rebuked a king, he recalled the sovereign's father:

---

[10] José Porfirio Miranda, *Marx and the Bible*, trans. John Eagleson (Maryknoll, N.Y.: Orbis Books, 1971), 56, emphasis original.

[11] Miranda, *Marx*, 57, emphasis original.

[12] Rafael Avila, *Worship and Politics*, trans. Alan Neely (Maryknoll, N.Y.: Orbis Books, 1981), 38.

[13] Abraham J. Heschel, *The Prophets*, vol. 1 (New York: Harper & Row, Publishers, 1962), 213–16.

[14] Miranda, *Marx*, 48.

Did not your father eat and drink
    and do justice and righteousness?
    Then it was well with him.
[16] He judged the cause of the poor and needy;
    then it was well.
Is not this to *know* me?
    says the LORD.   (22:15b-16, emphasis mine)

When we do injustice, we do not know God. Church labels do not make us invulnerable. Rather, claiming to be God's makes us vulnerable to God's demands. To understand Yahweh is to know that Yahweh is the One who acts "with steadfast love, justice, and righteousness in the earth" (9:24).

The seriousness of this is further emphasized if we let 7:16 "leak" into our considerations of 7:1-15.[15] Yahweh gave Jeremiah an astounding command: "As for you, do not pray for this people, do not raise a cry or prayer on their behalf, and do not intercede with me, for I will not hear you" (7:16). Although intercession is central to a prophet's vocation, here it is forbidden! (cf. also 11:14; 15:1).[16] The grim sense is that matters are beyond hope: "it is too late for any prayers to avail."[17]

Lent should prove a time of true faith, not petty piety. Our spiritual disciplines should help us see God, ourselves, and our relationship to the world more clearly. The question is whether we practice justice, mercy, and righteousness. Are our lives a testimony to the gospel, or a scandal? Are people hurt or alienated by us? Our Lenten disciplines should be occasions to deal with the hard questions of life. May the negative example of the temple worshipers (pun intended) warn us. Do we complacently settle for cheap grace?

---

[15] Verse 16 is part of a different pericope, yet 7:1–8:3 are integrally connected.

[16] Robert P. Wilson, *Prophecy and Society in Ancient Israel* (Philadelphia: Fortress, 1980), 240.

[17] Holladay, *Jeremiah*, 69.

These are not easy questions, but then Lent is not easy. Such questions are worth pursuing. At stake is nothing less than our knowledge and experience of God!

PALM SUNDAY
BLESSED IS THE ONE WHO COMES IN THE NAME OF THE LORD

Matthew 21:1-17; Jeremiah 27–28

Palm Sunday is one of the stranger Christian festivals. We proclaim with the crowd, "Hosanna in the highest!" Yet Passion Week also shows that a crowd not only praised Jesus but also condemned him. Why are the words of a fickle crowd noteworthy?

All the Synoptics link the triumphal entry and the temple cleansing. In Matthew, Jesus jubilantly enters Jerusalem and proceeds to the temple, where he "drove out all who were selling and buying in the temple, and he overturned the tables of the money changers and the seats of those who sold doves" (Matt. 21:12).[18] This raid is another example of Jesus' prophetic challenge to false religion. "Jesus is attacking prayer insofar as it is turned into an item of commerce and used to exploit others."[19] Referring to Jeremiah, he called the temple a veritable "den of robbers" (Matt. 21:13; cf. Jer. 7:11).

Jeremiah challenged the false prophets, who told two lies. They said the Exile would be short and that God had sanctioned rebellion against Nebuchadnezzar. Jeremiah pleaded over and again, "You, therefore, must not listen" (27:9, 14, 16). His counsel was politically subversive: Since God was using Nebuchadnezzar, the nation should submit to foreign occupation.

Jeremiah and Jesus dramatized their controversial messages with symbolic actions.

---

[18] The lectionary violates biblical accounts here: Palm Sunday is celebrated annually, but the temple clearance is remembered only one year in three and then disconnected from Palm Sunday. Yet the temple raid is recorded in all four Gospels.

[19] Sobrino, *Christology*, 150.

For antiquity, the sign, like the solemn word ... could not only signify a datum but actually embody it as well; ... it could act creatively, and in early cultures it probably had an even greater power to do so than the word.[20]

These actions were not *merely* symbolic but affected reality: God's future broke in and continues to break in to illustrate and even create new reality. Symbolic action reshapes paradigms and changes debates.[21]

The importance and power of Jeremiah's symbolic action is apparent in the virulence of Hananiah's attack. He not only refuted Jeremiah; he also broke Jeremiah's symbol, the yoke (28:10). Jeremiah did not merely brush off this violation but came back with a stronger symbol. He offered iron bars in place of the broken wooden bars (28:13).

Likewise, Jesus' symbolic action in the temple could not be ignored. No doubt the temple was soon back to business-as-usual after Jesus' raid. Yet Jesus' action made a deep impression and is one of few incidents included in all four Gospels. Some believe that this was a major catalyst behind the decision to execute Jesus.

Jeremiah and Jesus both gave their message in spite of great personal risk. Death threats were earlier invoked against both. Their messages compounded their risk of death. Both had opportunities to save themselves and both refused. Neither ameliorated, moderated, or abandoned his message.

---

[20] Gerhard von Rad, *The Message of the Prophets*, trans. D. M. G. Stalker (New York: Harper & Row, 1965), 74. John Bright notes that in "the mind of the day ... [a symbolic action] was not understood merely as the dramatic illustration of a point, or playacting, but as the actual setting in motion of Yahweh's destroying word" (John Bright, *Jeremiah* [New York: Doubleday, 1965], 133).

[21] Contemporary examples of the creative power of the symbolic act include the daring protests of civil rights advocates opposing segregation. Simple acts, such as attempting to eat in diners, reshaped the reality and the debate for many. At first complacent, many Americans realized the urgency of needed change only after seeing the protests on television.

Jesus' triumphal entry put him in trouble with the authorities. Had he paused to let the crowd calm down or to leave things ambiguous, he might have lived longer. Instead, he used the momentum to *heal* the temple by protest—and to heal blind and lame persons, too. Likewise, Jeremiah was offered respite when Hananiah broke Jeremiah's prophecy. If the dialogue had ended there, things might have been peaceful. Instead, Jeremiah, like Jesus, could not leave bad enough alone. He returned and prophesied more forcefully. He was not content to speak once or twice (20:9), and his compulsion was costly.

Here particularly we see the political import of Jesus' life, ministry, death, and resurrection. The church covers up such politics. Perhaps that is why the lectionary exorcises accounts of the temple raid from Holy Week. Yet the issues *are* political. Jesus was connected to a prophecy about kingship (Zech. 9). Jeremiah had the gall (chap. 27) to address not only his king, but foreign kings too. His prophetic word even had authority over foreign countries. False religion is not about trivial doctrinal differences. It has to do with the nitty-gritty of life, with oppressive politics.

Walter Brueggemann shows the intrinsic interrelation between the economics of affluence, the politics of oppression, and the religion of immanence.[22] His studies reveal the dynamic equivalence with our time. Modern-day rhetoric about deficit spending covers official antipathy toward the poor and oppressed. Politics is often false religion.

At the National Association of Evangelicals in 1983, Ronald Reagan fondly commended a father who believed in the importance of a nuclear holocaust option. He said, "I would rather see my little girls die now, still believing in God, than have them grow up under Communism and one day die no longer believing in God." But Jeremiah's recommendations of submission and surrender to the enemy refute such heresies.

---

[22] Walter Brueggemann, *The Prophetic Imagination* (Philadelphia: Fortress, 1978), 36.

Jeremiah claimed that sometimes the most faithful act is non-violent surrender. His option is not provided for in national security ideologies, which leave no room for the intervention of God in history. While the nuclear threat gets little press now, it still is real and its threat is simple: We demand that we either get things our way or we will blow the earth to hell. Lord, have mercy!

According to Millard Lind, the Torah and the prophetic word were the "ultimate authority in ... Judah's domestic and international relationships."[23] The prophetic word has little impact on our political institutions today. I do not necessarily lament this. But I do lament the fact that the prophetic word carries little political authority *among Christians*. I long for the day when the church forthrightly advocates, articulates, and creates a politics of God. Such a politics does not mean withdrawal from the world—far from it! Jeremiah and Jesus actively engaged the world, and we should do no less.

Let us work for God's reign in ways consistent with God's means. Let us call nations to pursue that reign in a manner consistent with God's ways. The false prophets avoided the hard words of God, making things easy for their listeners.[24] Thus Jeremiah urged his readers to be especially critical and suspicious of those who prophesy easy good news.

This is unsettling. We believe our faith is good news, "gospel." But it is not easy, quick, or optimistic good news. Jesus preached beatitudes, not "be-happy attitudes," Robert Schuller notwithstanding. Jeremiah and Jesus risked suffering and death. We cannot reach Easter without the tragic events that precede it. We do not get there through strength, might, power, or wisdom. "Do not let the wise boast in their wisdom, do not let the mighty boast in their might, do not let the wealthy boast in their wealth" (9:23). Jeremiah and Jesus counseled suffering patience. "It was the

---

[23] Millard C. Lind, *Monotheism, Power, Justice: Collected Essays* (Elkhart, Ind.: Institute of Mennonite Studies, 1990), 6.

[24] Hans Walter Wolff, *Confrontations with Prophets* (Philadelphia: Fortress, 1983), 70.

characteristic of the great prophets like Jeremiah ... that they ... learned to 'wait upon God.'"[25]

On Palm Sunday, when Jesus' sovereignty is proclaimed and celebrated, and when we recall Jeremiah's subversive political counsel and symbolism, we do well to remember how Zechariah (quoted in Matthew 21) described our sovereign.

> He will cut off the chariot from Ephraim
>> and the war-horse from Jerusalem;
> and the battle bow shall be cut off,
>> and he shall command peace to the nations;
> his dominion shall be from sea to sea,
>> and from the River to the ends of the earth. (Zech. 9:10)

HOLY WEEK
MY GOD, MY GOD, WHY HAVE YOU FORSAKEN ME?
Matthew 27:32-56; Jeremiah 20:1-18; Psalm 22

A trajectory in our canon embraces Psalm 22, Deutero-Isaiah's suffering servant songs, Jeremiah's laments, and Jesus' passion. We often assume that the Passion happened once for all to Jesus and that we are happily freed from redemptive suffering. But Jesus' passion, Jeremiah's pain, the suffering of Deutero-Isaiah's servant and the anonymous psalmist of Psalm 22 are models of how God works. Canonically, these texts point to the life and death of Jesus. But these texts also point to the way *we* are expected to live and, yes, even die. We too share in the redemptive suffering of the cross.

Jeremiah was unique as a prophet because of his laments and suffering, which were central to his message. Jeremiah's ministry marked a watershed. Before Jeremiah, "sufferings were only something incidental, having no intrinsic import of their own. Henceforward, the sufferings themselves began to rise into prominence."[26] A new theme emerged.

---

[25] Ernest W. Nicholson, *The Book of the Prophet Jeremiah, Chapters 26–52* (Cambridge: Cambridge University Press, 1975), 39.

[26] Martin Buber, *The Prophetic Faith* (New York: Harper & Row,

With Jeremiah a new element is announced in God's deal-
ings through prophets: Jeremiah serves God not only with
... harsh proclamations ... but also with his person; his life
becomes ... involved in the cause of God on earth. Thus ...
the prophet not only becomes a witness of God through ...
charisma, but also in ... humanity; but not as the one who
triumphs over the sins of [hu]mankind, not as one overcoming, but as a messenger of God, ... breaking under the
strain. Hence Jeremiah's life ... becomes a forceful witness,
his suffering soul and his life ebbing away in God's service
become a testimony to God.[27]

Prophetic intercession is here redefined.

Jeremiah not only confronts [hu]mankind in the manner of
Hosea or Isaiah, ... as intercessor, Jeremiah not only
endures the suffering that [people] ... caused him, but also
he has taken upon himself ... their misery.[28]

Jeremiah did not proclaim the redemptive efficacy of suffering. "These confessions know nothing ... of an atoning, redeeming
power."[29] He did not give an atonement theory. But the newness
in Jeremiah began a trajectory that embraced other aspects of the
Hebrew Scriptures and connects dramatically with Holy Week.[30]

Another Hebrew Scripture that explicitly relates suffering to
service is Second Isaiah's *ebed Yahweh* (עֶבֶד יְהֹוָה) songs. Many see
parallels between Jeremiah's laments and the *ebed Yahweh* songs.[31]

1949), 183.
    [27] Gerhard von Rad, "The Confessions of Jeremiah," in *A Prophet to
the Nations*, eds. Leo G. Perdue and Brian W. Kovacs (Winona Lake, Ind.:
Eisenbrauns, 1984), 346.
    [28] Von Rad, "Confessions of Jeremiah," 347.
    [29] Von Rad, "Confessions of Jeremiah," 347.
    [30] Even Jeremiah's elements are not completely new. Psalm 22—a
psalm with particular significance for observance of Holy Week—may
have been influential on Jeremiah.
    [31] Isa. 42:1-4; 49:1-6; 50:4-11; 52:13–53:12; cf. Holladay, *Jeremiah*, 104.

Their precise relationship is not clear. Perhaps Jeremiah as an exemplary prophet influenced *ebed Yahweh* songs.[32] Even with no causal relationship, one can see a canonical relationship.

Ebed Yahweh (the Servant of the Lord) is crucial to New Testament Christology. According to the traditions about Jesus' baptism, example, teaching, and death, this tradition was an important element in his self-understanding.[33] Particularly striking is Jesus' conscious identification with the Servant Song of Isaiah 52–53.[34]

Jeremiah, *ebed Yahweh*, and Jesus all spoke of the importance and significance of suffering in service to God. Jeremiah and Jesus' subversive recommendations will inevitably mean death. They endanger national and institutional security.

> Then the officials said to the king, "This man ought to be put to death, because he is discouraging the soldiers who are left in this city, and all the people, by speaking such words to them. For this man is not seeking the welfare of this people, but their harm." (38:4)

This bleak *Realpolitik* is echoed in John's Gospel.

> [47] So the chief priests and the Pharisees called a meeting of the council, and said, "What are we to do? This man is performing many signs. [48] If we let him go on like this, everyone will believe in him, and the Romans will come and destroy both our holy place and our nation." [49] But one of them, Caiaphas, who was high priest that year, said to them, "You know nothing at all! [50] You do not understand that it

---

[32] "We cannot know whether speculation about the meaning of Jeremiah's suffering is any part of the background to the Servant of Second Isaiah; but it is a possibility that must be considered" (David Jobling, *The Sense of Biblical Narrative: Three Structural Analyses in the Old Testament* [Sheffield: JSOT, 1978], 291).

[33] Oscar Cullmann, *The Christology of the New Testament* (Philadelphia: Westminster, 1959), 60–69.

[34] Cullmann, *Christology of the New Testament*, 64–65.

is better for you to have one man die for the people than to
have the whole nation destroyed." (John 11:47-50)

Jeremiah and Jesus walked into suffering with their eyes
open, knowing where they were headed. Just as Jeremiah recom-
mended surrender to Judah, so Jesus and Jeremiah accepted the
powerlessness of vulnerability before their enemies. Jesus
mourned how Jerusalem had abused its prophets, aware of his
own fate: "Jerusalem, Jerusalem, the city that kills the prophets
and stones those who are sent to it!" (Matt. 23:37).

In a war-ravaged city, Jeremiah kept initiating protest prophecies that guaranteed further persecution and suffering. He
became an outcast. He was beaten, insulted, imprisoned, and kept
in a cistern of mire. The prophet could have opted for a safer and
less-dramatic means of proclaiming his message. He had connec-
tions in high places. Nevertheless, he functioned primarily on the
edge of things and remained essentially peripheral.

The sufferings of both Jeremiah and Jesus culminated in despair and abandonment. Jeremiah was subjected to a range of sufferings.

> ¹⁴ Cursed be the day
>   on which I was born!
> The day when my mother bore me,
>   let it not be blessed!
> ¹⁵ Cursed be the man
>   who brought the news to my father, saying,
> "A child is born to you, a son,"
>   making him very glad.
> ¹⁶ Let that man be like the cities
>   that the LORD overthrew without pity;
> let him hear a cry in the morning
>   and an alarm at noon,
> ¹⁷ because he did not kill me in the womb;
>   so my mother would have been my grave,
>   and her womb forever great.
> ¹⁸ Why did I come forth from the womb

> to see toil and sorrow,
> and spend my days in shame?   (20:14-18)

This dramatic passage represents the climax of his sufferings. Since Jeremiah connected his birth to his call, this was a profound questioning of his call.[35]

Jeremiah and Jesus were abandoned, betrayed, and even attacked by those closest to them. Matthew detailed Jesus' betrayal at the hands of a disciple (Matt. 26:47-50). A prominent disciple, Peter, repeatedly denied him (26:69-75). Jeremiah also suffered at the hands of those close to him: "All my close friends are watching for me to stumble" (20:10b). "The phrase ... means literally 'every person of my peace,' ... a precise equivalent of our current phrase 'my support system.'"[36]

Jeremiah and Jesus both entered into suffering that was beyond explanation. For all their faithfulness, their proclamation of God's words was turned against them.

> [41] In the same way the chief priests also, along with the scribes and elders, were mocking him, saying, [42] "He saved others; he cannot save himself. He is the King of Israel; let him come down from the cross now, and we will believe in him. [43] He trusts in God; let God deliver him now, if he wants to; for he said, 'I am God's Son.'"   (Matt. 27:41-43)

Jeremiah laments,

> I have become a laughingstock all day long;
>   everyone mocks me.
> [8] For whenever I speak, I must cry out,
>   I must shout, "Violence and destruction!"
> For the word of the LORD has become for me
>   a reproach and derision all day long....
> [10] For I hear many whispering,
>   "Terror is all around!
> Denounce him! Let us denounce him!"   (Jer. 20:7b-8, 10a)

---

[35] Holladay, *Jeremiah*, 101.
[36] Holladay, *Jeremiah*, 102.

⁷ All who see me mock at me;
>   they make mouths at me, they shake their heads;
⁸ "Commit your cause to the LORD; let him deliver—
>   let him rescue the one in whom he delights!" (Ps. 22:7-8)

For false prophets, trust in God means security from threats. But trust in Yahweh is not so simple or reassuring. Betrayed by friends, they are apparently betrayed by God as well. Jeremiah, the faithful servant, cries out:

>   O LORD, Thou hast seduced me,
>   And I am seduced;
>   Thou hast raped me
>   And I am overcome. (Jer. 20:7)[37]

On the cross Jesus cried out to the God he served so faithfully, quoting Psalm 22: "My God, my God, why have you forsaken me?" (Matt. 27:46; cf. Ps. 22:1).

The suffering of God's faithful servants shocks us. What preacher dare speak of being seduced, raped, overcome, or abandoned by God? When we abandon idols and false gods, we have no security. Holy Week confirms that "to know Jesus as a [hu]man is to know him in terms of that concept by which he knew himself, … as *ebed Yahweh*, the suffering servant of God."[38] This is not easy to embrace, but it is central to the gospel. "The truth revealed in the *ebed Yahweh* is that salvation comes from suffering."[39] Anyone who would follow Jesus must also be willing to endure suffering servanthood.[40]

In Holy Week, we are challenged to endure, ponder, and plumb the depth of God's suffering in the world. Where will we wager our lives? With easy security or with the suffering God who

---

[37] Translation by Abraham Heschel, *Prophets*, 113.

[38] James W. Douglass, "A Non-Violent Christology," in *God, Jesus, and Spirit*, ed. Daniel Callahan (New York: Herder and Herder, 1969), 261.

[39] Douglass, "Non-Violent Christology," 261.

[40] James W. Douglass, *The Non-Violent Cross* (New York: Macmillan, 1966), 65.

gives all to be reconciled? In a story called, "Jeremiah, or God is a Downer," Daniel Berrigan notes, "Everyone dies. The question is, what do we leave behind for others? A gun (the definitive solution, the silencer) — or a vision?"[41]

EASTER SUNDAY
THEY DEPARTED FROM THE TOMB WITH FEAR AND GREAT JOY
Matthew 28:1-10; Jeremiah 32:1-5

Christ is risen! Christ is risen indeed! Amen!

Some Christians argue about the empty tomb, but the disciples were ambivalent about it. They responded with fear and joy. It proves nothing. Evidence of the resurrection is not in an empty grave but in how believers *live*. "The proof that God raised Jesus from the dead is not the empty tomb, but the full hearts of ... transformed disciples."[42]

Ultimately, a doctrinal profession about Jesus being raised needs to be accompanied by a life that reflects a new reality. The profession has converting power only if the proclaimer lives differently. Do we invest our lives, our selves, and our beings in God's future? Do we believe that God's future is also mysteriously present among us?

> On the morning of the resurrection, God put life in the present tense, not in the future. [God] gave us not a promise but a presence. Not a hope for the future but power for the present. Not so much the assurance that we shall live someday but that he is risen today. Jesus' resurrection is not to convince the incredulous nor to reassure the fearful, but to enkindle believers.[43]

Jeremiah is not all doom and gloom; there are many beautiful words in the book, and we are edified by such words. But now

---

[41] Daniel Berrigan, *A Book of Parables* (New York: Seabury, 1977), 123.

[42] Jordan, *Substance of Faith*, 29.

[43] Jordan, *Substance of Faith*, 29.

we look at an *action*, a *deed*. Jeremiah not only proclaimed a new reality; he also *invested* in it.

Jerusalem was besieged. The end Jeremiah had often predicted was near. His warnings would soon be fulfilled. He had been confined to the court of the guard because of his subversive proclamations. He had several options. Jeremiah could prepare for the takeover. Perhaps he could find ways to take care of himself during the occupation. Certainly he ought to lie low and not attract undue attention. (Attention never did him any good.) If he could stay alive, his chances for survival might improve.

Jeremiah had an opportunity to redeem familial land. God said that Jeremiah should do so. But why waste the money? Would the Babylonians honor Judean land transactions? To all intents and purposes, Jeremiah was throwing money away.

Why did God command such foolishness? "For thus says the LORD of hosts, the God of Israel: Houses and fields and vineyards shall again be bought in this land" (32:15). God gave a word of reassurance, a daring promise. Things looked tough: the end had arrived. But Jeremiah was not fooled. This was not the end. It was neither the final word nor the ultimate solution. It was only temporary. So Jeremiah invested in what would later be real. His symbolic action brought that future reality into his present. Thus, even while Jeremiah was predicting defeat (32:28), he was investing in God's future.

We do not find resurrection in Jeremiah. However, he informs our understanding of resurrection. He opted for resurrection reality. He bought land in Anathoth, his family village, where people earlier had sought to kill him. This prophetic sign, another symbolic action, not only points to hope but also sets in motion God's new reality. Ironically, even when he was not proclaiming doom he was accused of subversion!

The resurrection means God has the final word. Humans attempt final solutions, but God always has another word. God is not trapped by those who build temples, nor is God limited by a state that kills enemies. "By raising Jesus from the dead, God is refusing to take [humanity's] 'No' for an answer."[44] Jeremiah gave a word of hope at tremendous risk, which led to yet another official attempt to silence him (37:15).

People often tried to kill the prophet, but such attempts failed. Jeremiah would have the last word. He still has it. We hear him, not his enemies. What we know of *them* is in the book that bears his name.

> When [Jeremiah] tried to arrest the course of a nation, only to be thrown down and trampled underfoot, when he cried out in bitterness of heart against the inexorable Will that compelled a poet to become a prophet, and a lover of [humans] to be counted their enemy, he little knew that the … record of his own lonely experience of failure was to be a success of the highest rank and influence.[45]

Confidence in the resurrection frees us from fear. Once when President Reagan visited Las Vegas, local Catholic Workers brought a prophetic presence. A community member remembers:

> When we arrived, a large crowd had already gathered…. I was besieged by campaign vendors. Buttons, bumper stickers, hats, and flags were distributed to promote the contemporary conservative candidates. The band was on stage, entertaining the crowd with a few warm-up acts, while young and old scurried about finding their seats before the show began. The entire scene resembled a Ringling Brothers event.
>
> I glanced at our peace banner folded underneath my arm. Our message was so serious and so completely contrary to what most people here would welcome. A surge of anxiety swept over me. If we unfurled the banner, we would not

---

44 Jordan, *Substance of Faith*, 28.

45 H. Wheeler Robinson, *The Cross of Jeremiah* (London: SCM, 1925), 1.

only disrupt the contentment of the crowd, but would also provoke hostile reaction.[46]

They were not well received. But they were able to act from their confidence in the resurrection. Had they remained silent, they would be as ones who were dead.

> Christ came to liberate us from our fears. He gave us the gift of the resurrection so that we would be able to proclaim His message without hesitation, without doubt. Through an unfailing faith in the resurrection, we ... grow to become vibrant, outspoken witnesses to the gospel message.[47]

We do not preach naive optimism. Neither Jeremiah, Jesus, nor Catholic Workers promised quick results. The resurrection means being able to look beyond the present and thus see with new eyes. That is why Jeremiah gave incredible advice to exiles.

> [5] Build houses and live in them; plant gardens and eat what they produce. [6] Take wives and have sons and daughters; take wives for your sons, and give your daughters in marriage, that they may bear sons and daughters; multiply there, and do not decrease. [7] But seek the welfare of the city where I have sent you into exile, and pray to the LORD on its behalf, for in its welfare you will find your welfare. (29:5-7)

Jeremiah the celibate commended marriage and childbearing as a faithful act in a strange land. Gardens and childbirth can be conscious acts of resistance. Long before Jerry Falwell's Moral Majority, John Howard Yoder advocated a *moral minority*.

> What the world most needs is not a new Caesar but a new style. A style is created, updated, projected, not by a nation or a government, but by a people. This is what moral minorities can do — what they have done time and again.

---

[46] Julia Occhiogrosso, "Christ Came to Liberate Us from Fear," *Manna in the Wilderness* (Winter 1987), 1.

[47] Occhiogrosso, "Christ Came," 2.

> Liberation is the presence of a new option, and only a non-conformed, covenanted people of God can offer that. Liberation is the pressure of the presence of a new alternative so valid, so coherent, that it can live without the props of power and against the stream of statesmanship. To *be* that option is to be free indeed.[48]

I do not expect our exile to end soon. I do not expect the consummation of God's intention and reign today (although I could be wrong!). What I do expect and hope for is that we live in the reality and conviction of the resurrection today.

Latino Youth is an alternative high school for dropouts and push-outs in a troubled inner-city Chicago neighborhood. Richard Rutschman, a Mennonite, was its director. He had visions bigger than most people's imagination. In 1985, he eyed an abandoned 32-unit building. Condemned and decrepit, it was covered with graffiti and slated for demolition. On the border between two fierce street gangs, the Kents and Satan's Disciples, it was ravaged by both. Richard decided he wanted that building for Latino Youth. My most polite response was to consider this dream foolish.

This building was a huge tomb, representing the neighborhood's deterioration. But Latino Youth took it over, and today the graffiti is gone, replaced by stunningly vibrant murals. The building is repaired and has all new windows. The school is there and houses other charitable programs too: tutoring, job development, ESL (English as a second language) and GED (general equivalency diploma).

Maybe I was right: Richard was foolish or even worse. But only someone like Richard (or Jeremiah or Jesus) would take such a plunge. No one else would try. It was the craziness of the resurrection to attempt it.

Latino Youth took a building marked for demolition in a neighborhood overlooked by city officials. It invested in a future

---

[48] John Howard Yoder, "Exodus and Exile: The Two Faces of Liberation," *Cross Currents* (Fall 1973), 309.

that no one else saw or trusted. Appropriately, the building program was called "Building a Second Chance." It represented a second chance both for the building itself and for students who had not made it in regular schools.

May we all bet our lives on new realities revealed in Christ's resurrection. May our symbolic actions be investments in God's future. In this we find liberation.

> To become ... a beneficiary of the Resurrection of Jesus Christ means to live here and now in a way that upholds and honors the sovereignty of the Word of God in this life in this world, and that trusts the Judgment of the Word of God in history. That means freedom *now* from all conformities to death, freedom *now* from fear of the power of death, freedom *now* from the bondage of idolatry to death, freedom *now* to live in hope while awaiting the Judgment.[49]

As Jesus said, "I am the resurrection and the life. Those who believe in me, even though they die, will live" (John 11:25).

Christ is risen! Christ is risen indeed! Alleluia! Amen.

---

[49] William Stringfellow, *A Simplicity of Faith* (Nashville: Abingdon, 1982), 113.

6

Ezekiel on Fanon's Couch
A Postcolonialist Dialogue with David Halperin's *Seeking Ezekiel*

DANIEL L. SMITH-CHRISTOPHER

PROLOGUE

It is with great pleasure that I contribute the following study to honor Millard Lind. I am happy to express my gratitude for the contribution that he, with his colleague in Old Testament studies, Jacob Enz, made to my education and my understanding of the Bible. The enthusiasm and mastery of Professors Lind and Enz gave me a love for the Hebrew Bible.

Millard's creative enthusiasm and courage in facing the issue of war and peace in the Hebrew Scriptures inspired innumerable students. Although some of his students may not have entirely agreed with his views (a circumstance Millard is the first to affirm and enjoy!), all of us were and are challenged to take his lead and continue to struggle and work on the topic.

Millard's most important recent contribution to scholarship is a characteristically provocative commentary on the prophet Ezekiel. Thus, it seems only fitting that I dedicate my recent thoughts on Ezekiel to Millard and Miriam Lind on this occasion.

THE CONTEXT FOR READING EZEKIEL AS THE REFUGEE PROPHET:
HIS CRISIS AND OUR CRISIS

An anguished voice cries in pain across the centuries. He cries with the voice of the conquered, the voice of the refugee, the voice of the displaced and the forcibly ejected. It is a voice we know all too well in our day. It is possible to give a name to that voice: it is "Ezekiel" (ironically, "God strengthens"). The crisis that gave rise to his voice is now clear. As Walther Eichrodt states in his 1965–66 commentary, "It is so obvious as to be a certainty that Ezekiel was first and foremost a prophet for the exiles."[1]

Does Ezekiel, then, have a voice today? In a 1994 work issued by the International Labour Office in Geneva, Peter Stalker summarizes what we might today call "the voice of Ezekiel." Eighty million people now live in foreign lands. Each year one million people emigrate permanently from their native land, and another million seek political asylum. Eighteen million refugees are being impelled to move by natural disaster or war.

> Widening economic gaps between industrialized and developing countries, rapidly increasing populations, the penetration of poor countries by rich ones, the disruption caused by economic development, and the web of transport and communications systems — [these] all create the "structural conditions" that might encourage an individual to consider life elsewhere.[2]

Indeed, when we begin to think about the movement of people, whether voluntary or involuntary, we begin to realize that some sociologists and cultural historians are speaking of the emergence of a new world consciousness, a new world persona.[3] Homi Bhabha, for example, writes,

---

[1] Walther Eichrodt, *Ezekiel: A Commentary* (Philadelphia: Westminster, 1970), 9.

[2] Peter Stalker, *The Work of Strangers: A Survey of International Labour Migration* (Geneva: International Labour Office, 1994), 33.

[3] Stalker, *Work*, 3.

> The demography of the new internationalism is the history of postcolonial migration, the narratives of cultural and political diaspora, the major social displacements of peasant and aboriginal communities, the poetics of exile, the grim prose of political and economic refugees.[4]

Similarly, Pnina Werbner points out that

> what has evidently rendered holistic models of culture and society unviable is the reality of postwar population movements, transnational capitalism, global telecommunications, and the explosion of consumption. What now seems pressing is to theorize the problems of cultural translation and reflexivity, inter-ethnic communication and cross-cultural mobilisation, hybridity and creolisation.[5]

Clearly, it is a time to read Ezekiel, for the book calls to us not from Palestine, which is to say, not from "home," but from some unknown place in the southern region of the Neo-Babylonian empire, known only as "Tel Aviv." He is a stranger in a strange land. Who then is he? *What* then is he? It is no wonder that he envisions God's throne as equipped with the ability to move, with wings and wheels. Is God back home? Can God be with us in this strange place?

Ezekiel's opening vision reflects his struggle with this question, and his bizarre vision shows us his reflection on being in diaspora. All biblical books are products of a community of transmission, and the community of the book of Ezekiel is clearly a community struggling with mobile identities and transnational culture and theology. *That* is why Ezekiel's crisis is our crisis. And that is why we listen to Ezekiel today.

---

[4] Homi K. Bhabha, *The Location of Culture* (New York: Routledge, 1994), 5.

[5] Pnina Werbner, "Introduction: The Dialectics of Cultural Hybridity," in *Debating Cultural Hybridity, Multi-Cultural Identities and the Politics of Anti-Racism*, eds. Pnina Werbner and Tariq Modood (London: Zed Books, 1997), 6.

It was economics, control, and power that dragged Ezekiel to Babylon, and it is economics, control, and power that create our current situation. In his work on the internationalization of labor, *The New Untouchables*, Nigel Harris points out that population transfers in the nineteenth and twentieth centuries are the result of rich nations "penetrating" poorer nations for labor pools. Arabs find work in France, Turks in Germany, Mexicans in the U.S. Twenty-eight percent of London Underground workers, for example, are ethnic minorities. But internationalization has not spread its rewards equally.

The modern picture is not clear, however, until we see the driving economic and political forces in this massive globalization of population and business. Stalker writes that 1.2 billion live in absolute poverty. Another 700 million are unemployed or under-employed. Disparities of income continue. From 1960 to 1989, the richest 20 percent of world population increased control of global gross national products from 70 to 83 percent.[6]

What has all this to do with Ezekiel? With the typical Ezekiel of biblical studies, the answer is "Not much." But with a reading of Ezekiel, *the refugee*, "A great deal." Let us begin by examining the single most important historical reality for the book of Ezekiel — the Babylonian Exile.

ASSESSING THE BABYLONIAN EXILE IN THE TWENTIETH CENTURY

The twentieth century has seen a rough consensus develop with regard to the relative importance of the Babylonian Exile. My approach to the Babylonian Exile differs considerably from this emerging consensus among scholars of the exilic and Persian periods.[7] That consensus is constructed from both older and more recent contributions to the critical historiography of Israel.

---

[6] Stalker, *Work*, 23.

[7] I have most recently summarized my critical reflections on the conditions of the Exile in the opening essay of a volume dedicated to examining its impact and conditions. See my "Reassessing the Historical and Sociological Impact of the Babylonian Exile (597/586–539 BCE)," in

At the beginning of this century, for example, C. C. Torrey wrote that the Exile, "which was in reality a small and relatively insignificant affair, has been made, partly through mistake and partly by the compulsion of a theory, to play a very important part in the history of the Old Testament."[8] Thus there began a deem-phasizing of the Exile which would continue to express (albeit not in the extreme terms Torrey used) a scholarly consensus about the Exile. It is not that the Exile was not mentioned as an event. But as a critically important event in the history and development of the Hebrew people, the consensus appears more sympathetic to Tor-rey than, for example, Julius Wellhausen, whose assumption about the importance of the Exile as a transformative event was critical to his rewriting of the documentary hypothesis.[9]

However, there were signs of different opinions along the way. In his 1954 study of, notably, the book of Lamentations, Norman Gottwald gave an assessment of the Exile as a human tragedy which differed from his more recent emphasis on the socio-economic class of the exilic community:

> If the enduring memory of events and their impact upon succeeding generations is the major criterion of historical importance, then there can be no doubt that the sequence of happenings from 597 to 538 were among the most fateful in all Hebrew-Jewish history. It is not far wide of the mark to

---

Exile: Old Testament, Jewish and Christian Conceptions, ed. James Scott (Lei-den: Brill, 1997), 7–36. Having now read the recent work *Leading Captivity Captive,* ed. Lester Grabbe, JSOT Supplement Series, no. 278 (Sheffield: Sheffield Academic Press, 1998), I remain skeptical of recent trends to dis-count the importance of the Exile and to minimize its impact.

[8] C. C. Torrey, "The Exile and the Restoration," in *Ezra Studies* (Chi-cago: University of Chicago Press, 1910), 285.

[9] See John Barton, "Wellhausen's Prolegomena to the History of Israel: Influences and Effects," in *Text and Experience: Toward a Cultural Exegesis of the Bible,* ed. Daniel Smith-Christopher (Sheffield: Sheffield University Press, 1995), 316–29.

recognize in the sixth century BCE the severest test which Israel's religion ever faced?[10]

An excellent indication of the continued ambiguity in assessing the impact of the Exile is reflected in John Bright's influential *History of Israel*. On one hand, Bright claims, "Although we should not belittle the hardships and the humiliation that these exiles endured, their lot does not seem to have been unduly severe."[11] Yet two pages later, he writes, "When one considers the magnitude of the calamity that overtook her, one marvels that Israel was not sucked down into the vortex of history along with the other little nations of western Asia."[12]

In contrast, Herbert Donner in the influential history of ancient Israel edited by John H. Hayes and J. Maxwell Miller, says,

> It is easy … to overemphasize the drastic and debilitating consequences of the fall of Jerusalem and the triumph of Babylonian forces. Various aspects of life certainly were greatly modified, but Babylonian policy was not overly oppressive.... The exiles were not forced to live in inhuman conditions.... [They] remained free and certainly should not be understood as slaves. They would have been under no overt pressure to assimilate and lose their identities.[13]

This ambiguous assessment is shared by many of the recent commentators on the impact of the Exile on biblical literature, such as Peter Ackroyd, Thomas Raitt, Ralph Klein, and Raymond

---

[10] Norman Gottwald, *Studies in the Book of Lamentations* (London: SCM, 1954), 19.

[11] John Bright, *History of Israel*, 3d ed. (Philadelphia: Westminster, 1981), 345.

[12] Bright, *History*, 347.

[13] Herbert Donner, in *A History of Ancient Israel and Judah*, eds. J. Maxwell Miller and John H. Hayes (Philadelphia: Westminster, 1986), 421, 433.

Foster.[14] Ackroyd's work, still considered by many to be the major analysis of the Exile, was written in conscious awareness of the neglect of the exilic and postexilic periods in biblical analysis.[15] Yet in this important work, Ackroyd assesses the conditions of the exiles in Babylon by suggesting that there are indications "of reasonable freedom of settlement in communities—perhaps engaged in work for the Babylonians, but possibly simply engaged in normal agricultural life—of the possibility of marriage, of the ordering of their own affairs, of relative prosperity." Yet a few lines later, Ackroyd acknowledges that the "uncongenial nature" of the situation should not be "understated."[16]

While each of these writers attempts to present a balanced picture, the presumed "lack of evidence" seems to push the scholars toward a benign assessment of the human and social impact of the Exile. A more severe impact, it is presumed, would have left more evidence. Yet when stated in this stark manner, the working conclusion appears more clearly tendentious.[17]

More recent assessments of the Exile have taken an even more dramatic turn.[18] Now, the Exile is being seen not so much as

---

[14] Recent studies include Peter R. Ackroyd, *Exile and Restoration* (London: SCM, 1968); Raymond Samuel Foster, *The Restoration of Israel: A Study in Exile and Return* (London: Darton Longman & Todd, 1970); Thomas M. Raitt, *A Theology of Exile: Judgment/Deliverance in Jeremiah and Ezekiel* (Philadelphia: Fortress, 1977); and Ralph W. Klein, *Israel in Exile: A Theological Interpretation* (Philadelphia: Fortress, 1977).

[15] See, e.g., his "The Exilic Age," 1–16.

[16] Ackroyd, *Exile*, 32.

[17] One important essay challenged the prevailing assumptions about the generally light treatment of exiles. See J. M. Wilkie, "Nabonidus and the Later Jewish Exiles," *The Journal of Theological Studies* 2 (1951): 36–44. See also W. G. Lambert's descriptions of the violent claims of Nebuchadnezzar, "Nebuchadnezzar King of Justice," *Iraq* 27 (1965): 1–11.

[18] The literature is growing, but the "classic texts" of the debate include P. R. Davies, *In Search of Ancient Israel* (Sheffield: Sheffield University Press, 1992); T. L. Thompson, *The Origin Tradition of Ancient Israel, 1: The Literary Formation of Genesis and Exodus 1–23* (Sheffield: Sheffield

a political, human, and theological crisis, but rather as the geo-political maelstrom out of which the entire biblical "mythology" arises. In its most extreme forms, this view suggests that postexilic "Judaism" created, virtually ex nihilo, the entire biblical preexilic tradition, from the Patriarchs, through the Exodus, and even the monarchical period. The works of Thomas Thompson, John van Seters, and Philip Davies suggest that Israelite History *begins* after the rise of the Persian empire, and to write with any confidence about the historicity of events previous to this is questionable historiography at best.

In *Judaism in Persia's Shadow*,[19] Jon Berquist contends that the Torah is, for all intents and purposes, a creation of the court of Darius for an enthusiastically pro-Persian group of settlers who needed a basis for their claim to the Western coast of the satrap "Beyond the River." In this view, the Exile becomes not so much a crisis in the development of ancient Israelite identity and theology, as its cause! None of these more recent "radically skeptical" views of preexilic Israelite history, however, has much to say about the Exile itself. Again, the event seems unworthy of serious attention.

THE EXILE AND THE DESTRUCTION OF JERUSALEM IN 587 BCE

As a traumatic event, the Babylonian Exile begins with Neo-Assyrian imperial interests and military campaigns in Palestine over a century before the Exile itself.[20] Furthermore, the Babylon-

---

University Press, 1987); T. L. Thompson, *Early History of the Israelite People from the Written and Archaeological Sources* (Leiden: Brill, 1992); J. Van Seters, *In Search of History: History and Historiography in the Ancient World and the Origins of Biblical History* (New Haven: Yale University Press, 1983. Important responses include W. G. Dever, "'Will the Real Israel Please Stand Up?' Archaeology and Israelite Historiography: Part 1," *Bulletin of the American Schools of Oriental Research* 297 (1995): 61–80.

[19] Jon Berquist, *Judaism in Persia's Shadow* (Minneapolis: Fortress, 1995).

[20] Martin Noth, *The History of Israel*, 2d ed. (New York: Harper, 1960), 289. Bustenay Oded begins his analysis of the Exile by reviewing

ian Exile must be seen as a minor part of Nebuchadnezzar II's major campaign of pacification of the Levant and destruction of the Egyptian threat to his control of the area.[21]

The Exile itself took place in two major steps. For the initial surrender of 597, Nebuchadnezzar reflected on the regime's real interests, power, and resources. The famous inscription states that he appointed in Jerusalem "a king of his liking, took heavy booty from it, and brought it into Babylon" (*ANET*, 564; March 15/16, 597). According to 2 Kings 24, the number of exiles taken at this time was 10,000, along with 7,000 artisans and 1,000 "smiths" — in all, 18,000 (vv. 14, 16). Note the specificity with regard to merchants and skilled workers. This compares to Jeremiah 52:28, which notes that 3,023 persons were carried into captivity. Scholars have debated whether this number counts only men. If so, the total numbers of these initial exiles in 597 would have been considerable, perhaps 15,000–30,000. Even if Jeremiah's smaller number (3,023) is accepted, one must still multiply by an average family size! Oded notes that Assyrian sources clearly identify families accompanying exiles. There is little reason to doubt that Babylonian policies were the same, regardless of the historical reliability one places in Jeremiah's advice to "marry your sons and daughters" in Exile (Jer. 29).

The text does not even attempt to count the numbers killed and taken into exile in 587, but what we can know of the event suggests a horrific encounter with the full brunt of Nebuchadnezzar's militia. Furthermore, virtually all archaeological assessments of the destruction of 587 suggest that Jerusalem was treated severely. Nearby towns, such as Lachish and Beth-Shemesh, show total cessation of occupation. Donald Wiseman noted ash layers at

---

the events under the Neo-Assyrian empire: "Judah and the Exile," in *Israelite and Judaean History*, eds. John H. Hayes and J. Maxwell Miller (Philadelphia: Westminster, 1977), 435–88.

[21] Amelie Kuhrt, *The Ancient Near East c. 3000–330 BC*, vol. 2 (London/New York: Routledge, 1995), 590–92.

Gezer and Tell el Hesi,[22] indicating Babylonian battles. S. S. Weinberg writes:

> Excavations ... yield a picture of ruin and desolation that confronted the first returnees of 539/8. While some people had no doubt continued to live in Jerusalem, the archaeological picture is one of their squatting among the rubble, which increased as the terrace walls ... collapsed through lack of care and the debris accumulated in impassable piles on the lower slopes.[23]

Weinberg further considers it unlikely that in these circumstances any viable material culture could have been maintained. "We must think more in terms first of squatters and then of people able to maintain only a mere subsistence level."[24] More recent assessments concur. Gösta Ahlström states that the destruction of Jerusalem was thorough: "The walls were broken down and the city was plundered.... Arrowheads of northern origin and destroyed buildings that have been unearthed in excavations from this period bear witness to the disaster of the city."[25]

---

[22] Donald J. Wiseman, *Nebuchadnezzar and Babylon* (New York: Oxford University Press, 1991), 38.

[23] S. S. Weinberg, "Post-Exilic Palestine: An Archaeological Report," *Proceedings of the Israel Academy of Sciences and Humanities* 4 (1971) 80.

[24] Gösta Ahlström, *The History of Ancient Palestine* (Minneapolis: Fortress, 1993), 798. Note P. King's article on Jerusalem in *Anchor Bible Dictionary*: "Shiloh found evidence of the Babylonian destruction everywhere: thick layers of dark ash, scattered iron and bronze arrowheads, and collapsed structures" (P. King, "Jerusalem," *Anchor Bible Dictionary*, ed. David N. Freedman [New York: Doubleday, 1992], 3:757). Ephraim Stern cautions that the destruction seems to have been less severe in Benjamin than in Judah. He notes evidence suggesting that Bethel, Gibeon, and Tell en-Nasbeh continued to flourish. See Ephraim Stern, "Israel at the Close of the Period of the Monarchy: An Archaeological Survey," *Biblical Archaeologist* 38 (1975): 26–54.

[25] Weinberg, "Post-Exilic," 81.

What is clear is that the Babylonians moved the local administrative center of their conquered Palestinian territory north from Jerusalem to Mizpah, a further comment on the unviability of Jerusalem after the destruction. Whatever our assessment of the damage in Palestine, Ahlström warns that "the archaeological material has not yet been systematized in a way that provides a clear picture of how destructive the Babylonian campaigns (598–570 BCE) against Judah, Tyre, and Transjordan really were."[26] Ahlström also speculates about the possibility of Babylonian garrisons in many of the Judean locations, but there is no firm evidence of this.[27]

It is difficult to estimate the human extent of the crisis. Simply arriving at a credible number for the population of Jerusalem is controversial. Magen Broshi estimated that Jerusalem would have occupied 500–600 dunams in the seventh century, and that 40–50 inhabitants per dunam was a "reasonable" estimate. This results in a population estimate of around 24,000. William S. LaSor, however, notes that highly accurate population figures from ancient Ebla result in 446 persons per dunam, which would suggest a much higher estimate for Jerusalem if the two cities were in any way similar in population density.[28] Thus, LaSor concurs with William Albright's estimate of 250,000 before the Exile.

Obviously, these estimates vary so greatly as to make confident assessments of a quantitative impact on Judah extremely difficult. However, the archaeological evidence of destruction, combined with these population estimates, leads to a picture of horrific

---

[26] Ahlström, *History*, 805.

[27] Ahlström, *History*, 807.

[28] William Sanford LaSor, "Jerusalem," *International Standard Bible Encyclopedia*, ed. Geoffrey W. Bromiley (Grand Rapids: Eerdmans, 1982), 2:1001–30. Considerably smaller population estimates are provided by Charles Carter, "A Social and Demographic Study of Post-Exilic Judah," Ph.D. diss., Duke University, 1991. A dunam is one-fourth of an acre.

events that not surprisingly have become permanently etched into the historical lore of the Hebrew Bible.[29]

THE STATUS AND TREATMENT OF THE EXILE COMMUNITY

With regard to the actual life of the exiles, Martin Noth wrote in an ambiguous manner that is now typical of scholarly opinion on the Exile:

> The exiles were not "prisoners" but represented a compulsorily transplanted subject population who were able to move about freely in their daily life, but were presumably compelled to render compulsory labor service.[30]

More recently, Bustenay Oded suggests that the Exile community became land tenants of royal land, craftsmen were involved in projects, and religious personnel were able to conduct aspects of Jewish religious ritual at sites such as Casiphia (Ezra 8:15-20). In sum, Oded believes there is no evidence of suppression or religious persecution. The community members had "a certain internal autonomy and ... they enjoyed the freedom to manage their community life (Ezek. 33:30-33)."[31] Notable in Oded's sanguine picture of exilic life is his reference to the fifth-century Murashu texts, and his use of language like "assume," "presume," and "no clear and explicit evidence." It is precisely these tendencies to presume a tame, even if not entirely comfortable, existence that needs to be challenged in the light of an analysis of the experience of exiles throughout history and the evidence of trauma in the Hebrew literature after the experience.

One element in the prevailing consensus that is nearly obligatory in the literature about the Exile is the view that the exiles were not "slaves." This is hardly a precise observation, however, given the wide variety of slave systems in human history. Typic-

---

[29] See, e.g., Psalm 137; Lamentations; see also the Lachisch Ostraca, *ANET*, 322.

[30] Noth, *History*, 296.

[31] Oded, "Judah," 483.

ally, biblical scholars who use the term fail to define it.[32] For American authors, this presumably means that the exiles were not slaves in the sense that African-Americans were slaves in antebellum United States. To say, with Dandamaev, that they were not slaves in the technical Neo-Babylonian sense, furthermore, is only to describe a detail of Neo-Babylonian jurisprudence.[33] What matters, in short, is not their definition of the term *slave*, but a workable picture of actual conditions. For this, we must draw together the circumstantial evidence of biblical and nonbiblical texts.

In 1938, Weissbach discussed a cuneiform inscription of Nebuchadnezzar II that includes interesting references to the fate of those taken from lands that included "the Hattim" (Palestine and the coastal regions). Nebuchadnezzar writes of

> the whole of the races, people from far places, whom Marduk my Lord delivered to me—I forced them to work on the building of Etemenanki—I imposed on them the brick-basket.

The terms used in this inscription—"I forced them to work"—certainly refer to corvée labor, and *e-mi-id-su-nu-ti tu-up-si-ik-ku* ("I imposed on them the brick basket") implies clear subservience.[34]

In his recent monograph, *Social Justice in Ancient Israel and in the Ancient Near East*, Moshe Weinfeld relates the Akkadian *tup-*

---

[32] It is important to see the wide diversity in slave systems as carefully documented in Orlando Patterson, *Slavery and Social Death* (Cambridge: Harvard University Press, 1982).

[33] Among many of Dandamaev's sources, one may cite "Social Stratification in Babylonia 7th to 4th Centuries BC," *Acta Antiqua* 22 (1974): 437: "The forced labour sector in Babylonia, in contrast to Greek and Roman antiquity, was not able to absorb such masses of captives."

[34] The translation from Weissbach's German is my own. Cf. the older translation in Stephen Langdon, *Building Inscriptions of the Neo-Babylonian Empire, Part 1: Nabopolassar and Nebuchadnezzar* (Paris, 1905), 59, 149. I wish to thank my Loyola Marymount University colleague, Fr. William Fulco, S.J., for his helpful advice on many of the linguistic features of this text.

sikku to the Hebrew term סֵבֶל ("bearing burdens"; see 1 Kings 11:28 and 5:27ff. of Solomon's forced labor). Weinfeld points out that the terms *ilku* and *tupsikku* are two variants of forced labor. *Ilku* involves travel (connecting with the verb *alaku*, "to go"), while *tupsikku* "refers specifically to bearing burdens and construction work done locally."[35] Similar differentiation in the types of forced labor are seen in Hittite and Egyptian nomenclature. The two terms, however, are used interchangeably of corvée labor. Kuhrt, for example, noted that

> the most spectacular evidence of Nebuchadnezzar's extraordinary military successes can be found in the remains of his building-works in Babylonia. All the great old cities were extensively rebuilt, their shrines repaired and beautified. Most notable in this massive effort at reconstruction is the development of Babylon into the immense and beautiful city of legend.... The many lengthy, royal inscriptions and stamped bricks show that most of this building was the work of Nebuchadnezzar during his long reign of forty-three years (605–562).[36]

It is significant how often labor is associated with rule over varied peoples in the Neo-Babylonian inscriptions. R. M. Adams's archaeological survey of the central flood plain of the Euphrates in 1981 led him to conclude,

> There is no doubt about the rapid, continued growth that got under way, during, or perhaps even slightly before, the Neo-Babylonian period. This is most simply shown by the rising number of sites.... The total increases from 143 in the Middle Babylonian period to 182 in the Neo-Babylonian period, to 221 of Achaemenid date.... The available documentary evidence suggests that large masses of people were involuntarily transferred as part of intensive Neo-

---

[35] Moshe Weinfeld, *Social Justice in Ancient Israel* (Minneapolis: Fortress, 1995), 85.

[36] Kuhrt, *Ancient*, 593.

Babylonian efforts to rehabilitate the central region of a domain that previously had suffered severely.[37]

Such evidence should not be overlooked when considering the impact and conditions of the Babylonian Exile (Jer. 51:34-35). When this is combined with biblical references to "slavery" and conditions of Exile, the emerging picture is dark, even if we must depend upon the use of metaphors and allusions rather than precise historical observation. For example, J. M. Wilkie argued already in 1951 that we may need to reassess the treatment of Babylonian exiles in the light of Deutero-Isaiah's concept of the suffering of the famous image of the "suffering servant."

> There is independent evidence to suggest that Second-Isaiah's language is neither metaphorical nor at variance with the actual conditions, but is an accurate description of conditions which he knew only too well.[38]

Further insight can be gained from a study of the lexicography of trauma in the Hebrew Bible. For example, consider the biblical terminology of chains and prison. Chains and bonds are spoken of in at least three different major terms. They are frequently associated with the Babylonian conquest, whether literally or figuratively:

1. מוֹסֵר n.m., from אָסַר, "to tie, imprison." It is usually translated "bonds," as in Nahum 1:13. "And now I will break off his yoke from you and snap the bonds that bind you." Significantly, it is used of the Babylonian Exile in Isaiah 52:2, "Shake yourself from the dust, rise up, O captive Jerusalem; loose the bonds from your neck." And in Psalm 107:14, "He brought them out of darkness and gloom, and broke their bonds asunder."

2. זִק, "fetter" (always in plural, זִקִּים). "Yet she became an exile, she went into captivity.... All her dignitaries were bound in

---

[37] R. M. Adams, *Heartland of Cities: Surveys of Ancient Settlement and Land Use on the Central Floodplain of the Euphrates* (Chicago: University of Chicago Press, 1981), 177.

[38] J. M. Wilkie, "Nabonidus and the Later Jewish Exiles," 40.

fetters" (Nah. 3:10). Isaiah 45:14 speaks of foreigners coming as prisoners, a reversal-of-fortune motif. They "shall come over in chains and bow down to you." Psalm 149 echoes the treatment of the dignitaries. The captors "bind their kings with fetters and their nobles with chains." A fourth term, כֶּבֶל, is used of Joseph in Psalm 105:18.[39] Note the form in Jeremiah 40:1, "when he took him bound in fetters." The LXX has χειροπέδαις, "foot shackle" (47:1, LXX).

3. בַּנְחֻשְׁתַּיִם, "... with/in bronze fetters," from the root נְחֹשֶׁת, "bronze, copper." Notably, this term is used Jeremiah 39:7 to refer to the bonds on Zedekiah (cf. 2 Kings 25). Second Chronicles 36:6 speaks of such fetters on Jehoiachin. Finally, Lamentations 3:7 speaks of siege and *chains* in reference to post-event reflections on the conquest of Jerusalem.

Further insights can be gained from a brief examination of three terms for "imprisonment."

1. כָּלוּא, "confined," from the verb כלא, "to hold back," appears in Jeremiah 32:2; 1 Samuel 25:33; Psalm 119:101, and notably of exiles in Isaiah 43:6.

2. בּוֹר אֵין מָיִם, "pit with no water," occurs in the late Joseph material in Genesis 37; but see Jeremiah 38:6 and Zechariah 9:11, where the reference is closer to exile.

3. בֵּית עֲבָדִים, "house of bondage," is the image used of Egyptian bondage in Exodus 13:3, 14; 20:2; Deut. 5:6; 6:12; 7:8; and elsewhere. Note also Jeremiah 34:13 and Micah 6:4.[40]

---

[39] Note, however, the significance of the Joseph stories being post-exilic, see D. B. Redford, *A Study of the Biblical Story of Joseph (Genesis 37–50)* (Leiden: Brill, 1970).

[40] Serious questions can be raised about the application of this terminology to the Egyptian bondage before the Exodus. If Redford is correct that the tradition of the Hebrew "slaves" working in Pithom and Raamses can be no older than late 6th century BCE, then we cannot discount an "exilic" redaction of the Exodus traditions that may well reflect the Babylonian experience with more accuracy than the Egyptian experience. See Redford, *A Study of the Biblical Story of Joseph*, but

This linguistic evidence clearly shows that various forms of the Hebrew terms normally rendered "imprisonment" turn up as metaphors for exile, along with the various use of terms of binding and fetters. Can *all* of this be dismissed as mere metaphor?

In another frequently occurring biblical motif, "sight to the blind" and "release of prisoners" appear as metaphors of exile. This is found in many exilic and postexilic passages, such as Psalm 146:7-8; Zechariah 9:12; and Isaiah 42:7; 61:1.

Reversal-of-fortune motifs may reveal further important insights. For example, treatment of foreigners in Isaiah 45:14 may reflect memories of the writer's own treatment, or treatment of his people. And the famous "Exile Psalm" (Ps. 137) concludes with the chilling sentiment, "Happy shall be they who take your little ones and dash them against the rock!" (v. 9).

The immediate context suggests the sort of reciprocal retributive justice best represented by the emphasis, "Happy shall they be who take *your* little ones and dash them against the rock." This raises the grim possibility that the writer of this bitter psalm observed precisely this treatment of his own people by the Babylonians during the executions noted in 2 Kings 25. After all, the Neo-Assyrian texts are famous for their frightfulness: "I built a pillar over against his city gate, and I flayed all the chief men who had revolted, and I covered the pillar with their skins.... Ahiababa I took to Nineveh.... I spread his skin upon the wall of Nineveh."[41] In light of the calculated terrorism of the Near Eastern regimes, there is no real basis for assuming that the Neo-Babylonian empire's military tactics were any less severe.[42]

How then might we reread Ezekiel in the light of the Babylonian Exile? First and foremost, Ezekiel is traumatized by *state-sponsored terrorism*. The noted medical researcher and theorist who

---

especially his *Egypt, Canaan, and Israel in Ancient Times* (Princeton: Princeton University Press, 1992).

[41] D. D. Luckenbill, *ARAB*, 145, noted in H. W. F. Saggs, "Assyrian Warfare in the Sargonid Period," *Iraq* 25 (1963).

[42] Note Kuhrt, *Ancient*, 514–18.

has worked for years on treatment of terror and torture victims, Caroline Gorst-Unsworth, defines state-sponsored terrorism as

> the act of a state against an individual or group, with the aim of achieving specific psychological changes (directly) in their victims and often (indirectly) in their communities.... The survivor of torture has not merely been the accidental victim of physical injury or threat of death such as might occur, for example, in a natural disaster or accident.... He or she has received the focused attention of an adversary determined to cause the maximal psychological change.... Neither is it the individual who suffers. For every person tortured, there are mothers and fathers, wives, husbands and children, friends and relatives who wait in uncertainty and fear.... Torture has effects on communities and on whole societies.[43]

Do we have any substantive reason to excuse Mesopotamian regimes from the accusation of state-sponsored terrorism merely because it is ancient history rather than twentieth-century events? In reference to the Neo-Assyrian empire, Amelie Kuhrt writes of reliefs depicting its kings reclining near the severed heads of enemies. Assyrian inscriptions boast of the dead rebels draped on their city walls, or rebellious rulers entrapped in cages with wild animals, cages then suspended at the entrance to cities. The king, she writes,

> was awe-inspiring; the fear that filled his enemies was the terror of those knowing that they will be ruthlessly, but justly, punished. The royal power to inspire fear was visualized as a shining radiance, ... a kind of halo, that flashed forth from the royal face.... It made him fearsome to behold, and it could strike his enemies down, so that they fell to their knees before him, dazzled by the fearful glow.[44]

---

[43] Caroline Gorst-Unsworth, "Psychological Sequelae of Torture: A Descripture Model," *British Journal of Psychiatry* 157 (1990): 475–76.

[44] Kuhrt, *Ancient*, 517.

The legendary suddenness of executions demanded by the "mad king" is an essential element in the drama of the tales in Daniel 1–6, even if we are dealing with late-Persian-period collective memories of the Neo-Babylonian experience.

What are the implications of this for reading Ezekiel? One way to approach this issue is through a discussion of the frequent theme of Ezekiel's psychological state, which has once again been raised by David Halperin in his 1993 work, *Seeking Ezekiel: Text and Psychology*.[45]

EZEKIEL ON THE COUCH

Halperin's work is a fascinating contribution to the collection of efforts by scholars—whether in biblical or psychological disciplines—to analyze the behavior and attitudes of the priest-prophet Ezekiel through a close examination of selected texts. Halperin himself states that his work is an attempt to revise, correct, and renew the psychoanalytical suggestions originally made by E. C. Broome in his 1946 article, "Ezekiel's Abnormal Personality."[46] Although Halperin acknowledges that psychological interpretations of Ezekiel go back at least as far as A. Klostermann's 1877 essay, it is Broome's more Freudian approach that Halperin is particularly interested in revising and reviving.

Psychological interpretations of Ezekiel are resisted by many scholars. For example, Walther Eichrodt protests,

> Never at any point ... do we find any trace of mental abnormality or even disease. In spite of all his frequently bizarre symbolic actions and the often overstrained excitability of his speech, Ezekiel's message is everywhere seen to be well thought out and directed towards a single end, which is in

---

[45] David Halperin, *Seeking Ezekiel: Text and Psychology* (University Park, Pa.: Pennsylvania State University Press, 1993).

[46] E. C. Broome, "Ezekiel's Abnormal Personality," *The Journal of Biblical Literature*, 65 (1946): 277–92.

keeping with his conception of God, of the world, and of human nature.[47]

In his massive *Introduction to the Old Testament as Scripture*, Brevard Childs notes,

> Various theories have been suggested to explain the peculiarities of Ezekiel's ecstatic behavior in terms of psychological disturbances or physical illness, ... but in general these attempts have met with little positive reception by critical commentators and have left only an indirect influence on the history of research.[48]

Even those who reject specific psychological explanations struggle to explain what Georg Fohrer designated as the twelve "sign-actions" of the prophet. These twelve "sign-actions" include Ezekiel's famous enacting of the silent tableau scenes of Jerusalem, packing an "exiles' bag," cutting his own hair for symbolic purposes, and binding his own hands.

Walther Zimmerli sees these actions variously as conscious efforts to "set forth in a visible action the event announced by Yahweh as something already begun,"[49] or merely as the results of events that "overtake him and which make him appear to be overpowered by these experiences, ... [such as] the tragic loss of his wife."[50] In other words, such events challenge our ability to avoid some kind of psychological or psycho-theoretical matrix for fully appreciating Ezekiel.

As Halperin himself acknowledges, anyone voyaging into the study of Ezekiel today must steer a steady course between Walther Zimmerli and Moshe Greenberg, and is likely to need to

---

[47] Eichrodt, *Ezekiel*, 26.

[48] Brevard S. Childs, *Introduction to the Old Testament as Scripture* (Philadelphia: Fortress, 1979), 359.

[49] Walther Zimmerli, *Ezekiel*, vol. 1 (Philadelphia: Fortress, 1979), 29.

[50] Zimmerli, *Ezekiel*, 29.

do so for some time to come.[51] Zimmerli, on one hand, has provided us with a commentary deeply informed by the history of Christian critical studies in the book of Ezekiel in the twentieth century. He is particularly conscious of reading the Hebrew consistently, pointing out the various layers of textual emendations, and occasionally eliminating selected sections of text as later intru-

[51] Among the works consulted for this essay are Leslie C. Allen, *Ezekiel 20–48*, Word Biblical Commentary (Waco, Tex.: Word Books, 1990); Ellen Frances Davis, "Swallowing Hard: Reflections on Ezekiel's Dumbness," in *Signs and Wonders*, ed. J. Cheryl Exum, Biblical Texts in Literary Focus (Decatur, Ga.: Scholars Press), 217–37; William H. Brownlee, *Ezekiel 1–19*, Word Biblical Commentary (Waco, Tex.: Word Books, 1986); Meindert Dijkstra, "The Glosses in Ezekiel Reconsidered: Aspects of Textual Transmission in Ezekiel 10," in *Ezekiel and His Book: Textual and Literary Criticism and Their Interrelation*, ed. Johan Lust, Bibliotheca Ephemeridum Theologicarum Lovaniensium 74 (Leuven: Leuven University Press, 1986), 55–77; J. Van Goudoever, "Ezekiel Sees in Exile a New Temple-City at the Beginning of a Jobel Year," in *Ezekiel and His Book*, ed. Lust, 344–49; Moshe Greenberg, "What Are Valid Criteria for Determining Inauthentic Matter in Ezekiel?" in *Ezekiel and His Book*, ed. Lust, 123–35; R. E. Clements, "The Ezekiel Tradition: Prophecy in a Time of Crisis," in *Israel's Prophetic Tradition: Essays in Honor of Peter R. Ackroyd*, eds. Richard Coggins, Anthony Phillips, and Michael Knibb (Cambridge: Cambridge University Press, 1982), 119–36; Daniel Block, *The Book of Ezekiel, Chapters 1-24*, New International Commentary on the Old Testament (Grand Rapids: Eerdmans, 1997); Iain M. Duguid, *Ezekiel and the Leaders of Israel*, Vetus Testamentum Supplements 56 (Leiden: Brill, 1994); Leslie C. Allen, *Ezekiel 20–48*, Word Biblical Commentary (Waco, Tex.: Word Books, 1990); Joseph Blenkinsopp, *Ezekiel*, Interpretation (Louisville: John Knox, 1990); Bernhard Lang, "Street Theater, Raising the Dead, and the Zoroastrian Connection in Ezekiel's Prophecy," in *Ezekiel and His Book*, ed. Lust, 297–316; Susan Niditch, "Ezekiel 40–48 in a Visionary Context," *Catholic Biblical Quarterly* 48 (1986): 208–24; Georg Fohrer, *Ezechiel* (Tübingen: Mohr, 1955); Walther Zimmerli, *Ezekiel: A Commentary on the Book of the Prophet Ezekiel*, trans. R. E. Clements, Hermeneia (Philadelphia: Fortress, 1979, 1983); Moshe Greenberg, *Ezekiel 1–20*, Anchor Bible (New York: Doubleday, 1983); Moshe Greenberg, *Ezekiel 21–37*, Anchor Bible (New York: Doubleday, 1997).

sions. On the other hand, Greenberg takes a more cautious approach and avoids frequent recourse to tearing into the fabric of the present text. The general tendencies of these two modern Ezekiel scholars serve as helpful counter-weights in analyzing the text.

HALPERIN'S ANALYSIS: SOME SAMPLE ARGUMENTS

Halperin states that the "centerpiece" of his arguments about the psychological nature of Ezekiel is Ezekiel 8:7-12. In this section Ezekiel "digs through the wall" during a visionary return to Jerusalem. This narrative occupies one of the most important "visions" of the first half of the book, chapters 8–11. Halperin's central assertion is that this digging in the wall "is a symbolic representation of sexual intercourse." His entire psychoanalytical interpretation of Ezekiel and the related issues of sexuality follow from this initial interpretation.

Three Hebrew terms appear to be the center of Halperin's argument about sexuality and Ezekiel's digging in walls. The term חֹר, "hole," appears in Ezekiel 8:7 as well as the relatively rare verb חָתַר, "to dig, bore through," and the noun פֶּתַח, "opening, entrance." Part of the interest in this passage is, of course, the great difference between the Masoretic and Septuagint texts. The Greek text is shorter.

Halperin translates the Hebrew text of Ezekiel 8:7-8 as follows: "And he brought me to the opening of the court. And I looked, and behold, one hole in the wall. And he said to me, 'Son of man, dig in the wall.' And I dug in the wall, and behold one opening." But he translates the Greek as follows: "And he led me in to the entry spaces of the court. And he said to me, 'Son of man, dig.' And I dug, and behold one door."

Some problems are already evident here. Halperin translates פֶּתַח אֶחָד as the specific "one opening." But here is an example of the use of אֶחָד as an indeterminate: "a hole." Gesenius lists Ezekiel 8:8 as an example of precisely this phenomenon of אֶחָד as indeterminate (125c [p. 401]). The Greek reflects the same phenomenon, so פֶּתַח need not refer to an actual door, but may also be the more ambiguous "opening" or "entryway." פֶּתַח can be something other than a door, as in Psalm 77:23, and we see similar phenomena with the Greek in the New Testament. F. C. Conybeare and George Stock note several examples of the indeterminate use of the numeral εἷς, whose use and meaning evolved "under the influence of Hebrew idiom."[52]

What did Ezekiel actually see? In English, *door* is hopelessly ambiguous. This can well be illustrated with the English translation of Genesis 19:6: "Lot went out of the door to the men, [and] shut the door after him." The first use of *door* is פֶּתַח, or "entryway," while the second is דֶּלֶת, the actual device of closure—presumably a wooden door on some kind of hinges. Halperin, not catching the indeterminate use in both the Greek and Hebrew, appears to presume that Ezekiel sees a door (he translates "one door") rather than an opening, a hole in the wall.

The more generalized view of a hole in the wall invites speculation. Halperin earlier argues with Howie:

> Let us grant, for the sake of argument, Howie's rather curious assertion that digging holes in walls was a "common process" in Ezekiel's time. (It is hard to imagine who, aside perhaps from a burglar, would have had use for such an operation).[53]

Another occasion for holes in walls has not occurred to Halperin: the events surrounding the Exile itself might be relevant factors in his psychological assessments of Ezekiel. Let us begin with a series of other uses for the term חֹר. When we read these occasions, we should be asking, "What are the occasions for digging holes?"

Some of the uses of the term are as follows:

---

[52] F. C. Conybeare and St. George Stock, *Grammar of Septuagint Greek* (Peabody, Mass.: Hendrickson Publishers, 1988, from 1905 edition), 25.

[53] Halperin, *Seeking*, 22.

1. 2 Kings 12:10 — A hole is made in a box to collect money.
2. 1 Samuel 13:6 — The Hebrew people hid themselves in holes, caves, rocks, tombs, etc., for fear of the Philistines.
   3. 1 Samuel 14:11 — Hebrews come out of "holes" where they had hidden themselves.
   4. Job 30:6 — People hide in holes from poverty and disaster.
   5. Nahum 2:13 (Heb.) — A reference to caves and dens (holes).
   6. Zechariah 14:12 — On the day of the Lord, eyes will rot in their "holes."
   7. Isaiah 11:8 — The nursing child shall play over the hole of the asp.

Note especially Isaiah 42:22:

But this is a people robbed and plundered,
   all of them are trapped in holes
   and hidden in prison;
they have become a prey with no one to rescue.

Halperin is on somewhat stronger ground when he claims a sexual association with the somewhat rare term חָתַר, "to dig, bore through." Adultery is nearby in two cases: Job 24:16 and Jeremiah 2:34, but so is the "digging" of thieves or the poor. Amos 9:2 mentions digging to Sheol to escape judgment, rather like the uses of חֹר noted above. Note that the term חָפַר is translated into Greek as ὀρύσσω, which is generally used for hew or dig (tombs, wells, graves, etc.; Gen. 21:30; 26:15, 18, 19, 21; Exod. 7:24; 2 Chron. 16:14; Tobit 2:7; 8:9).

Halperin cites only one other use of the term חֹר for hole in a decidedly sexual context: Song of Solomon 5:4. But a broader survey of the use of the term suggests strong associations with disasters — judgments of God, confrontation with military enemies, or poverty. These "holes" were more often places of refuge or safety in times of disaster than they were sexual allusions. I am not arguing here that "digging holes" is a technical term always associated with warfare or disasters. Rather, I am stating that the primary allusion for this in the Bible is precisely wars and disasters, whether real or threatened. Surely attention to this would have suggested something other than repressed sexuality in a reading of Ezekiel 8:7-8.

When we consider the historical and social context of Ezekiel, other associations suggest themselves. By most modern estimates, Ezekiel was among the first exiles taken from Jerusalem. This Exile occurred after a siege of the city by Nebuchadnezzar. In the Bible, sieges involved siege-engines and battering rams from at least as early as the Assyrian empire. Amos speaks of defeat by the Assyrians in 4:3. He says, "Through breaches in the wall you shall leave." See also Psalm 144:14, which compares breach with exile. Isaiah 30:13 goes into graphic detail:

> Therefore this iniquity shall become for you
> like a break in a high wall, bulging out, and about to collapse,
> whose crash comes suddenly, in an instant.

Second Kings 25:4, of course, attests directly to battering rams in the Babylonian arsenal during the siege of 587. In two separate texts, Ezekiel also refers to battering rams (כָּרִים) — in his tableau where he sets up the model of the siege of Jerusalem in 4:2-3; and in pronouncing the disaster in 21:22 (27, Heb.). They are implied in Ezekiel 26:9, where the walls of Jerusalem are being "struck" and its towers broken down. Thus, an image of Ezekiel digging through walls ought to suggest damage done to Jerusalem's walls in a siege, and all Ezekiel must do is dig a bit further, and "behold," an opening!

Which wall are we talking about? Ezekiel says only that he is placed on the north entrance to the temple court. This implies that Ezekiel imagines himself standing outside the city of Jerusalem. This view is shared by Iain Duguid in his recent study of Ezekiel and the elders, suggesting that the sequence of moving inward toward the temple supports this reading.[54]

Estimates of Jerusalem's perimeter wall before the Exile vary, but the temple court clearly represents the extreme northern

---

[54] Iain M. Duguid, *Ezekiel and the Leaders of Israel* (Leiden: Brill 1994), 112.

end. Second Chronicles 25:23 suggests that King Joash of Jerusalem broke down 400 cubits of north/western wall and then immediately seized "vessels of the House of God." No further destruction of walls appears to be necessary. The "Sheep Gate," argues William LaSor, is so named because here sheep were brought in from outside the city wall in preparation for sacrifice at the temple.[55] It seems clear, then, that the northeastern segment of the city wall was also the northeastern wall of the temple complex. It was therefore the most likely to show the damage of the siege of 597, when Ezekiel was taken into exile.

In his discussions of Nehemiah's survey of the damaged walls of Jerusalem almost 150 years later, Joseph Blenkinsopp points out that the northern and eastern sections of Jerusalem would have born the brunt of attacks by Mesopotamian regimes. Nehemiah finds these sections in the greatest state of destruction. Thus, more workers are employed in this section than at the other sections.[56]

As Zimmerli and others note, the Hebrew text's additional discussion of digging in the walls does, in fact, relate to 12:1-16, where allusions are made to Zedekiah's attempted escape from Jerusalem. Most scholars see 12:13 as a post–587 insertion regarding Zedekiah's blindness and capture, and our reading of the text makes this a natural association.

One can argue similarly with other examples in Halperin's analysis. For example, Halperin believe that Ezekiel's turning a sword on himself to shave the hair of his beard is a veiled reference to pubic hair, so off we go into an analysis of the psychosexual implications of this. However, swords are used throughout the prophetic literature as metaphors for conquering armies, as Halperin concedes when he says: "Let us grant that Ezekiel, ... inspired by a still earlier prophet, turned Isaiah's razor on himself.

---

[55] LaSor, "Jerusalem," 1019.

[56] Joseph Blenkinsopp, *Ezra and Nehemiah* (London: SCM, 1989), 232. See also the emphasis on foes from the "north" in Jeremiah 1:13-15.

What might have driven him to [do this]?"[57] What drove him indeed!

What appears to have driven Ezekiel to act out the horrors of conquest—the scattering of refugees in fear, the butchering of prisoners captured, and the taking of exiles? The answer is what drives thousands of traumatized humans to relive memories that can literally drive them to despair, alcoholism, silence, and suicide. If we may paraphrase the apocryphal remark of Freud, surely a sword is sometimes actually a sword.

The point is, however, that reading Ezekiel in the context of the sociopolitical events of the time suggests that his behavior and observations can and probably should be read in the light of these actual traumatic circumstances. Such a reading should, in fact, be a prerequisite to any assessments of Ezekiel's behavior, much less the textual reconstruction of a problematic passage.

The results of Halperin's analysis of Ezekiel the man are not pleasant. Halperin himself states,

> Ezekiel "as he really was"—as I imagine him—is very far
> from being a lovable person. He emerges in these pages as
> an extreme exemplar of a morbidity that afflicts many and
> perhaps all human societies.[58]

Furthermore, Halperin ends his analysis of Ezekiel by stating that the prophet "died as he had lived: wretched, hateful, tormented by rages and longings which he could not possibly have understood." I would argue strongly, and quite to the contrary. Ezekiel knew at least one major source of his torment, and so do we: he had experienced the tortuous brutalities of ancient warfare and the trauma of destruction. Yet Halperin mentions the Exile—and then only in passing—precisely two times in his entire book.

Such tendencies to read the psychological state of Ezekiel totally apart from the social and political experiences he suffered are symptoms of the same avoidance in other biblical scholarly

---

[57] Halperin, *Seeking*, 27.
[58] Halperin, *Seeking*, 5.

analyses—an avoidance of the Exile as a real event where human beings deeply suffered. Any psychological assumptions about Ezekiel derived apart from serious attention to the Exile are thus tantamount to blaming the victim.

POSTTRAUMATIC STRESS DISORDER AND EZEKIEL THE REFUGEE

Attention to the social, economic, and traumatic causes of stress at work in circumstances of subordination, disaster, warfare, or political oppression (either individually in or a group) has led in recent years to increased attention to Posttraumatic Stress Disorder (PTSD).[59] It was only in 1980 that the Diagnostic and Statis-

---

[59] Among the works consulted for this study are the following, in alphabetical order of authors' names: A. Bleich, S. Kron, C. Margalit, G. Inbar, Z. Kaplan, S. Cooper, and Z. Solomon, "Israeli Psychological Casualties of the Persian Gulf War: Characteristics, Therapy, and Selected Issues," *Israel Journal of Medical Sciences* 27:11–12, 673–76; J. Borkan, P. Shvartzman, S. Reis, and A. Morris, "Stories from the Sealed Rooms: Patient Interviews During the Gulf War," *Family Practice* 10/2 (1993): 188–94; I. Bownes, E. O'Gorman, A. Sayers, "Assault Characteristics and Posttraumatic Stress Disorder in Rape Victims," *Acta Psychiatrica Scandinavica* 83/1 (1991): 27–30; Daniel Brom and Eliezer Witztum, "When Political Reality Enters Therapy: Ethical Considerations in the Treatment of Posttraumatic Stress Disorder," in Kleber et al., *Beyond Therapy*, 237–48; E. Carlson and R. Rosser-Hogan, "Cross-Cultural Response to Trauma: A Study of Traumatic Experiences and Posttraumatic Symptoms in Cambodian Refugees," *Journal of Traumatic Stress* 7/1 (1994): 43–58; C. Classen, C. Koopman, and D. Spiegal, "Trauma and Dissociation," *Bulletin of the Menninger Clinic* 57/2 (1993): 178–94; J. Davidson and E. Foa, "Diagnostic Issues in Posttraumatic Stress Disorder: Considerations for the DSM-IV," *Journal of Abnormal Psychology* 100/3 (1991): 346–55; P. Dixon, G. Rehling, R. Shiwach, "Peripheral Victims of the Herald of Free Enterprise Disaster," *British Journal of Medical Psychology* 66 (1993): 193–202; C. Figley, and R. Kleber, "Beyond the Victim: Secondary Traumatic Stress," in *Beyond Trauma: Cultural and Societal Dynamics*, R. Kleber, C. Figley, and B. Gersons (New York: Plenum, 1995), 75–98; A. Fontana, R. Rosenhoeck, and E. Brett, "War Zone Traumas and Posttraumatic Stress Disorder Symptomatology," *The Journal of Nervous and Mental Disease* 180/12 (1992): 748–55; B.

Gersons, and I. Carlier, "Post-Traumatic Stress Disorder: The History of a Recent Concept," *British Journal of Psychiatry* 161 (1992): 742–48; A. Goenjian, L. Najarian, R. Pynoos, A. Steinberg, P. Petrosian, S. Setrakyan, L. Fairbanks, "Posttraumatic Stress Reactions after Single and Double Trauma," *Acta Psychiatrica Scandinavica* 90 (1994): 214–21; B. Green, J. Lindu, M. Grace, and A. Leonard, "Chronic Posttraumatic Stress Disorder and Diagnostic Comorbidity in a Disaster Sample," *The Journal of Nervous and Mental Disease* 180/12 (1992), 760–66; E. Hauff and P. Vaglum, "Vietnamese Boat Refugees: The Influences of War and Flight Traumatization on Mental Health on Arrival in the Country of Resettlement," *Acta Psychiatrica Scandinavica* 88 (1993): 162–69; D. Lukoff, F. Lu, and R. Turner, "Toward a More Culturally Sensitive DSM–IV," *The Journal of Nervous and Mental Disease* 180/11 (1992): 673–82; Susan Mattson, "Mental Health of Southeast Asian Refugee Women: An Overview," *Health Care for Women International* 14 (1993): 155–65; C. Molgaard, K. Poikolainen, J. Elder, A. Nissinen, J. Pekkanen, A. Golbeck, C. deMoor, K. Lahtela, and P. Puska, "Depression Late After Combat: A Follow-Up of Finnish World War Two Veterans," *Military Medicine* 156/5 (1991): 219–22; John B. Murray, "Posttraumatic Stress Disorder: A Review," *Genetic, Social, and General Psychology Monographs* 118/3 (1992): 315–38; Richard H. Rahe, "Acute Versus Chronic Post-Traumatic Stress Disorder," *Integrative Physiological and Behavioural Science* 28/1 (1993): 46–56; S. Robinson, M. Rapaport-Bar-Sever, and J. Rapaport, "The Present State of People Who Survived the Holocaust as Children," *Acta Psychiatrica Scandinavica* 89 (1994): 242–45; Derek Summerfield, "Addressing Human Response to War and Atrocity: Major Challenges in Research and Practices and the Limitations of Western Psychiatric Models," in *Beyond Trauma*, eds. Kleber, Figley, Gersons, 17–30; P. Sutker, M. Uddo, K. Brailey, A. Allain, and P. Errera, "Psychological Symptoms and Psychiatric Diagnoses in Operation Desert Storm Troops Serving Graces Registration Duty," *Journal of Traumatic Stress* 7/2 (1994): 159–71; R. Ursano, C. Fullerton, Tzu-Cheg Kao, and V. Bhartiya, "Longitudinal Assessment of Posttraumatic Stress Disorder and Depression after Exposure to Traumatic Death," *The Journal of Nervous and Mental Disease* 183/1 (1995): 36–42; John P. Wilson, "The Historical Evolution of PTSD Diagnostic Criteria: From Freud to DSM–IV," *Journal of Traumatic Stress* 7/4 (1994): 681–98; U. Yaktin and S. Labban, "Traumatic War Stress and Schizophrenia," *Journal of Psychosocial Nursing* 30/6 (1992): 29–33; R. Yehuda, B. Kahana, S. Southwick, E. Giller, "Depressive Features in

tical Manual of Mental Disorders (DSM) of the American Psychiatric Association listed a symptomology of "Posttraumatic Stress Disorder." Among the indications of PTSD appearing in the latest edition of DSM, we find

> recurrent and instrusive distressing recollections of the event, including images, thoughts, or perceptions, ... recurrent distressing dreams of the event, ... acting or feeling as if the traumatic event were recurring (includes a sense of reliving the experience, illusions, hallucinations, and ... flashbacks), ... intense psychological distress at exposure to internal or external cues that symbolize or resemble an aspect of the traumatic event, ... efforts to avoid thoughts, feelings ... associated with the trauma, ... [and a] feeling of detachment or estrangement from others.[60]

In the sixteen years since this symptomology has entered DSM, interest in trauma studies and related psychological and sociological studies have increased dramatically. This interest has not come without a serious backlash. To suggest that warfare— both shooting and being shot at, for example—can have serious and debilitating psychological consequences has obvious implications for governments and industries. These two institutions are usually eager to devote as many resources as possible to the causes of destruction and as few as possible on its human and environmental results.

In a recent review of the history of PTSD, Wilson points out,

> Viewed from a historical perspective, the emergence of widespread interest in PTSD by the medical and behavioural sciences as well as in legal arenas of litigation is quite understandable and, perhaps, expectable when examined by a retrospective look at some major events of the twentieth century: two World Wars; the atomic bombing of Hiro-

---

Holocaust Survivors with Post-Traumatic Stress Disorder," *Journal of Traumatic Stress* 7/4 (1994): 699–704.

[60] Cf., Murray, "Posttraumatic," 316.

shima; scores of nationalistic and colonial wars; widespread civil violence; mass genocide.... When it is considered that hundreds of millions of human lives have been adversely effected by such traumatic events, it only stands to reason that sooner or later scientific inquiry would accumulate enough momentum to began examining the multifaceted aspects of what traumatization means, and the potential long-term impact [on] human lives of such events.[61]

By now PTSD has been thoroughly documented as resulting from a variety of traumatic experiences, both natural and produced by human intervention. Its central symptoms, intrusive memory and debilitating depression, have been documented in an impressive variety of cultures around the world. Studies have been conducted of Armenians who survived the massive earthquake of 1988 (25,000 dead), Vietnamese and Cambodian refugees in the USA and Norway, Sri Lankan survivors of disaster, and Israelis, Russians, and Indians. The work continues, particularly on nuancing cultural variations in symptoms and in the expression of symptoms.

A sampling from recent literature on PTSD is suggestive. As B. Gersons and I. Carlier point out in their review article in the *British Journal of Psychiatry* (1992), PTSD has its origins as a new diagnosis in response to the unique psychic consequences of war in the twentieth century — particularly the war in Vietnam.[62] War continues to provide significant sources of research. In the Gulf War, missiles were fired at Tel Aviv neighborhoods, for example.[63] What was the psychosocial impact of this violence? A high incidence of PTSD symptoms (over 50 percent) occurred among military personnel who worked with identifying the dead. One worker reported crying out the name of the first identified body while sleeping.[64]

---

[61] Wilson, "Historical," 682.
[62] Gersons and Carlier, "Posttraumatic."
[63] Borkan, Shvartzman, Reis, and Morris, "Stories."
[64] Sutker, Uddo, Brailey, Allain, and Errera, "Psychological."

Ezekiel's vision of the valley of bones in chapter 37 may have been intended to depict a battlefield strewn with dead.

John Murray further notes that "combat exposure, its duration, witnessing the death of comrades, and participating in atrocities were the most frequent factors associated with PTSD."[65] Guilt associated with participation in the atrocities of the Vietnam War appears to be a prominent feature among those who experienced that conflict.[66] J. Davidson and E. Foa concur, stating that "physical injury, bereavement, participation in atrocities, exposure to grotesque death, and witnessing or hearing about death were ... often associated with the development of PTSD."[67] Note here the suggestions about Ezekiel's hearing of the fall of Jerusalem, with the accompanying news of his wife's death.

Particularly important in PTSD research is the fact that symptoms can persist or even turn up years after the events that triggered the symptoms.[68] Disaster workers reported symptoms three years following the sinking of the Herald of Free Enterprise ferry in the English Channel in 1987.[69]

Research has discovered specific factors when dealing with children, such as prolonged exposure to violence in poor, urban neighborhoods,[70] but also with women, particularly in cases of rape.[71] Notable for our study of Ezekiel, Murray reports that "the interval between rape and presenting for treatment was about eight years for a woman who had lost her ability to speak in the meantime."[72] Note that the text indicates that Ezekiel was struck mute for the duration of most of his symbolic actions, and he

---

[65] Murray, "Posttraumatic," 316.

[66] Murray, "Posttraumatic," 317.

[67] Davidson and Foa, "Diagnostic," 347. See also Ursano, Fullerton, Kao, and Bhartiya, "Longitudinal," 41.

[68] Murray, "Posttraumatic," 324.

[69] Dixon, Rehling, and Shiwach, "Peripheral."

[70] Fitzpatrick and Boldizar, 1993.

[71] See Bownes, O'Gorman, and Sayers, 1991.

[72] Murray, "Posttramatic," 327.

became able to speak only with the news of the fall of Jerusalem and the death of his wife. Research indicates that PTSD symptoms are found in those reacting to natural disasters as well.[73]

Research on specific symptoms is intriguing. For example,[74] C. Classen, C. Koopman, and D. Spiegel report the symptoms of feeling detached, as if one is an observer of one's own mental or bodily processes:

> Rape victims often speak of feeling as though they are float-ing above their own body, feeling sorry for the woman suf-fering the sexual assault. A car accident survivor said her experience "was as though I was separate from myself and watching, like in a dream when you are watching your-self." ... A Vietnam combat veteran said, "I felt myself separating from myself and looking down at the person who was in combat, and feeling sorry for him."[75]

Such specifics give us pause when thinking of Ezekiel's famous vision of being miraculously and bodily transported back to Jeru-salem to witness the heresies of the temple in chapters 8–11.

The application of PTSD symptomology and literature to his-torical cases is not new. In a 1994 issue of *Psychological Medicine*, Parry-Jones and Parry-Jones apply PTSD terminology to an eighteenth-century avalanche disaster. Drawing on accounts from those who witnessed and survived this disaster, they were able to observe classic PTSD symptoms. Most important, however, is Jonathan Shay's study *Achilles in Vietnam*.[76]

Of particular interest to us is the PTSD research conducted with refugees. Psychologists and medical scholars have been inter-ested in cross-cultural differences in exhibiting PTSD symptoms, and in the length of time that symptoms are reported or persist

---

[73] Murray, "Posttramatic," 326.

[74] Classen, Koopman, and Spiegel, "Assault."

[75] Classen, Koopman, and Spiegel, "Trauma," 181.

[76] Jonathan Shay, *Achilles in Vietnam: Combat Trauma and the Undoing of Character* (New York: Atheneum, 1994).

among, for example, Cambodian refugees and Vietnamese refugees in the United States and Norway.[77]

Scholars are moving toward a profound recognition that PTSD is allowing for a much greater depth in our understanding of the psychological and even spiritual impact of warfare and refugee life. The loss of one's way of life, one's entire world, may itself trigger such symptoms. As D. Lukoff, F. Lu, and R. Turner argue, "Cultural bereavement may exemplify a psychospiritual problem occurring within a non-Western ethnic group."[78] When this loss is connected to violent loss, as with refugees created by warfare or state-sponsored terrorism, we begin to hear new tones in the voice of Ezekiel.

Sociologists are now beginning to analyze the psychological and even spiritual impact of state-sponsored terrorism against whole peoples and cultures. Frantz Fanon, the Martinique-born psychiatrist, worked on the side of the Algerian resistance from 1953 until his untimely death in 1961. Though Fanon is often remembered for his political philosophy, he was also a pioneer in the exploration of the psychological impact of colonization and of the sociopolitical context of psychological illness.

In *Frantz Fanon and the Psychology of Oppression*, Hussein Bulhan writes,

> To lock up a person in a cell, left to his fantasies and hurts, is simply to sanction and intensify the very "pathology" to be cured. It is also to reenact, in the name of science and care, the very sadomasochism, rejection, and violence prevalent in his social life. Moreover, it is not enough to search for a "cure" by conjuring up imaginary roles and concocting artificial groups when real aspects of the person and his

---

[77] Carlson and Rosser-Hogan, "Cross-Cultural"; Hauff and Vaglum, 1993; Mattson, "Mental Health."

[78] Lukoff, Lu, and Turner, "Toward," 676.

social milieu can be engaged, confronted, and changed in the real society.[79]

Attention to the social, economic, and traumatic causes of stress at work in circumstances of subordination, disaster, warfare, or political oppression (either individually or a group) has led in recent years to increased attention to PTSD as a means of understanding cultural groups who suffer as entire peoples. Eduardo and Bonnie Duran's brilliant work, *Native American Postcolonial Psychology*,[80] is an excellent move in this direction and has obvious relevance to a fuller reading of Ezekiel.

In their work, the Durans note the specific social impact of the First Contact period, the Invasive War Period, the Subjugation and Reservation Period, the Boarding School Period, and finally the Forced Relocation and Termination Period. They refer to the cross-generational aspects of PTSD symptomology, as noted in children of Holocaust survivors, and discuss dreams as places of pain and groping for understanding in Native culture and practice.

These avenues of research suggest interesting new directions in assessing the social values of Ezekiel's "visions," including the more egalitarian Israel projected in the great vision of restoration in chapters 40–48.

THE "SIGN-ACTIONS" OF EZEKIEL: TOWARD A NEW READING

The PTSD literature forces us to ask serious questions about the adequacy of any psychological assessment of Ezekiel that does not appreciate the historical and social implications of the siege of Jerusalem, the deportations, and the executions by the Babylonian armies in the Exile.

---

[79] Hussein Abdilahi Bulhan, *Frantz Fanon and the Psychology of Oppression* (New York: Plenum Press, 1985).

[80] Eduardo and Bonnie Duran, *Native American Postcolonial Psychology* (Albany: State University of New York Press, 1995).

Furthermore, PTSD literature notes the presence of secondary trauma, the symptoms of which are widely documented. One need not be present at the death of a loved one — merely the news can be sufficiently traumatic. Furthermore, proximity to the time of the disasters or traumas is clearly an interesting aspect of PTSD studies, some of which document symptoms twenty to forty years after the events themselves.

Has the psychological exegesis of Ezekiel tended toward blaming the victim? A synoptic reading of the Exile through Ezekiel and the book of Lamentations forces us to take a fresh look at the actions and behavior of Ezekiel. Lamentations consists of poetic memories of the fall of Jerusalem. Reading Ezekiel with an eye to Lamentations suggests that many of Ezekiel's "bizarre" actions modeled the trauma of the fall of Jerusalem. This can be true whether Ezekiel was acting on personal knowledge, on the knowledge brought to him by recent refugees, or whether the texts were redacted to reflect these realities. Let us consider some of the famous "sign-actions" in this way:

First, in 3:22-27, Ezekiel sits confined in his home with his hands tied by cords. We see similar images of confinement in Lamentations 3:7-9, with its suggestive language of chains.

Second, in Ezekiel 4:1-3, the siege of Jerusalem forces some people to eat impure foods, or foods prepared in an impure manner. Lamentations 1:11; 2:12; and 4:4, 9-10 speak about hunger, leading to suggestions of cannibalism (cf. Jer. 37:2; 52:6, 24; and possibly 2 Kings 25:3).

Third, in 5:1-17, Ezekiel acts out the threefold punishment of Jerusalem. A third of the city's inhabitants are burnt, a third die by the sword, and a third are exiled, or "scattered to the wind." Similarly, Lamentations 1:1 and 2:21 speak of those who have "fallen by the sword."

Fourth, in chapter 12 Ezekiel prepares "an exile's bag" and is led through a hole in a wall to exemplify being taken as a prisoner of war. He is reliving the events, both his own past experience, and his image of events to come. In Lamentations 1:3, 18 we read, "Led into exile," while Lamentations 2:8 refers to destroyed walls.

Fifth, in Ezekiel 21, Babylonian forces are modeled by a sword. Compare Lamentations 2:21 and 5:9, where the "sword" refers to foreign rule.

There is, of course, a tendency to dismiss historical references to the suffering of exile in Lamentations as well. Iain Provan, for example, speaks of "stereotypical" or "pattern-types" for historical texts such as Lamentations. If Lamentations, so the argument runs, was written in a stereotypical pattern for laments, then the specific details are not the result of historical observation or experience. Rather, they are to be dismissed as a literary invention after the style of a lamentation.[81] However, such literary analysis renders chains and fetters, swords and suffering, into sanitized metaphors that insulate the modern reader from the trauma of the Exile as an event in the life of the Hebrews.

Such exclusively literary approaches are similar to questioning the sanity of Ezekiel. They also question how seriously "symbolic actions" should be taken as reflecting social realities of the exilic experience and impact. Thus, when Halperin ignores the social circumstances and realities of the Exile in order to read Ezekiel as struggling with sexuality, he is blaming the victim.

When Halperin confidently concludes at the end of his engaging study that "at last we can hear Ezekiel," I would argue that we cannot hear Ezekiel clearly unless we also hear the imperial voice of Nebuchadnezzar the conqueror. Studies of Ezekiel and other exilic-period biblical literature will need to understand something of the trauma of the Exile if they are to be sufficiently historical and critical and if modern readers of faith are to garner valid theological fruit from this prophet.

---

[81] Iain W. Provan, *Lamentations* (Grand Rapids: Eerdmans, 1991). I argue, however, that even stereotypical language of trauma and suffering can hardly be intended to describe benign events.

7

Power in Wisdom
The Suffering Servant of Ecclesiastes 4

Douglas B. Miller

Millard Lind introduced me to the importance of the servant poems of Isaiah, which then became the inspiration for this treatment of Ecclesiastes 4. Millard himself has been even more of an inspiration, especially for his scholarship, his care for students, and his service to the church. It is a joy to honor him in a small way by contributing to this collection of essays.

Perceptions of Qohelet's attitude toward social and political power have been unavoidably shaped by the assumption that Qohelet is a cynical pessimist, and that he wrote Ecclesiastes primarily to vent his personal frustrations.[1] It is sometimes claimed

---

[1] Early Jewish and Christian exegetes, assuming the author to be Solomon, largely took one of two positions regarding the book: that the speaker was confessing the vain deeds of his youth as a warning, or that he was urging people to eschew the vain things of this world in preparation for the eternal realm (sometimes both). With the Enlightenment came a reevaluation of both authorship and message, and an appreciation for the complexity of Qohelet's thought. The author was then read as a critic of Israel's faith—a critic who refused to ignore the absurd realities of life. Apparent tensions in the work were generally ascribed to later editors and/or redactors who sought to soften Qohelet's statements in the direction of orthodoxy (see e.g., George A. Barton, *The Book of Ecclesiastes* [Edinburgh: T & T Clark, 1908]). Some have argued that Qohelet, while acknowledging life's inherent absurdity, nevertheless emphasizes certain hopeful possibilities (e.g., R. N. Whybray, "Qoheleth, Preacher of Joy,"

that he views human suffering primarily as an intellectual dilemma,[2] or mentions it only as an isolated exception to an otherwise self-centered focus.[3] While he advises his readers to escape misfortune as best they can, so the scenario continues, he has little hope for change and certainly no proposal for actually doing anything about life's tragedies.

There are good reasons, however, for concluding that Qohelet's purpose in writing was not simply to vent his own disappointments, and that the advice he gives is not simply cynical. Here we will reassess Qohelet's teaching with regard to power and the oppression that may be associated with it.

In this essay I will argue that Ecclesiastes 4:1-16 should be read as a unit in which Qohelet points to individualism (lack of a community orientation) and materialism (the drive to accumulate) as key factors in the persistence of oppression. In their place, he promotes a lifestyle that counteracts rather than perpetuates systems of oppression. I will begin with some prefatory comments about the book of Ecclesiastes and a rationale for the structure and

---

Journal for the Study of the Old Testament 23 [1982]: 87–98). In recent decades, there has been a renewed attempt to account for the book's perceived tensions as either misunderstandings or as intentional on the part of the author. The work of Michael V. Fox (*Qohelet and His Contradictions* [Sheffield: Almond, 1989]) has been especially significant in the effort to read the book essentially as received, even if some editorial work may still be granted (e.g., at 1:1; 7:27; and 12:9-14). I also work from this position, but additionally insist that Qohelet is not declaring all of life to be absurd, vain, or meaningless, even though life's limitations are at the heart of his instruction. Those who take a similar approach include Daniel C. Fredericks, *Coping with Transience: Ecclesiastes on Brevity in Life* (Sheffield: JSOT, 1993); Kathleen A. Farmer, *Who Knows What is Good?* (Grand Rapids: Eerdmans, 1991); and C. L. Seow, *Ecclesiastes*, Anchor Bible 18C (New York: Doubleday, 1997).

[2] E.g., Fox, *Contradictions*, 201. In contrast, Barton cites 4:1-3 as indicative of Qohelet's "profound sympathies with the lower classes" (*Ecclesiastes*, 114).

[3] E.g., James L. Crenshaw, *Ecclesiastes*, Old Testament Library (Philadelphia: Westminster, 1987), 106.

unity of chapter four. I then will present an exposition of the chapter that reveals the interrelationship of the issues raised by Qohelet. I will conclude by relating Ecclesiastes 4 to the rhetoric and ethics of the book as a whole.

THE BOOK OF ECCLESIASTES

Ecclesiastes is rightly identified as wisdom literature: its purpose is persuasive, it argues primarily on the basis of regular and observable human experiences, and it instructs its readers on making the best of their present existence. I understand the book in its final form to be essentially the work of one author/editor.[4] Since there are few difficulties of a textual nature, the interpretive task may be devoted to the message of the book in its received form.

It is especially vital to assess properly Qohelet's use of the term *hebel* (הֶבֶל), which appears nearly forty times in the book. Literally, the word means "vapor" or "fumes," but it is often translated as "vanity" (KJV, NRSV, NASB), as "meaningless" (NIV), or with other terms of negative assessment. However, *hebel* is better understood, in the artistry and design of Qohelet, as a symbol with several metaphorical referents: some things are transient, others are insubstantial, and still others are foul or wrong. So "all is *hebel*" (1:2; 12:8).[5] Thus, Qohelet is realistic about the inequities of life,

---

[4] It is difficult to assess with confidence the relationship between the first-person statements at the heart of the book and the occasional presence of a third-person narrator (1:1-2; 7:7; 12:8-14). Michael Fox raises the possibility that the narrator's voice is used by the author to reflect the style of ancient Near Eastern instructional literature. See Michael V. Fox, "Frame-Narrative and Composition in the Book of Qohelet," *Hebrew Union College Annual* 48 (1977): 83–106. I conclude that the book's coherence requires either that Qohelet is responsible for all—or nearly all—of the book as we have it, or that an editor has collected and arranged his teachings essentially in this form.

[5] See Douglas B. Miller, "The Symbolic Function of *Hebel* in the Book of Ecclesiastes" (Ph.D. diss., Princeton Theological Seminary, 1996), and "Qohelet's Symbolic Use of הבל," *Journal of Biblical Literature* 117 (1998): 437–54. Assessments of *hebel* with some similarity to my position

and is critical of false confidence in the potential of wisdom, toil, and attempts to achieve pleasure; yet he is not declaring life *as a whole* to be empty, futile, or meaningless. Rather, he is dismantling these false hopes in order to establish a viable orientation in which work, pleasure, and wisdom find their proper place.

Another complication for the interpretation of Ecclesiastes is the matter of its organization. Some commentators have decided that the book has no identifiable pattern. Beginning with the seminal work of Addison Wright, however, it has been recognized that many of Qohelet's literary devices have a structural significance.[6] These include the repetition of key phrases,[7] inclusio,[8] and chiasm.[9] In short, the book may be divided into two halves, though themes overlap between the two. The focus of the first half of the book (1:2–6:9) is upon human effort as manifested in work, pleasure, and wisdom, while the second half (6:10–12:8) emphasizes the limits of human knowledge.

---

may be found in Fredericks, *Coping with Transience* and Farmer, *Who Knows What is Good?*

[6] Addison G. Wright, "The Riddle of the Sphinx: The Structure of the Book of Qoheleth," *Catholic Biblical Quarterly* 30 (1968): 313–34. Respect for Wright's insights in no way requires one to embrace his entire proposal.

[7] Key repeating phrases include, in the first half, "(*hebel* and) chasing after wind," and in the second, "who can find" and "do not know" or "no knowledge."

[8] The work's theme statement prominently frames the first-person instruction (1:2; 12:8). In addition, the book both opens and closes with poems that concern human limitations and that allude also to the limitations of the cosmos.

[9] Daniel Fredericks has argued convincingly for a chiastic arrangement in Eccles. 5:6 [English, 5:7]–6:9 ("Chiasm and Parallel Structure in Qoheleth 5:6–6:9," *Journal of Biblical Literature* 108 [1989]: 17–35; cf. C. L. Seow, *Ecclesiastes*, 215–18). In general, interpreters have continued to grow in their respect for the book's closing assessment that Qohelet was a sage who wrote words of truth with care and felicity (12:9-10).

THE LIMITS AND STRUCTURE OF ECCLESIASTES 4:1-16

We turn now to Ecclesiastes 4:1-16, found in the midst of Qohelet's focus on human effort. There is little question about the boundaries and thematic unity of the preceding and following units. Ecclesiastes 3:1-22 begins with the "time" poem (3:1-8), followed by a reflection on the sovereignty of God in the determination of events (3:9-15). The implications of time for God's testing of human beings are developed in 3:16-22.[10] The section that follows our passage, 4:17–5:6 (in English, 5:1-7), is also concerned with the deity — in this case, with warnings concerning perilous speech.

It remains, then, to determine whether the verses in between, Ecclesiastes 4:1-16, are interrelated and united in theme. Commentators generally agree regarding the boundaries of smaller units in this chapter: verses 1-3, 4-6, 7-8, 9-12, 13-16.[11] One striking feature

---

[10] The conclusion of the unit in 3:22 parallels that of 2:24-26, the ending of the royal experiment section. This, the reference to "time" in 3:17 and the continued development of God's role connect 3:16-22 with 3:1-15, making it unlikely that the comments on oppression in 4:1-3 are a continuation of 3:16-22 (Fox, *Contradictions*, 199–200). Although 3:16, like 4:1-3, concerns corrupted power, the focus in chap. 3 continues to be upon the role of God.

[11] A diversity of proposals for the interrelationship or nonrelationship of these subunits has been made by commentators, e.g., Robert Gordis, *Koheleth: The Man and His World* (New York: Schocken, 1968), 238–46, who considers 4:1-3 part of the previous section; J. A. Loader, *Ecclesiastes* (Grand Rapids: Eerdmans, 1986 [1984]), 47–57; Barton, *Ecclesiastes*, 113–22, who isolates vv. 13-16; and R. N. Whybray, *Ecclesiastes* (Grand Rapids: Eerdmans, 1989), 81–91, who isolates both 4:1-3 and 4:13-16. Fox is one who does see some pattern among the subunits, calling them "a loose thematic cluster" (*Contradictions*, 199). Graham Ogden, who would also isolate 4:13-16, argues that 4:1-12 be divided into three sub-sections, ending in a "better"-saying (4:1-3, 4-6, 7-9), with vv. 10-12 an explanatory addition to the third sub-section ("The Mathematics of Wisdom: Qoheleth IV 1-12," *Vetus Testamentum* 34 [1984]: 446–47). Dominic Rudman has recently defended the thematic unity of the entire chapter ("A Contextual Reading of Ecclesiastes 4:13-16," *Journal of Biblical Literature* 116 [1997]: 57–73).

of these smaller units, suggestive of some pattern of association, is the use of the term *tôb* (טוֹב, "good, better") in each section. The first two subunits *end* with a "better-saying," the final two *begin* with a better-saying, while the center section, framed by two *hebel* statements, asks the rhetorical question "Why am I depriving myself of good (*tôb*)?"

Another stylistic feature in chapter four is the use of numbers. The word "one" (אֶחָד) is found six times here (out of seventeen in Ecclesiastes). The terms שֵׁנִי (3x) and שְׁנַיִם (5x), "second" and "two" respectively, occur here and only one other time in the entire book (11:6). As he uses these numbers, Qohelet incorporates them into unique variations of the better-saying pattern (4:3, 6, and 9).[12]

Granted a unity of style and some association with numbers, the task remains to determine whether this arrangement also has a thematic focus. Commentators propose various topics around different combinations of the subsections in chapter four, such as the divisiveness of humanity or a challenge to the value of hard work.[13]

Verses 13-16, however, are problematic in several ways. Most commentators isolate them as unrelated to what comes before or after. Yet certain repetitions of vocabulary connect this final section to 4:1-12: "prison" (v. 14, which may be compared to oppressions in vv. 1-3), "the living" (vv. 2, 15), "second" (vv. 8, 10, 15), "no end" (vv. 8, 16), "under the sun" (vv. 1, 3, 7, 15), "I saw" (vv. 1, 4, 7, 15), and the *hebel* phrase (vv. 4, 7, 8, 16).

Of course, the *hebel* phrase serves as the prime motif throughout Ecclesiastes, while "under the sun" and "I saw" are

---

[12] These provide an interesting comparison with typical "numerical sayings" in wisdom literature. Traditionally, numbers are used simply for counting, as in Prov. 6:16, "There are six things which the LORD hates, seven which are an abomination to him." Qohelet finds additional uses for numbers in his rhetoric. Cf. Graham Ogden, "Mathematics of Wisdom," 446–53.

[13] Dominic Rudman, "Contextual Reading," 58; and Robert Gordis, *Koheleth*, 240, respectively.

also pervasive. Yet it is worth noting that the latter two phrases do not occur again until the end of Ecclesiastes 5 (vv. 12, 17 [English, vv. 13, 18]). Furthermore, the other vocabulary repetitions in 4:13-16 coincide with the previously noted marks of affinity (use of *tôb* and numbers) and the cohesive units which precede and follow chapter four. These considerations invite an attempt to incorporate the message of verses 13-16 with that of the rest of the chapter.

The structure of Ecclesiastes 4 proposed here is chiastic:

A The oppressed abandoned (4:1-3)
  B Toil in competition; advises contentment (4:4-6)
    C Toil for no purpose (4:7-8)
  B' Toil alone; advises cooperation (4:9-12)
A' The oppressed wise youth abandoned (4:13-16)

The employment of *tôb* and the numbers one and two are thus not simply catchwords in this chapter.[14] Their configuration draws attention to the thematic unity of these verses: a concern for self-centered toil framed by discussions of oppression. Qohelet demonstrates in this unit how certain kinds of toil result in the loss of good (*tôb*) for the many.

AN EXPOSITION OF ECCLESIASTES 4

4:1-3 *The Oppressed Abandoned*

1 Furthermore,[15] I saw[16] all the oppressions that are worked under the sun. Look, the tears of the oppressed[17]—with no

---

[14] Fox perceives a kind of thematic "chaining" involving *tôb* from one subunit to the next rather than an artificial *Stichwort* connection (*Contradictions*, 200).

[15] The verb שַׁבְתִּי (4:1, "Furthermore") signals the start of this new section. See discussion at 4:7 below. Unless otherwise indicated, the translations here and elsewhere in this essay are my own.

[16] The verb רָאָה ("to see") is one of several verbs by which Qohelet emphasizes his direct encounter with topics of current focus. In this unit it occurs again in vv. 3, 4, 7, and 15.

[17] The term הָעֲשֻׁקִים is employed in this verse to express both "oppressions" and "the oppressed" (cf. Jer. 50:33; Ps. 103:6), while the

one to comfort them! Power[18] comes from the hand of their oppressors—with no one to comfort them.[19] **2** And I congratulated the dead who have already died more than the living who are still alive, **3** but better than both of them is the one who never has been and has not seen the evil work that is worked under the sun.

The previous section (3:1-22) ended with Qohelet's conclusion that nothing is better for humans than to enjoy their work (הַמַּעֲשֶׂי). Now he points out that some people's work is devoted to oppressing others (הַמַּעֲשֶׂה הָרָע אֲשֶׁר נַעֲשָׂה), "the evil work which is worked"). He will proceed to describe how one's work can truly be enjoyed (4:4-6, 9-12). R. N. Whybray rightly observes the way Qohelet crafts his words to achieve the effect of high emotional intensity:

> The threefold repetition of the same root in "oppressions … oppressed … oppressors," the use of the dramatic "behold" and of emotive words like "tears" and "comfort," the

---

active participle indicates the oppressors (עֹשְׁקֵיהֶם). The root עשק is used of such things as exploiting a debtor who is unable to pay (Deut. 24:14) and of political or social tyranny (Deut. 28:29, 33). Cf. also Job 35:9 and Amos 3:9, where this term is used of "oppressions" that are specific actions, the latter with the verb רָאָה.

[18] The word כֹּחַ refers to strength and ability in general, whether of individuals or groups; cf. Eccl. 9:10.

[19] Some commentators have removed the second occurrence of this phrase as a dittography, while others have proposed various emendations. For instance, R. B. Y. Scott reads מְנַקֵּם ("avenger") for מְנַחֵם (*Proverbs, Ecclesiastes* [Anchor Bible 18; New York: Doubleday, 1965], 222). Others propose words that have dropped out, and still others suggest alternate meanings of verbal roots with the extant text. However, the repetition is meant for emphasis (so, e.g., ad loc., Crenshaw, *Ecclesiastes*; Seow, *Ecclesiastes*; and Roland Murphy, *Ecclesiastes*, Word Bible Commentary 23A [Dallas: Word, 1992]), and formally displays a theme of this section: the superiority of two over one.

change from prose to poetical form and the repetition of "and they had/there was no one to comfort them."[20]

It is particularly important to notice the verb נחם in the Piel ("comfort"), employed twice in this verse. It indicates an act of verbal encouragement, such as when David expressed regret to Hanun upon the death of his father Nahash (2 Sam. 10:2). However, for those in situations of oppression, the verbal declaration expresses confidence in deliverance (Isa. 40:1). Sometimes the term refers to the deliverance itself.[21] The speaker in Lamentations 1:16 longs for a "comforter" (as in 4:1, מְנַחֵם, a Piel participle of נחם) who will bring strength in the aftermath of an enemy's victory. The term רַע ("bad, evil"), which exhibits a partial synonymity with *hebel* in Ecclesiastes, expresses Qohelet's evaluation that these oppressive deeds done under the sun are wrong and disgusting.[22]

Qohelet concludes by lamenting the power that the oppressors have over their victims, and considers the dead—and even more, those who were never born—to be better off than such afflicted ones.[23] Qohelet has now introduced the three primary

---

[20] Whybray, *Ecclesiastes*, 81. Whybray goes on to point out how these verses give ample evidence of the inaccurate charge against Qohelet that he is content merely to point out injustice without proposing action to put it right.

[21] Cf. Pss. 23:4; 71:21; 86:17; 119:82; Isa. 49:13; 51:3, 12; 52:9; Jer. 31:13; Zech. 1:17.

[22] Compare the correspondence between *hebel* ("vapor") and רַע ("bad, evil") in Eccl. 1:12-15; 2:12-17; 2:18-23. The word רַע, usually translated as "evil," "adversity," "disaster," and the like, indicates either what is harmful or what is unacceptable, whether from a divine or a human perspective. Injustices are included among those matters Qohelet declares to be רַע, an affront to his sense of what is right. See Fox, *Contradictions*, 39-40; and Miller, "Qohelet's Symbolic Use of הבל," 449-52.

[23] The apparently contrary comment by Qohelet in 9:4 that a live dog is better than a dead lion is ironic in context. Qohelet's use of a better-saying here recalls his advice in 2:24; 3:12; and 3:22 that "there is nothing better than" to enjoy oneself, and it anticipates his deliberation on the knowledge of goodness (*tôb*) in 6:10-7:14.

parties who are his concern in Ecclesiastes 4: (1) the oppressed; (2) their oppressors; and (3) those called to give comfort. This third group, composed of Qohelet and his audience, are present in this subunit only by their absence: "no one to comfort."

4:4-6 Toil in Competition

> **4** Then I saw all toil and all gain[24] in work that it comes from a person's rivalry[25] with their friend. This indeed is vapor (*hebel*) and a pursuit of wind. **5** Fools fold their hands[26] and eat their flesh. **6** Better is a handful with peacefulness[27] than two handfuls with toil and a pursuit of wind.[28]

Up to this point in his treatise (Eccl. 1–3), Qohelet has repeatedly stressed that hard effort accomplishes nothing of permanent or significant value. The effort is as futile as chasing after wind. The second subsection of this unit, like 4:1-3, ends with a bettersaying and takes up a dimension of the toil issue which Qohelet

---

[24] The term כִּשְׁרוֹן may sometimes indicate "gain" and other times "skill." It may indicate the latter in Eccl. 2:21, but the former in 5:10 [English, 5:11]. Here in 4:4, the sense of "gain" appears more appropriate to the context than "skill" (so RSV). Qohelet presents the irony of those who lose and cause loss through their attempts to acquire.

[25] The term קִנְאָה, often translated "envy," indicates rivalry or competition. It is used both negatively (Prov. 14:30) and positively elsewhere (to refer to that which motivates greater accomplishment or zeal), as in Isa. 37:32.

[26] The phrase "folding the hands" is idiomatic for idleness, an idleness that brings poverty, according to Prov. 6:10; 10:18; 24:33; and others.

[27] The term נַחַת does not indicate inactivity, but rather the absence of strife or danger (cf. Isa. 30:15; Prov. 29:9; Eccl. 6:5; 9:17). Thus, it does not refer to the fools who "fold their hands" in 4:5.

[28] The Targum explains this verse to mean that a handful of food with enjoyment is better than toil. However, Prov. 15:16; 16:8; and 17:1 employ a similar construction to praise having a small amount of material things rather than a large amount along with some particular problem, such as trouble, lack of justice, or strife (Seow, *Ecclesiastes*, 188).

has not yet addressed: the rivalry which motivates those who labor.[29]

He is now focused directly upon his middle group, those who might help the ones "with no one to comfort them" (4:1). He finds them busy toiling in competition with others. Note the irony of the word *friend* here, which refers not to one who is supporting, but one who is attempting to outperform the other. People thus motivated do not help those in need nor—another irony—do they accomplish anything for their own benefit: "it is vapor and pursuit of wind" (v. 4).

An important phrase for understanding this subunit is 4:5b, וְאֹכֵל אֶת־בְּשָׂרוֹ, "and eats or consumes his flesh").[30] In one understanding of verse 5, Qohelet is declaring that even a sluggard, who folds the hands and refuses to work, has something to eat.[31] When Qohelet concludes with a plea for contentment in verse 6, he is elevating the fool—one otherwise not to be praised—as being in this regard superior to the one who toils fruitlessly.

Seow argues against such an interpretation on the grounds that elsewhere in Ecclesiastes *basar* (flesh) refers to the human body. In addition, the noun *basar* with a suffix in the Hebrew Bible never refers to one's food, but to the body or part of a body. Exam-

---

[29] As Seow points out, the grammatical construction קִנְאַת־אִישׁ may be taken two ways: as the motivation for toil and gain, or as the result of toil and gain (*Ecclesiastes*, 179). See the use of קִנְאָה to mean rivalry in Isa. 11:13 and *b.B.Bat.* 21a; cf. Eccl. 9:6. In either case, Qohelet is commenting upon an unhealthy dissatisfaction with what one has (see also Job 5:2; Prov. 6:34; 14:30; 27:4).

[30] It is possible, as some have proposed, that v. 5 is an instance of Qohelet adapting a traditional saying to his own purposes. This could explain some of the interpretive ambiguity.

[31] So Norbert Lohfink, *Kohelet*, 4th ed., Die Neue Echter Bibel, Altes Testament (Würzburg: Echter, 1993), 36–37. The verb אכל is commonly used with בשׂר in reference to humans eating food (Exod. 12:8, 46; 16:12; 29:32; Lev. 7:18; Num. 14:11; Deut. 12:20; Ezek. 4:14).

ples include the attack of an enemy (Ps. 27:2) and self-cannibalism during siege (Isa. 49:26).[32]

Thus, it is more likely that in 4:4-5 Qohelet has juxtaposed two extremes — obsessive competition and the poverty of slothfulness — in order to present a third and better option in verse 6. Better, he says, is the little one has in one's hand with peaceful rest than *either* self-destructive sloth *or* to have two full hands accompanied by exhaustive labor, which amounts to futility. In this way, Qohelet urges his reader to contentment in material things.[33]

4:7-8 Toil for No One Else

7 Furthermore,[34] I saw vapor (*hebel*) under the sun: 8 the case of one, without a second, who has not even son or bro-

---

[32] Seow, *Ecclesiastes*, 179.

[33] Cf. other treatments of toil without rest or satisfaction at Eccl. 1:8, 18; 2:22-23; 5:9-11 (English, 5:10-12); and 6:3-9.

[34] The term שׁבתי, used adverbially, is employed twice elsewhere in Ecclesiastes (4:1; 9:11) to indicate the beginning of a new thought. Though introducing a new focus, it is incorrect to conclude, as do some commentators (so Whybray, *Ecclesiastes*, 85), that it must always serve as a strong disjunctive beginning a major new unit (see, correctly, Fox, *Contradictions*, 201, 203; cf. also Seow, *Ecclesiastes*, 177, 188). Note *b.Ta'an.* 17a (Soncino translation):

> Hence the Sages have declared that any priest who can identify his *Mishmar* and his particular *Beth-ab* and who also knows definitely [*wywdc sbty*] that the members of his *Beth-ab* were participating in the service of the temple is forbidden to drink wine on the whole of that day ... [and twice more similarly in this passage; cf. *b.Shabb.* 88b; *b.Nid.* 47a].

The term is transitional, but it indicates connection with what was discussed previously. When שׁבתי is used in 4:1, Qohelet is picking up a subject treated previously in 3:16. At 9:11, Qohelet begins a section that meditates upon time and chance (cf. Eccl. 3), but the situation of inappropriate rewards described in that verse has also been mentioned previously, notably in 9:1-3 (also 2:14-21; 6:8; 7:15; 8:14). Thus, here in 4:7, Qohelet uses שׁבתי to introduce a new aspect of the same subject he has been discussing.

ther; and there is no end to that person's toil, yet their eyes are never satisfied with riches. "For whom am I toiling and depriving myself of good?" This indeed is vapor (*hebel*) and an evil business.[35]

Qohelet is again concerned with his would-be comforter group. First, he describes a person who toils without "end" (קֵץ) and without "satisfaction" (שָׂבַע) in riches. Then as he continues, Qohelet extends the analysis: the toiler, while accomplishing neither personal benefit nor good for anyone else, seems unable to stop.[36] The situation, more broadly evaluated, then, is (v. 8b) "vapor and an evil business" (הֶבֶל וְעִנְיַן רָע).[37]

The reference to riches anticipates the discussions in 5:9-11 and 5:12-16. But the focus in this subsection, as with the unit as a whole, is on self-serving effort as opposed to work that is of benefit to others. Again there is irony: in pursuit of riches, the toiler has been deprived of good, the good that Qohelet is about to describe in 4:9-12. But no one else has benefited from it either, particularly

---

[35] Both occurrences of *hebel* in 4:7-8 refer to the insubstantiality of vapor to describe work that is futile. The addition of "evil (רָע) business" in v. 8 communicates that Qohelet is not only being descriptive, but is pronouncing a negative evaluation. The רָע phrase echoes 1:13, with allusions also to 2:23, 26; 3:10; and in anticipation, 8:16. The phrase is also used in 5:13, where it appears to be a reference to a specific incident rather than a general evaluation of human existence.

[36] As elsewhere in the book, a rhetorical question is employed. The speaker is not identified—possibly it is Qohelet (Barton, *Ecclesiastes*, 64, 115). Most commentators agree, however, that this is a statement by the toiler or a question which Qohelet is challenging the toiler to make (see Gordis, *Koheleth*, 97). Perhaps by keeping the speaker unidentified, the reader is subtly invited to make the question one's own (Raymond E. Johnson, "The Rhetorical Question as a Literary Device in Ecclesiastes" [Ph.D. diss., Southern Baptist Theological Seminary, 1986], 160). In any case, the answer to the question is a negative one.

[37] Qohelet now declares toil to be *hebel* when done for personal benefit, just as previously he used *hebel* for toil that results in benefit for another (2:18-23).

the oppressed ones with which Qohelet introduced this section
(4:1-3), who experience their own dose of evil (רָע, v. 3).

An additional irony is that the question in 4:8 is asked in the
singular ("I, myself"). The person is working alone ("one, without
a second"), which reflects a significant aspect of the problem Qohelet is addressing and for which he now provides an answer.

4:9-12 Toil in Cooperation

> 9 Better are two than one, because they have a good reward
> for their toil. 10 For if either should fall, the one will lift up
> the other; but woe[38] to the one who falls and does not have
> a second to assist. 11 Also, if two lie together, they keep
> warm; but how can one keep warm alone? 12 And though
> one might prevail against another, two will withstand one.
> A threefold cord is not quickly broken.[39]

Here again Qohelet targets his middle, comforter group, now
building his positive case. Here he advocates "life in community"
in contrast to the futility of "toil for self," which he has disparaged
in 4:4-8. In verse 9, as in verse 6, Qohelet is not simply describing
life and pronouncing an evaluation. He is using the better-saying
type of wisdom sentence to give implicit advice. One may choose
to live a solitary life, with its deficiencies and potential woe. Or
one may live and work communally, which is "better" and brings

---

[38] Reading אִילוֹ as אִי לוֹ (woe to the one), and understanding אִי as
an alternate spelling of אוֹי, as does the Septuagint, the Syriac, the Vulgate
and several other Hebrew mss. (cf. Eccl. 10:16; Isa. 6:5). The Targum reads
it as conditional, like the other conditionals with עִם in this section (cf.
Eccl. 6:6). See the discussion in Antoon Schoors, *The Preacher Sought to
Find Pleasing Words* (Leuven: Peeters, 1992), 149; and Seow, *Ecclesiastes*,
182.

[39] A proverb involving the numbers one through three and, in particular, a "three-ply cord" shows up in an Akkadian fragment of the Gil-
gamesh Epic, where it likewise indicates strength in numbers. See A.
Shaffer, "The Mesopotamian Background of Qoh 4:9-12," *Eretz Israel* 8
(1967): 247–50; and idem, "New Light on the 'Three-Ply Cord,'" *Eretz
Israel* 9 (1969): 159–60.

a "good reward." Note that Qohelet does not declare this advice to be *hebel*.

When two are toiling together, they achieve a good reward (שָׂכָר טוֹב; v. 9) in three ways: (1) they help one another in mishaps, (2) they help one another keep warm, and (3) they provide greater resistance against adversity. Raymond Johnson points out Qohelet's devices for clinching each of these three points: a woe-saying for the first, a rhetorical question for the second, and a proverb for the third.[40] The woe-saying in 4:10b and the rhetorical question in verse 11b promote a tone of urgency as they develop the inadequacy of solitary existence.

This subunit is sometimes understood to reflect the setting of a journey during which one might fall, sleep in the night cold, and encounter bandits. However, nothing specifically suggests a journey in the passage.[41] Another setting in which such things might happen has already been provided in 4:1-3: the powerful oppress the weak as they toil. If one oppressed person falls, either in the exhaustion of labor or by being struck down, another can lift that person up. The poor who are cold at night need companions to keep warm. And when the oppressed are attacked, they require numbers, lest they be "broken."

Yet, the three circumstances Qohelet provides are general enough to embrace more than just those who are oppressed. Thus, they also serve as an appeal to those of other economic classes who are vulnerable to seduction by the solitary life.

4:13-16 The Oppressed Youth Abandoned

13 Better is a youth, a commoner but wise, than a king who is old but foolish, who no longer knows to take warning. 14

---

[40] "Rhetorical Question," 161–62.

[41] So Barton, *Ecclesiastes*, 115; and Rudman, "Contextual Reading," 68. In greater affinity with the theme of toil in this section, it is possible to construe the "journey" setting in economic terms, perhaps toiling on the way to market one's goods or otherwise to conduct business.

For out of prison[42] he[43] came forth to the king,[44] although[45] in his kingdom[46] he was born poor. **15** I saw all the living walking under the sun with the youth, the "second" (שֵׁנִי) who will replace him. **16** There was no end to all who were before them. Yet those who come later will not rejoice in him. Surely this indeed is vapor (*hebel*) and pursuing wind.

---

[42] This reading is supported by the ancient versions (except for the Targums). Nearly all commentators take הסורים as a bi-form for האסורים. Elsewhere an omission of *aleph* may be noted by comparing 2 Kgs. 8:28 with 2 Chron. 22:5.

[43] It is unclear whether the referent of the pronoun *he* is the youth or the king. In favor of the former is the possible connection between the youth's common status and his time in prison, and Qohelet's use elsewhere of clauses beginning with כִּי ("for") to provide the rationale for his better-sayings (e.g., 2:25; 3:22; 6:4), although none of them are so defended in chap. 4 (cf. Whybray, *Ecclesiastes*, 88–89). I understand both the one leaving prison and the one born poor to be the commoner introduced in v. 13a (so Fox, *Contradictions*, 207). However, it is also possible that v. 14a contrasts the young commoner (who came forth from prison) with the old king (v. 14b), who was "born into his kingship" and then "impoverished." The latter reading takes the form רָשׁ as a perfect 3ms verb rather than as a participle (so Seow, *Ecclesiastes*, 184).

[44] The interpretive options for לִמְלֹךְ are as follows: (1) an infinitive, "to reign," or (2) "to counsel" (from מלךְ II); or (3) a preposition with noun, "to the king."

[45] The sense of the phrase כִּי גַּם here is concessive. The function of these two particles in combination has several distinctive senses, but often the addition of גַּם serves simply to strengthen a common use that כִּי has by itself, such as "for (indeed)," Deut. 12:31; "yet (indeed)," Eccl. 8:12; "that (indeed)," Eccl. 8:16. For the concessive use of כִּי, cf. Jer. 49:16; Ps. 37:24.

[46] The late term מַלְכוּת with the preposition בְּ generally refers to the reign of the king and all his government, but occasionally also to its geographical dimension (Dan. 11:9; Ezra 1:1). The possessive *his* could refer either to the youth (his birth in the geographical region over which he would later rule) or to the old king (unknown to him and in his own kingdom, his successor was born poor).

As the structure of 4:1-16 returns to the issue of oppression with which it began, all three parties of Qohelet's concern again become evident: (1) those in power who oppress (the foolish king), (2) those are oppressed (the commoner youth once imprisoned), and (3) those others ("who are before them," and "those who come later," v. 16) who have potential to bring comfort.[47]

The subject-less verbs and third masculine singular pronouns in this subunit make for an ambiguity that has greatly challenged the interpretive skills of commentators. In addition, there is the question whether this tale has historical or legendary roots.

Essentially two proposals for this story have been offered. Both agree that 4:13 presents a contrast between a young, wise commoner and an old, foolish king. The first reads that the youth came from prison, usurped the royal office, and ruled wisely in his place, yet later was dishonored by a fickle public.[48] Variations on this thesis propose that the wise youth was himself deposed by a second youth (שֵׁנִי, v. 15b),[49] or that the wise youth succeeded the king without usurping his place (שֵׁנִי as "successor").[50]

The other proposal sees the wise youth as coming from prison to a position of adviser to the king before succeeding him.[51] As with the first proposal, this youth who gave much to his people

---

[47] Here Qohelet again picks up the issue of wisdom, a major theme of the "royal pursuits" section early in the book (1:12–2:26). This is its first mention since then.

[48] I.e., there was only one youth. Some, such as E. Podechard (*L'Ecclésiaste* [Paris, 1912]), ad loc., would delete שֵׁנִי ("second") as a gloss.

[49] E.g., ad loc., Fox, *Contradictions*, and Seow, *Ecclesiastes*.

[50] So Gordis, *Koheleth*, 245. This variation differs from the second proposal by not allowing that king and successor reign together for a time.

[51] Rudman, "Contextual Reading," develops the work of Graham Ogden, "Historical Allusion in Qoheleth IV 13-16?" *Vetus Testamentum* 30 (1980): 309–15. So also Addison G. Wright, "The Poor But Wise Youth and the Old But Foolish King (Qoh 4:13-16)," in *Wisdom, You Are My Sister*, ed. Michael L. Barré (Washington, D.C.: Catholic Biblical Association of America, 1997), 149–50.

was largely unappreciated and his memory unheralded. It suggests plausible allusions to biblical figures such as Joseph and Daniel.[52]

The advantages of this latter position are several, and it is reflected in the translation above. First, emending the vowels of Masoretic Text for לִמְלֹךְ to read "to the king" in 4:14a allows a less awkward reading of the pronoun in "his kingdom" (v. 14b, a reference to the king).[53] Second, it makes the best sense of שֵׁנִי in verse 15 (a reference to the youth as successor to the king).[54] Third, supposing that both the king and his successor remain for a time together makes best sense of the plural pronoun in verse 16a, "before them."

In either proposal, Qohelet tells of a poor one who came to royal office and ruled wisely, yet the public he served failed to give him appropriate honor. Whether or not the tale involves allusion to legend or history, most agree it is best read as a parable or an example story of the rags-to-riches type.[55] We will now look more closely at its details.

Starting with a better-saying, Qohelet tells of this young but wise commoner who had been incarcerated.[56] Both his youth and

---

[52] Other biblical and postbiblical possibilities have also been suggested, even by those who advocate the first proposal.

[53] In addition, all other instances of the *mlk* root in Ecclesiastes are the noun "king" (12x); the verb is never used.

[54] In 4:8, שֵׁנִי indicates companion or successor, and in v. 15 the combination הַחַיִּים הַמְהַלְכִים ("the living who were walking [or living]") is syntactically similar to הַיֶּלֶד הַשֵּׁנִי. So it is natural to read the latter also as appositional: the youth who was the "second" or successor.

[55] So Murphy, *Ecclesiastes*, 42. It is part of Qohelet's rhetoric to allude to various life situations, whether those of himself or of others.

[56] The term מִסְכֵּן (in the Hebrew Bible only here and in 9:15-16; cf. מִסְכְּנֹת in Deut 8:9) in post-biblical Hebrew indicates a person of lower social status, though it refers only secondarily to impoverishment in terms of wealth (cf. Marcus Jastrow, *A Dictionary of the Targumim, the Talmud Babli and Yerushalmi, and the Midrashic Literature*, 2 vols. [Brooklyn, N.Y.: Traditional, 1903], 807–8). The Akkadian *muskenu/maskenu*, from

his lack of social status make his characterization as "wise" (4:13) unexpected. His description as poor (רָשׁ, v. 14) suggests experiences of oppression (note esp. 5:7 [English, v. 8]) as does his time in prison (v. 14), for prisons were often the repository for economic and political outcasts.[57]

Furthermore, to ascribe wisdom to one assuming political power is to anticipate positive government. Ideals of kingship in the ancient Near East prominently included not only wisdom but also the establishment of justice within the king's realm.[58] Law codes such as that of Lipit Ishtar (Sumerian) reflect the importance of both justice and wisdom, and both are frequently mentioned in royal propagandistic literature.

The Babylonian Hammurabi announces in the prologue to his law code that the gods Anum and Enlil have named him "to cause justice to prevail in the land, to destroy the wicked and the evil, that the strong might not oppress the weak." He goes on to describe himself as a pious, wise, and strong warrior.[59] Qohelet

---

which it is likely borrowed, indicates a status of dependency upon the state (E. A. Speiser, "The Muskenum," in *Oriental and Biblical Studies*, ed. and intro. J. J. Finkelstein and M. Greenberg [Philadelphia: University of Pennsylvania, 1967], 332–43). The term יֶלֶד is used most often of a young child, so that here youth is contrasted with old age, common status with royalty, and wise with foolish (so Rashbam).

[57] On the character of ancient prisons of this region, see Karel van der Toorn, "Prison," *Anchor Bible Dictionary*, ed. David Noel Freedman and Gary A. Herion (New York: Doubleday, 1992), 5:468–69.

[58] See, e.g., Keith Whitelam, "King and Kingship," *Anchor Bible Dictionary*, 4:42-47. See also the texts cited in C. L. Seow, "Qohelet's Autobiography," in *Fortunate the Eyes That See*, ed. A. Beck, *et al.* (Grand Rapids: Eerdmans, 1995), 275–87.

[59] Theophile J. Meek, "The Code of Hammurabi," *Ancient Near Eastern Texts Relating to the Old Testament*, ed. James B. Pritchard (Princeton: Princeton University Press, 1969), 162. Cf. also the Epic of King Keret (Ugaritic) in which Keret's son rebukes him because (vi. 44-50) "You do not judge the cause of the widow, you do not try the case of the importunate. You do not banish the extortioners of the poor, you do not feed

implies, therefore, that this wise commoner has a concern for oppressed ones like those mentioned in the initial subunit of this
chapter (4:1-3). If the biblical Joseph is in mind here, his deliverance of the masses from starvation would provide a model combination of wisdom with justice.

In 4:15, Qohelet describes all "the living" who are "under the
sun." Both expressions are found in 4:1-3 and refer in general to
those who are presently alive. But in verses 1-3, these living ones
are either experiencing oppression, seeing the "evil work" in life,
or both. These folks are further described in 4:15 as "walking (or
living) with" (עם ... המהלכים) the king's successor. As Rudman
notes, the verb הלך in the Piel pattern with preposition עם occurs
also in Sirach 13:13, where it indicates companionship.[60] The story
line thus is going well at this point; the people are manifesting the
companionship and support for which Qohelet campaigned in 4:9-
12, and the lack of which he lamented in 4:1-3. Furthermore, the
"second," missing in 4:7-8, is now present.

Again in 4:16, a positive situation is described. There was
"no end" to all the people "before them." Unlike 4:7-8, where there
was "no end" to toil, and 4:4-6, where envy motivated workers to
grab for two handfuls, here *people* are the main concern. These
people are "before them," loyal servants of the king and his successor.[61] The most apt parallels to this expression occur in 1 Samuel 19:7, where David serves Saul, and in 1 Samuel 29:8, where
David protests his good service "before" Achish.

Despite this pleasant picture, those who are "after" will not
rejoice in "him" — presumably, that is, in the youth who has been
the primary focus in this unit. If those who sense historical allusion
in this tale are correct, one might think of both Joseph, whose con-

---

the orphan before your face (nor) the widow behind your back" (J. C. L.
Gibson, *Canaanite Myths and Legends* [Edinburgh: T & T Clark, 1977], 102).

[60] Rudman, "Contextual Reading," 68. The text of Sir. 13:13 reads,
הֹשָּׁמֶר וֶהְיֶה זָהִיר וְאַל תֵּהֲלֵךְ עִם אַנְשֵׁי חָמָס: "Watch and be warned, and let
not yourself walk with men of violence."

[61] See Rudman's discussion of the possibilities for the antecedents
of the plural pronoun here ("Contextual Reading," 69–71).

tributions to Egypt were later forgotten (Exod. 1:8), and Daniel, whose exalted status before Nebuchadnezzar was not maintained by either Belshazzar (Dan. 5) or Darius (Dan. 6).

Fickle followers thus easily cast aside the royal figure presented here. His attempts to promote a just community end in expulsion from that community, whether only figuratively or also physically. His wise and just efforts accomplish no lasting legacy for him. As Qohelet insisted early in his work (1:11) and will describe yet again (9:14-16), popular memory is transient. Though wisdom is better than strength, the wisdom of the poor man of 9:15-16 is also despised.[62]

Oppression cannot be alleviated alone; there must be a concerted "three-fold" effort. Because the endeavors of such a wise one are of no lasting result and because his memory dissipates, Qohelet declares these things to be *hebel* (vapor) and a "chasing after wind."

Herein lies a call to justice that recognizes the grief coming to those who take up such a call. Qohelet's suffering-servant ruler is thus reminiscent of the similar figure in Second Isaiah.[63] Qohelet, however, forecasts no eventual vindication for this person, divine or otherwise.

Summary of Ecclesiastes 4:1-16

Qohelet observes the situation of the oppressed, which is so horrible that he congratulates those who were never born (4:1-3). As he looks around, he sees no one attempting to assist the oppressed. Instead, they are toiling to achieve "two handfuls" out of rivalry and competition with others. Although sloth, a second lifestyle option, is self-destructive, Qohelet admonishes contentment as a third and best way (4:4-6).

Further, Qohelet sees people obsessively toiling for no one's benefit (4:7-8, center of the unit). He then commends life in com-

---

[62] The man in 9:15 is described as אִישׁ מִסְכֵּן חָכָם, while the youth of 4:13 is יֶלֶד מִסְכֵּן וְחָכָם.

[63] Cf. Isa. 42:1-4; 49:1-6; 50:4-9; 52:13–53:12.

panionship (cooperation) for its many advantages (4:9-12). Thus, in the paradoxical mathematics of Qohelet, more is not always to be preferred. With regard to comrades, two is better than one (vv. 9-12), but in material things one may be better than two (v 6).[64]

Qohelet concludes his meditation with an episode about an oppressed youth who came forth to reign with wisdom (4:13-16). But this royal one is merely rejected and abandoned. He remains unappreciated. By this arrangement of subunits in Ecclesiastes 4, Qohelet suggests the complex interrelationship among individualism, materialism, toil, and oppression.

QOHELET'S RHETORIC

Before assessing the ethics of Ecclesiastes 4, we need to understand the rhetoric of Qohelet's work. Qohelet is best described as a realist who is addressing persons in the middle classes of postexilic Israel.[65] These times harbor a certain economic opportunity, but they also are subject to sudden reversals and the capriciousness of those in positions of political power. Qohelet's audience is particularly vulnerable to discouragement and cynicism.

In response, Qohelet offers his audience a way of coping with these realities, highlighting three themes in particular. Pleasure, he admonishes, will never provide complete satisfaction, but

---

[64] Ogden, "Mathematics," 453.

[65] I use the term *realist* for one who is aware of life's problems, tragedies, and mysteries, but who refuses to declare all of life absurd or meaningless. The traditional ascription of Ecclesiastes to Solomon, although his name does not occur in the book, has been rejected by most scholars on linguistic and other grounds. While many would date the book to the period of the Ptolemies in the third century BCE, recent arguments for a fifth-century, Persian provenance are persuasive (James L. Kugel, "Qohelet and Money," *Catholic Biblical Quarterly* 51 [1989]: 47; Seow, *Ecclesiastes*, 11–36). Either setting provides a time of social and economic volatility. Although a middle "class" did not exist, precisely speaking, various groups had more options and privileges than those who were impoverished and/or slaves, but at the same time had less means and privilege than the wealthy and those who ruled.

enjoyment is a dimension essential to worthwhile living. Toil (and wealth) ultimately cannot accomplish security, but one ought to find fulfillment in one's toil. Wisdom does not guarantee success, but there is a wisdom that knows how to make the best of this life.

The rhetoric of Ecclesiastes — the particular strategy by which Qohelet seeks to persuade his audience of these truths — may be outlined briefly as follows. To be heard at all, Qohelet first establishes his credibility (ethos) as one who recognizes the injustices of life. He then calls into question several of the assumptions, values, and practices of his audience (destabilization). Finally, he advocates an approach to living that embraces the good gifts of God while recognizing God's apparent arbitrariness (restabilization).[66]

This pattern is evident in chapter 4, where Qohelet first establishes ethos, his own credibility as author. The audience is confronted with Qohelet's competence, for he has seen "all the oppressions that are worked under the sun" (4:1) and "all toil and all gain" (v. 4). He is also benevolent. He grieves for the oppressed (v. 1), cares for those who struggle without satisfaction (vv. 6, 8), and is concerned for the unfortunate (vv. 10-11). These attributes motivate the audience's willingness to hear what he has to say.[67]

On the basis of his established credibility, Qohelet then works to challenge, or destabilize, the belief system of his audience. This he does carefully and largely indirectly in order to protect himself from rejection by his readers.[68] In the second subunit

---

[66] For further discussion of rhetoric in the book of Ecclesiastes as a whole, see my dissertation, "The Symbolic Function of *Hebel*," 193–206; and "The Rhetoric of Ecclesiastes: What the Preacher Forgot," *Catholic Biblical Quarterly* (forthcoming). On the terms *destabilization* and *restabilization*, see Leo G. Perdue, *Wisdom in Revolt: Metaphorical Theology in the Book of Job* (Sheffield, England: Almond, 1991), 22-27.

[67] In addition to competence and benevolence, the book elsewhere establishes Qohelet's status (a third aspect of ethos) as a venerable and trustworthy sage (e.g., Eccl. 12:9-11).

[68] For example, Qohelet employs wisdom sayings rather than direct imperatives to urge his audience to action — particularly in the early chapters of the book. His use of the imperative mood comes primarily in the

of chapter 4 (vv. 4-6), Qohelet juxtaposes the oppression raised in 4:1-3 with a lament about toil motivated by rivalry. He thus calls into question one significant type of motivation: the drive to better oneself, to achieve and even to surpass the good things enjoyed by others. He anticipates the defensive response that the alternative to hard work is to impoverish oneself like the fool. So he acknowledges the folly of sloth (v. 5), then proposes a third way: contentment.

He continues his destabilization of values by citing the obsessed worker. By presenting a rhetorical question without designating a speaker, he allows the reader to ask the question for oneself: "For whom am I toiling and depriving myself of good?" (v. 8). Qohelet firmly declares his own assessment of such activity by labeling this an "evil business." Thus, in chapter 4, Qohelet works primarily with the related issues of toil and wealth (one of his three main targets in the book), although he also addresses pleasure, to which he alludes with the term *good* in verse 8, and wisdom (vv. 13-16).

Qohelet's third and final rhetorical movement is to restabilize or reconstruct, to present an alternative value system. His first action of this sort is the third option in the second subunit (4:4-6): contentment. His most significant advocacy for an alternative ethic is found in the fourth subunit, 4:9-12, where he outlines three reasons for working in cooperation.

The final subunit (4:13-16) plays at least two roles rhetorically. On one hand, it reinforces what Qohelet has said about the limitations faced by single individuals: only together can a "good reward" be accomplished. Only a community that is wise can accomplish justice. On the other hand, it serves as a caution to those who would take up the cause Qohelet champions, to counter the oppression of the weak. Consistent with his realism throughout, he insists that wisdom, though the "better" way, never guarantees

---

latter part of the book's second half, after his credibility has been well-established.

results even in the most just of endeavors.[69] People are fickle, and those who are wise expose themselves to failure and rejection.

CONCLUSION

Qohelet on Power and Oppression

Before summarizing the ethical issues raised in Ecclesiastes 4, it is instructive to note Qohelet's treatment of power and oppression issues elsewhere in the book. When Qohelet next raises the problem of oppression, in 5:7-11 (English, 5:8-12), he urges his readers not to be surprised by it. The comments that immediately follow reiterate the instruction we have seen in Ecclesiastes 4: money will not satisfy, and the sleep of the honest laborer is to be preferred over the insomnia and false satisfaction of the rich.[70]

As for relations with the powerful, Ecclesiastes 8:1-5 and 10:16-20 counsel prudence in relations with the king. One must be careful, Qohelet cautions, for their power can be devastating.[71] The strength of wisdom in relation to political might is also treated in 9:13-18. Through wisdom a wise man was able to overcome a powerful king, yet the wise man was not remembered. As in 4:13-16, Qohelet highlights both the value and the vulnerability of wisdom, particularly the fickleness of those who receive benefit from it.

Qohelet's address of power issues may thus be considered along two axes. The first is that of the oppressor (power) and the oppressed (no power). He was certainly not the earliest to recognize this scenario and the human factor in injustice.[72] The second axis provides the response of wisdom. There is power in wis-

---

[69] Wright, "Poor but Wise Youth," 150, notes that in this case, the "second" does not help (cf. 4:9-12).

[70] Note also his parody of Solomon. His pleasure, wisdom, wealth, and accomplishments (1:12–2:26) are all declared to be *hebel,* wasted and futile effort.

[71] Note Qohelet's similar admonitions concerning respect for the deity in 4:17–5:6 (English, 5:1-7); 11:9 (cf. 12:14); and 8:12-13.

[72] Cf. Job 24; Prov. 13:23; 14:31; 18:23; 28:15.

dom—power great enough to enable a small city to withstand a great army (9:13-15). Wisdom also has power enough to go to the root of problems, including those of oppression. But this wisdom is vulnerable. Those who have it may neglect to activate it, and it provides no security for its possessor (9:16).

A Community Lifestyle

We turn now to the wisdom ethics of Ecclesiastes 4, aspects of which are echoed elsewhere in the book. For wisdom's power to be activated, Qohelet's audience will need to embrace the alternative community lifestyle he proposes. This way of being is characterized by simplicity and by working with others to meet common needs. Living contentedly requires that one be willing to accept a "handful with rest" rather than to strive for "two handfuls" with toil and dissatisfaction. It means resisting the desire to accumulate, whether motivated by competition or obsession, and therefore being available to assist those in need.

Because Qohelet connects these admonitions with the problem of societal abuse *and* proposes an alternative, it is evident that he is not a fatalist. He does not accept the realities of injustice as unchangeable. The author of Ecclesiastes is not throwing up his hands in despair, nor is he pointing out problems in order to scoff at them cynically. Yet neither is he a crusader or a social revolutionary.

Conservative or Radical?

Qohelet's instruction is both conservative and radical. It is conservative because it urges a prudent attitude toward those in power in order to avoid unnecessary trouble. It thus echoes the teachings of Torah not to curse one's ruler (Exod. 22:28) and anticipates the admonition of Paul in Romans 13:3: "Do you wish to have no fear of the authority? Then do what is good, and you will receive its approval" (NRSV).

Qohelet is conservative also because he refuses to advocate the overthrow of unjust government. He does not counsel revolution, but provides a caution to those who would. He recognizes that no individual, however wise and rightly motivated, can resolve the problems of an entire society. This presents a challenge to those concerned with getting "just the right person" into a key power position.

Yet Qohelet's proposal is also radical because it pursues the two root causes of suffering and oppression. On one hand is the problem of individualism, long recognized as both the vitality and the scourge of the modern West. It frames and infuses our outlook on life and our sense of accountability to it. Our dearest goals tend to be individual goals; our sense of evil and responsibility is expressed in terms of the individual. We even conceive of health and wholeness as a matter of what is best for individuals, whether experienced separately or in groups.

Qohelet asks us to consider two instead of one, to think of the whole, of cooperative togetherness. If we do so, we will chart our goals more in terms of group success. We will recognize when distortions are of a systemic nature, and we will ask what is best for "all of us," and not only what is best for "me." In this way, Qohelet is in line with Abraham's call to be a people who are a blessing to others (Gen. 12:1-3), and with Israel's prophets who exhorted against self-centeredness. For example, Amos cries against upper-class women: "Hear this word, you cows of Bashan who are on Mount Samaria, who oppress the poor, who crush the needy, who say to their husbands, 'Bring something to drink!'" (Amos 4:1, NRSV).

It is unclear what Qohelet would have to say to the tribalism of our present time that seeks what is best for "my group." Although he resents the intrusion of the "foreigner" (6:2), he does not couch his call to community in nationalistic terms.

On the other hand is the problem of materialism, a focus on acquisition and possession. Again Qohelet follows in the steps of the prophets: "Woe to those who join house to house, who add field to field, until there is no more room, and you are made to dwell alone in the midst of the land" (Isa. 5:8, RSV).

Additional prophets come to mind, along with the Decalogue's exhortation to reject coveting (cf. Micah 2:1-3; Exod. 20:17;

Deut. 5:21). With regard to the concern both for material goods and for community relationships, Qohelet's work is also reminiscent of the admonitions in Leviticus 19:13-18 to care for the needy, reject thievery, and love one's neighbors rather than rob or intimidate.

Qohelet challenges us to release our grip upon things we hold in our hands, to relax our tremendous drive to work more in order to have more, and to distinguish our needs and our wants better. He urges contentment with one instead of the desire for two. If we can make this change, we will spend our time differently. We will work less and love more. We will support and protect. And in winter we will keep warmer in the bargain.

Qohelet Addresses the Middle Classes

Qohelet is no Machiavelli, counseling the prince how to gain and then hold onto power. In this way he differs also from numerous ancient Near Eastern wisdom texts that counsel rulers on the proper use of their position.[73] But neither does Qohelet have advice for the lower classes. He appears disturbed by the prospect of social role reversal (Eccles. 10:5-7), and his common youth who came to power (4:13) does not constitute a symbol of hope.[74]

Any confidence he has for the resolution of oppression lies with the middle classes, who are his audience. It is a matter of speculation why this is true. Perhaps it is because their cooperation is crucial to any full-scale societal shift. At any rate, Qohelet does have a vision for change. He believes people can live in

---

[73] Examples include a text known as "Advice to a Prince," from the libraries of Ashurbanipal (Assyrian), dated to the early first millennium BCE; and, "The Instruction Addressed to King Merikare" (Egyptian), dated to the late third millennium.

[74] The lament over social class reversal—the poor and ruling class switching roles—is common in wisdom literature. Proverbs alludes to it and it receives extensive treatment in several Egyptian wisdom texts. See Raymond C. Van Leeuwen, "Proverbs 30:21-23 and the Biblical World Upside Down," *Journal of Biblical Literature* 105 (1986): 599–610.

wholesome ways that get at the heart of the destructive patterns pervading his world.

The middle classes do not know that their "salvation" is connected with the redemption of both the oppressed and the oppressor. So Qohelet attempts to convince them of the irony and paradox of the values they hold. It may not be too much to assume that, like the oppressed, the middle classes are both fearful and jealous of the oppressor. But like the oppressor, they are both fearful and disdainful of the oppressed. The suffering royal servant figure in 4:13-16 becomes a representative of those who will take up Qohelet's way of living: to pursue justice and contentment at the risk of failure and rejection.

Qohelet's strategy is to address oppression by taking on the futility of the oppressor as well as the futility of those middle groupers who imitate oppressor values. The wise will embrace community and simplicity even though there is no guarantee of success against oppression. Theirs is a way that knows no power in the conventional sense. Yet within them is the hope for change: they alone have found the proper motivation for their toil, the true source of pleasure and satisfaction in their lives, and the true path of wisdom in this world.

8

Power, Love, and Creation
The Mercy of the Divine Warrior
in the Wisdom of Solomon

TOM YODER NEUFELD

The relationship between power and love, most particularly in how it comes to expression in the motif of the Divine Warrior, has been a leitmotif in Millard Lind's writing. Such issues have also occupied my own scholarly attention.[1] The Wisdom of Solomon represents a point along the way between early understandings of Yahweh as warring on behalf of an oppressed powerless people — or against them when rebellious — and late biblical understandings of God as a lover of enemies. Wisdom of Solomon raises the question as to whether these concepts are fundamentally at odds with each other. The following investigation is offered as an expression of respect, gratitude, and deep affection to Millard Lind — teacher, mentor, and model of grace and peace.[2]

---

[1] See my *Put on the Armour of God: The Divine Warrior from Isaiah to Ephesians*, JSNTSS 140 (Sheffield: Sheffield Academic Press, 1997); revision of "God and Saints as War: The Transformation and Democratization of the Divine Warrior in Isaiah 59, Wisdom of Solomon 5, 1 Thessalonians 5, and Ephesians 6" (Th.D. dissertation, Harvard University Divinity School, 1989).

[2] This paper was first presented in similar form at the Society of Biblical Literature Annual Meeting in Kansas City, November 26, 1991, in the Study of Peace and the Bible group, with Millard Lind present.

INTRODUCTION

The intimate relationship between creation and divine warfare as arenas for the exercise of divine power is everywhere evident in the Bible.[3] So also is the notion that the phenomena of creation are mechanisms or expressions of divine grace and love—the flip side of divine warfare, as the cloud and fire, water and manna of Israel's desert wanderings illustrate. In late texts this tradition of creation as pliable tool in the hand of a sovereign Creator or

---

[3] See, e.g., such classic texts as Exod. 15, Deut. 32, Ps. 18, or Hab. 3, and attendant literature. Besides Millard Lind's *Yahweh Is a Warrior: The Theology of Warfare in Ancient Israel* (Scottdale, Pa.: Herald Press, 1980), see also, e.g., Bertil Albrektson, *History and the Gods: An Essay on the Idea of Historical Events as Divine Manifestations in the Ancient Near East and in Israel* (Lund: GWK Gleerup, 1967); Frank Moore Cross, *Canaanite Myth and Hebrew Epic: Essays in the History of the Religion of Israel* (Cambridge: Harvard University, 1973), 79–144; Norman K. Gottwald, "War, Holy," *Interpreter's Dictionary of the Bible*, suppl. vol. (Nashville: Abingdon, 1976), 942–44; Theodore Hiebert, *God of My Victory: The Ancient Hymn in Habakkuk 3*, HSM 38 (Atlanta: Scholars, 1986); Hiebert, "Warrior, Divine," *Anchor Bible Dictionary* (New York: Doubleday, 1992), 6:876–80; Patrick D. Miller, *The Divine Warrior in Early Israel* (Cambridge: Harvard University, 1973); Miller, "El the Warrior," *Harvard Theological Review* 60 (1967): 411–31; Gerhard von Rad, *Holy War in Ancient Israel*, trans. and ed. Marva J. Dawn (Grand Rapids: Eerdmans, 1991); Lawrence E. Toombs, "War, Ideas of," *Interpreters Dictionary of the Bible* (Nashville: Abingdon, 1962), 4:796–801; Moshe Weinfeld, "Divine Intervention in War in Ancient Israel and in the Ancient Near East," in *History, Historiography and Interpretation: Studies in Biblical and Cuneiform Literatures*, eds. H. Tadmor and M. Weinfeld (Jerusalem: Magus, 1983), 121–47.

While the roots of this tradition lay in the ancient Near Eastern mythologies of cosmogonic warfare, in Israel this tradition became an integral part of the narrative of God's actions on behalf of his people and then also against them. This breaking of the myth through historicization has been an especially important component of the Wright, Cross, and Hanson line of analysis. See Cross, *Canaanite Myth and Hebrew Epic*; Paul D. Hanson, *The Dawn of Apocalyptic* (Philadelphia: Fortress, 1975); G. Ernest Wright, "God the Warrior," in *The Old Testament and Theology* (New York: Harper and Row, 1969), 121–50.

warrior Judge comes to expression most forcefully in apocalyptic texts, in which the apparent solidity and order of creation gives way in the end to divinely ordered chaos.[4] But it is present as well in other less eschatologically oriented sapiential texts,[5] such as, for example, Sirach 39:16-35.

In Sirach, creation performs "with delight" the express purposes of God for both wrath and blessing (ἐν τῇ ἐντολῇ αὐτοῦ εὐφρανθήσονται; Sir. 39:31), having been created for a particular purpose, to be served at the appropriate time. But nowhere in the sapiential literature, with the possible exception of Job,[6] is this notion developed more thoroughly than in the Wisdom of Solomon, a document that emerged within a highly Hellenized Judaism at or around the turn of the era.[7]

---

[4] Ezek. 32:7, 8; Zeph. 1:14-18; Matt. 24:29//Mark 13:24//Luke 21:25-26; Rev. 8-9.

[5] For our present purposes, we need not determine whether apocalyptic is a subspecies of wisdom, as claimed by Dieter Georgi ("Das Wesen der Weisheit nach der Weisheit Salomos," in *Gnosis und Politik*, ed. Jacob Taubes, Religionstheorie und Politische Theologie 2 [München/ Paderhorn: Fink/Schoningh, 1984]); and others. See also the brief summary of discussion and literature in John J. Collins, "Cosmos and Salvation: Jewish Wisdom and Apocalyptic in the Hellenistic Age," *History of Religions* 17 (1977): 121-23.

[6] Note the excellent study of Job by Leo G. Perdue, *Wisdom in Revolt: Metaphorical Theology in the Book of Job* (Sheffield: Sheffield Academic Press, 1991). Perdue sees the motif of *Chaoskampf* as the predominant one in Job.

[7] See discussions of this in John J. Collins, *Between Athens and Jerusalem: Jewish Identity in the Hellenistic Diaspora* (New York: Crossroad, 1983), 182; Dieter Georgi, *Weisheit Salomos: Jüdische Schriften aus hellenistisch-römischer Zeit*, Unterweisung in lehrhafter Form, Band 3 (Gütersloh: Gütersloher Verlagshaus/Gerd Mohn, 1980), 394-97; cf. Georgi, "Wesen der Weisheit," 66-68; and the earlier "Der vorpaulinische Hymnus, Phil 2,6-11," in *Zeit und Geschichte: Dankesgabe an Rudolf Bultmann zum 80. Geburtstag*, ed. Erich Dinkler (Tübingen: Mohr, 1964), 269, n. 30; M. Gilbert, "Wisdom Literature," in *Jewish Writings of the Second Temple Period*, ed. Michael E. Stone (Philadelphia: Fortress, 1984), 301-13, esp. 312; James M.

In the following study I will explore the relationship between power and love as it comes to expression in the relationship between creation, divine warfare, and divine love in the Wisdom of Solomon. First, I will focus on the role of creation as ally and arsenal in divine warfare on behalf of victimized just or righteous persons.

Second, that creation was assigned such a role begs for an explanation of the constancy of creation in light of the ongoing oppression of the righteous. "Solomon" proffers the explanation that God's love and mercy are acts of sovereign power no less manipulative of creation than is divine warfare.

Third, such sovereign love and mercy are to be mimicked by the just as vice-regents of God, even at the price of their own victimization. Last, the date and provenance of the Wisdom of Solomon place this document in close proximity to sapiential texts now canonized within the New Testament. This provides a means of comparison and contrast with the more frequently surveyed terrain. At the conclusion of the study, I will thus throw a sidelong glance at Matthew 5:45, where sun and rain serve as examples of God's love for enemies—a God who is to be imitated by would-be sons and daughters of God.

Reese, *Hellenistic Influence on the Book of Wisdom and its Consequences* (Rome: Biblical Institute, 1970); George W. E. Nickelsburg, *Jewish Literature Between the Bible and the Mishnah: A Historical and Literary Introduction* (Philadelphia: Fortress, 1981), 184; David Winston, *The Wisdom of Solomon: A New Translation with Introduction and Commentary*, Anchor Bible 43 (Garden City, N.Y.: Doubleday, 1979), 12–14, 20–25. Most take the Hellenistic character of the document to signal an Alexandrian provenance, while Georgi opts for a Syrian context (*Weisheit*, 396), though he correctly observes that the pervasiveness of Hellenism makes any determination difficult if not impossible (*Weisheit*, 395).

THE WISDOM OF SOLOMON

The Wisdom of Solomon is by common agreement pseudepigraphical. The choice of Solomon as purported author[8] suggests that the author wants this book to be seen as a work of wisdom; that is, as general moral instruction for those aspiring to wisdom and righteousness. Just as importantly, however, this document presents itself as a word by a king for kings who have it within their power to exercise authority within the public sphere, as 1:1 and 6:1, 2 make explicit.[9] The fictional author and audience imply that these words are directed not at the margins of society, but at the center. This is true even if Wisdom is self-consciously diasporic literature.

A distinct feature of Wisdom is the deletion throughout of explicit identifiers of persons, places, or events. These remain easily recognizable to the scripturally literate, but their anonymity forces readers to reflect on persons and events as generalizations, as paradigmatic abstractions. Most striking is that persons and events that are singularly unique in the tradition become paradigmatic, such as Enoch, or the events surrounding the Exodus from Egypt. The intended effect is, in my view, to subvert confidence in the cosmos as an immutable, well-ordered, and thus predictable whole. To state it ironically, God typically or characteristically responds to evil through the direct manipulation of the phenomena of creation (e.g., 16:24).[10] Although Sophia is the ultimate teacher of science (7:15–8:1), of creation as a measurable, predictable whole (11:20b), she also appears as the warring Logos (10:1–

---

[8] See Walter A. Brueggemann's study of the relationship of Solomon to the wisdom tradition, "The Social Significance of Solomon as a Patron of Wisdom," in *The Sage in Israel and the Ancient Near East,* eds. John G. Gammie and Leo G. Perdue (Winona Lake, Ind.: Eisenbrauns, 1990), 117–32.

[9] Citations to the Wisdom of Solomon are, from here on, given only by chapter and verse numbers.

[10] In "conventional" wisdom, creation is a well-ordered moral whole, sustained by a loving God whose will and greatness is readable from the phenomena of creation. See the discussion in Collins, "Cosmos and Salvation," 125–28; and Perdue, *Wisdom in Revolt,* 12–22.

11:10; 18:14-20), whose killing spree is stemmed only by the logos of the "perfect man" (ἀνὴρ ἄμεμπτος) in 18:20-25.

THE ROLE OF CREATION IN DIVINE WARFARE

The role of creation and cosmos in divine warfare comes to forceful expression in the hymn to the Divine Warrior in 5:15-23.[11] The warrior rises in response to the conflict between the impious and the just, depicted in chapters 2-5 in a fashion highly dependent on the motif of the servant or son of God in the Fourth Servant Song of Isaiah 52:13-53:12.[12] The just one is victimized to the point of murder by impious rulers who mistake their might as right (2:11).[13] They have made a pact with death, and thus consider themselves immune.[14] More, they have entered into a relationship of friendship with death and have made death their ally (2:12-20). They test the claims of the righteous one that he is a "servant of the Lord" (παῖς κυρίου, 2:13) and a "son of God" (υἱὸς

---

[11] Fuller discussion is in my *Put on the Armour*, 48-72.

[12] Cf. M. Jack Suggs, "Wisdom of Solomon 2:10-5: A Homily on the Fourth Servant Song," *Journal of Biblical Literature* 76 (1957): 26-33; Joachim Jeremias, "παῖς θεοῦ," *Theological Dictionary of the New Testament* (1976), 5:684; recently also Georgi, "Vorpaulinischer Hymnus," 266; Georgi, *Weisheit*, 405-406; Georgi, "Wesen der Weisheit," 73; George W. E. Nickelsburg, *Resurrection, Immortality, and Eternal Life in Intertestamental Judaism*, Harvard Theological Studies 26 (Cambridge: Harvard University Press, 1972), 58-68; Jane Schaberg, "Major Midrashic Traditions in Wisdom 1,1-6,25," *Journal for the Study of Judaism in the Persian, Hellenistic and Roman Period* 13 (1982): 75-101. For a contrary view, see Reese's criticism (*Hellenistic Influence*, 113) that while Isaiah traditions clearly play a role in these chapters of Wisdom, this is not an interpretation (midrash) of Isaiah 52-53.

[13] The pretensions to divinity on the part of these impious (we should see them as oppressive) rulers becomes obvious when one compares their "might is right" stance with that of God in 12:16.

[14] Cf. Isa. 28:15. There, too, rulers are the ones who claim such immunity.

θεοῦ, 2:16, 18), that is, a monarch with full credentials. They do so by killing him — or so they think (3:2-4).

Against these oppressors and on behalf of the just rises now the Divine Warrior. This time "Solomon" draws on Third Isaiah, specifically the depiction of the Divine Warrior in Isaiah 59:15b-20.[15] No doubt the already highly abstract treatment in Isaiah commended it to the author. It is well-suited to elaboration, and the author does so by expanding especially the motif of creation and cosmos as arsenal and ally (cf. flood and wind in Isa. 59:19). The Divine Warrior makes creation a weapon with which to punish enemies (ὁπλοποιήσει τὴν κτίσιν εἰς ἄμυναν ἐχθρῶν, 5:17). The cosmos itself will join God as an ally in the war "against those who are out of their minds" (συνεκπολεμήσει δὲ αὐτῷ ὁ κόσμος ἐπὶ τοὺς παράφρονας, 5:20). Hereupon follows a brief inventory of the cosmic arsenal: shafts of lightning like arrows drawn from a well-drawn bow (5:21); hailstones of wrath as from a catapult; sea water, violent rivers, powerful winds, and tempests (5:22-23).

This highly abstracted and mythologically colored motif anticipates the role that "creation" (κτίσις) and "cosmos" (κόσμος) are given in divine warfare in chapters 10-19. As indicated earlier, the events surrounding the Exodus — most particularly the plagues in Egypt — are referred to frequently as typical of the divine response to oppression and idolatry. Further implications of such a role for creation are summarized succinctly in 19:6-21. The whole creation is said to have been "created anew" or "from above" (ὅλη γὰρ ἡ κτίσις ἐν ἰδίῳ γένει πάλιν ἄνωθεν διετυποῦτο; cf. John 3:3) at God's command (ὑπηρετοῦσα ταῖς σαῖς ἐπιταγαῖς) for the sake of God's servants (ἵνα οἱ σοὶ παῖδες φυλαχθῶσιν ἀβλαβεῖς, 19:6). The constant renewal or recreation of the cosmos (*creatio continua*) becomes at such times *creatio de novo*. Note that in response to idolatry, a major interest of the author, God not only turns the creatures that have become objects of worship against the impious as punishment; God also adds to them beings never before seen

---

[15] Fuller discussion of this passage is in my *Put on the Armour*, 15–47.

(11:15-20a). This again is a witness to the strategic element in the creative energies of the Divine Warrior.

In 16:16-29 the "mighty arm" of God with which God flogs the ungodly is identified as unusual rains, hail, relentless storms, and fire. The cosmos is the "superwarrior (ὑπέρμαχος) of the just" (ὑπέρμαχος γὰρ ὁ κόσμος ἐστὶν δικαίων, 16:17).[16] Creation punishes the unjust and in kindness goes easy on those who trust God (16:24). The author pushes such dualistic language even further:

> For the whole world was illumined with brilliant light, and went about its work unhindered, while over those people [the impious] alone heavy night was spread, an image of the darkness that was destined to receive them; but still heavier than darkness were they to themselves.   (17:20-21)

The clear impression is that in the hand of God creation serves up two quite different sets of experience, and both are something other than what they appear to be on the surface. Whereas on one level the just are vulnerable to the oppression of the impious (chap. 2), and clearly dependent on the intervention of the Divine Warrior (5:15-23; cf. 2:19-20), at another they are impervious to the murderous intentions and acts of the oppressors. They only *seem* to have died at the hands of the wicked (2:21–3:4). Conversely, the impious only seem to have had power and success (5:6-14). On one hand we see the ironic figures of the fruitful barren woman in 3:13, the blessed eunuch in 3:14-15, or of the well-

---

[16] There is, of course, nothing new in the idea that the phenomena of creation play a role in divine warfare. See, e.g., Exod. 15, which speaks of floods, fury as fire, breath, and wind. Like Isa. 59, Deut. 32 is postexilic and speaks of hunger, heat, and pestilence. Deut. 33:1-2, a fragment of one of the oldest war hymns, speaks of flaming fire. Second Sam. 22:9-16, which parallels Ps. 18:8-15, speaks of smoke, fire, darkness, brightness, wind (spirit), lightning, and breath. Ps. 77:16-18 mentions thunder, lightning, and whirlwind; Hab. 3, pestilence and plague; Isa. 28:2, hail, tempest, and a storm of waters; Isa. 29:3-10, thunder, earthquake, great noise, whirlwind, tempest, and flame; Isa. 66:15-16, chariots like the storm wind and flames of fire.

aged pious youth (4:7-9). On the other hand, we see the rueful insight of the oppressors that the sun did not really shine on them (5:6b) and that their life was really no life at all (5:13a), whatever their wealth and power (5:8). In fact, their pact with death has excluded them from the cosmos (1:14; 2:24).

So when the ostensibly victimized just one meets the oppressors as regal judge (5:1),[17] their "repentance" (μετανοοῦντες, 5:3) is not repentance so much as it is "second thoughts," insight or hindsight into the true nature of reality (cf. 11:11-14; 12:27; 18:2). Pseudo-Solomon's use of this bewildering metaphysical mix serves the strategy of destabilizing a sense of the cosmos as a unified, well-ordered, and predictable reality.

Given such evidence, it is difficult if not impossible to read this document as protoscientific, as John Collins does in his important article, "Cosmos and Salvation."[18] Collins claims that Wisdom reflects a kind of protodeism in which God recedes behind the inexorable relationship of cause and effect as it plays itself out in creation. Collins' stress on wisdom as mediator of a "scientifically" predictable universe, with the experience of God as only indirect, renders the Divine Warrior encountered in chapter 5 and elsewhere as anomalous, and the paradigmatic use of the plagues of Egypt as inexplicable. In my view the presence of the Divine Warrior, most especially the explicit arming of creation to serve the warrior's strategies, renders the universe anything but "fixed," "essentially impersonal," functioning predictably according to "natural laws."

For pseudo-Solomon, creation is malleable in the extreme, functioning at the immediate behest of an engaged deity. Thus the fixedness of creation (7:17-22; 11:20b) is in the end a foil for its malleability (notice what precedes 11:20b). On one hand, creation

---

17 Georgi (*Weisheit*, 416) translates παρρησία as the "sovereign freedom" of heavenly beings. I see here first and foremost the confidence and freedom accorded kings in their function as judges (so also Georgi earlier in "Vorpaulinischer Hymnus," 274, especially n. 39). The salvation of 5:2 is thus also exaltation to the status of royal judge over the tormentors.

18 Collins, "Cosmos and Salvation," 128–31.

is celebrated as good and whole (11:20b), one in which Sophia as architect can act as guide and instructor (7:17-22). On the other hand, creation is so closely tied to the active sovereignty of God that, given the presence of death, accompanied by oppression and rebellion, creation "comes to the aid of Yahweh," as it were. Creation ceases to be open to the "science" of prediction and taxonomy. It "forgets its native power" (τῆς ἰδίας ἐπιλέλησται δυνάμεως, 16:23; cf. 19:20) and serves the ingenuity of God. Therein lies the attractiveness for pseudo-Solomon of the events surrounding the Exodus as grist for his paradigmatic mill.

GOD'S MERCY AND FORBEARANCE TOWARD THE IMPIOUS

All this invites and urges the central question: if this is how creation should be counted on to function in response to evil and oppression, why are the impious still around, free to oppress the just, free to victimize those who would rule and judge with justice and love?

Wisdom's author is not as perturbed by this question as is Qohelet (Ecclesiastes). After all, the just have their future as regents at the right hand of God assured (5:15-16). The sufferings of the present are either only apparent or no more than a test—one the just pass with flying colors (3:5). Nor is the author as troubled by what happens to the impious as is the composer of Isaiah's fourth Servant Song, to whom the author has listened in chapters 2–5, but apparently with only one ear.[19] Even so, the axiom of the sovereignty of God requires some accounting for the presence of the impious—more specifically, why the cosmos has not caved in on them. The sovereignty of God also requires that the explanation reside finally in God. "How would anything have endured if you had not willed it?" (11:25).

The explanation is as simple as it is crucial: "You love all things that exist, and detest none of the things that you have

---

[19] The appropriation of the fourth Servant Song does not include any explicit attention to the notion that the servant suffers for and on behalf of the oppressors.

made" (ἀγαπᾷς γὰρ τὰ ὄντα πάντα καὶ οὐδὲν βδελύσσῃ ὧν ἐποίησας, 11:24). "You spare all things, for they are yours, O Lord" (φείδῃ δὲ πάντων, ὅτι σά ἐστιν, δέσποτα φιλόψυχε, 11:26). Out of this love flows mercy toward all (ἐλεεῖς δὲ πάντας, 11:23), a mercy intended to keep the door open for "repentance" (μετάνοια, 11:23; 12:2, 10, 20). To be sure, such mercy shows itself less in forgiveness than in measured and restrained punishment ("little by little," κατ᾽ ὀλίγον; 12:2, 8-10), punishment intended to lead to repentance. Such merciful restraint is no less grounded in love, however.

"Solomon" reminds God that the odds against the success of such a strategy are finally insurmountable, since it is unlikely that those who are congenitally evil (πονηρὰ ἡ γένεσις αὐτῶν καὶ ἔμφυτος ἡ κακία αὐτῶν, 12:10) will repent. If in the end they do, it will be too late. It will then mean no more than coming to an awareness of their own folly (5:3-13). Meanwhile, the impious will predictably mistake such divine mercy and forbearance, expressed in the *apparent* solidarity of the cosmos (2:6-9), as impunity, or even as evidence of their own divinity (2:11).[20]

Yet, Wisdom's author knows that the continuance of creation can nonetheless be explained only as evidence of the finally inexplicable patience, love, mercy, sparing, and preservation of God — a patience that might therefore also run out at any time. The crucial point for the author is that such mercy, restraint, forbearance, and patience are not a matter of divine disinterest, evidence of fear (12:11), or lack of power (12:17). Rather, mercy is derived directly from the power of the Divine Warrior/Creator, as 11:21-22 illustrates clearly:

[21] For it is always in your power to show great strength,
and who can withstand the might of your arm?
[22] Because the whole world before you is like a speck that
tips the scales,
and like a drop of morning dew that falls on the ground.

---

[20] The pretensions to divinity in the "might is right" disposition of impious rulers is illustrated in 12:16, where God's might is the source of right.

We can add to this 12:18:

> Although you are sovereign in strength, you judge with
>   mildness,
> and with great forbearance you govern us,
> for you have power to act whenever you choose.

Mercy grows out of God's care for all (12:13), including presumably his enemies and those of his servants and sons. Mercy
thus becomes a specific act of divine power, and it provides as
much evidence as does punishment of its "completeness" or "perfection" (δυνάμεως τελειότης, 12:17). We might even say that
mercy becomes part of the arsenal of the Divine Warrior. After all,
the mending of all that God has brought into being ultimately
motivates the Divine Warrior's engagement in the first place.
Locating mercy in that initiative explains the continuity between
mercy and restrained punishment, and why its rejection as an invitation to repentance leads to the warfare of creation against the
impious. The *metanoia* ("repentance," "change of mind") that
awaits the intransigent is thus no longer restorative change, but
hindsight into the nature of divine power, into the fate of the just
and of the impious (5:17-23; 12:26-27).[21]

The author's essential contention is that whatever constancy
creation has can be explained only as specific and deliberate acts
of divine mercy — acts of power no less than the disassembling of
order in divine warfare. In view of the presence of rebellion,
oppression, and hubris, such mercy is "disorderly conduct." Given
that destruction and judgment *should* occur, the mercy that is
expressed in the nurturing and sustaining face of creation shows
itself to be a free and sovereign act of power.

THE IMITATION OF GOD IN MERCY AND SOVEREIGNTY

The Wisdom of Solomon is intended to warn, encourage,
and advise those with the responsibilities of servants of God —

---

[21] The depiction of the divine warrior in 5:17-23 can be read as part
of the speech of recognition on the part of the impious.

first, judges and monarchs; and second, those who by virtue of their fidelity to and friendship with Sophia enjoy such status. The commoners and even the marginalized who "overhear" these words from outside the palace as intended for them,[22] are themselves implicitly invested with sovereignty and elevated to the status of regal sons and daughters of God (2:16, 18; 12:19). It may be, as I shall shortly suggest, that the marginalized are the freshly marginalized by virtue of their fidelity to their sovereign calling. In any case, we see an implicit connection between monarchs and sages, between monarchs and the just.[23]

However, Isaiah's fourth Servant Song exerts some control over the author's portrait of the just and their fate at the hands of rival rulers. This might leave the impression that the servant of God is essentially a passive victim rather than a royal *vicarius Dei*. The good monarch disappears into the pauper and the widow (2:10). True, the pauper and widow reappear as sovereigns and judges in 5:1, 15-16.[24] But their co-regency with God is apparently

---

[22] They surely constitute an essential component, if not the majority, of the actual audience.

[23] On the democratization of royal wisdom and the implicit elevation of the righteous to the status of vice-regent for God, see Perdue, *Wisdom in Revolt*, 63.

[24] It is difficult to be certain when pseudo-Solomon understands this reappearance to take place. I have argued that the eschatological timetable in Wisdom of Solomon is an exceedingly difficult one to ascertain (*Put on the Armour*, 66–68; see also Nickelsburg, *Resurrection*, 88–89). I agree to a considerable degree with Georgi's assessment that the author does not mean for the reader to figure it out. Georgi has made it a leitmotiv in his various studies of the Wisdom of Solomon to show that Wisdom is marked by discontinuities, contradictions, and repetitions, with no apparent desire on part of author or redactor to resolve them. Georgi contends that these peculiarities are central to its strategy (*Weisheit*, 393–94; cf. also "Wesen der Weisheit"). Georgi's theory sees pseudo-Solomon's discombobulating of time and metaphysics as an assault on a consciousness rooted in this world, as an early expression of gnosticism (e.g., "Wesen der Weisheit," 80). This may be going too far, but it has the virtue

obscured in the early chapters of Wisdom by their victimization. Or is it?

In 12:19-22 the nature of the co- or vice-regency—the *imitatio Dei*—of the just is made explicit. As servants and children of God (12:19-20), the just are to judge as God judges (12:22).[25] They are to subject evil to "radical critique" in life and word (ἔλεγχος, 2:12-16). That will ensure the hostility of the regal bullies, whose own claims to status and legitimacy are questioned publicly, not least by the preposterous claim of the apparent victim that God is *his* father—that he, the suffering just one, is the true regent. More, the just are to judge in mercy, forbearance, and preservation—in love. Their imitation of God is called "philanthropy." "It is necessary for the just one to be a lover of humans" (δεῖ τὸν δίκαιον εἶναι φιλάν-θρωπον, 12:19; my translation). Just as God's patience and mercy are characteristically mistaken by the impious for weakness or divine cowardice,[26] so presumably can the mercy and patience of his servants. As the impious rulers say in 2:11, "Let our might be our law of right, for weakness is exposed as useless" (my translation).

One might then well ask whether the portrait of the just in the early chapters of Wisdom is less that of a victim than that of a monarch imitating a God who lets the sun shine and the rain fall on the impious. That such "rule" would be mistaken for powerlessness is a predictable part of the scenario. Nothing changes the fact, however, that the *philanthropia* of the servant/son/king is an act of power—that it presupposes the sovereignty of God's children, even if it exposes such a ruler and judge to the abuse of rival

of warning against too quick an ordering of what might be quite intentional disorder.

We might thus understand the turnabout to come in the fate of the just *whenever* the Divine Warrior chooses to intervene. The last shall be first, but they may not need to wait for a final conclusive reckoning.

[25] Cf. also the designation of rulers as judges in 6:1.

[26] Note that the term for divine love in 11:26 is "love of life" (φιλό-ψυχος). Usually if not always it means cowardice as in "love of *one's own* life" (*A Greek-English Lexicon*, compiled by Henry George Liddell and Robert Scott, 9th ed. [Oxford: Clarendon Press, 1940], s.v. φιλόψυχος).

rulers. Therefore, just as the mercy of God is finally a strategy of power, so also is the vulnerability of the just a deliberately taken stance, the exercise of sovereignty.

Of course the appropriation of both the fourth Servant Song and the paradigmatic events of the Exodus recognizes the suffering of the just as true suffering—suffering not chosen for its own sake. That does not obscure, however, that the call to *philanthropia* in 12:19-22 is a call to a disposition that exposes the regent to abuse in a world of persistent oppression and violence. Even God's mercy, as expressed in the constancy of creation, can be and is mistaken by oppressors as divine weakness and powerlessness—or worse, as evidence of their own divinity.

For Wisdom's author, this implies necessarily that *philanthropia* remains only one possible strategic response to evil—for God as for God's coregents. And nothing tests divine mercy like persistent refusal to see it as an invitation to repentance (12:17). The freedom to respond with something other than mercy must be open to the sons and daughters of God in their function as administrators of public justice as well, if there is to be mercy and not simply forgetfulness, disinterest, irresponsibility, or powerlessness. Indeed, one might wonder whether the effectiveness of their "rule" may lie in part on the unpredictability characterizing the public exercise of responsibility that itself is patterned after a God who does what God wills—by a Sophia who can create, teach, and lose her temper.[27]

LOVE FOR ENEMIES AS THE EXERCISE OF SOVEREIGNTY

Now for the sidelong glance at a more or less contemporaneous sapiential text, Matthew 5:45. The divine sonship of the "superjust" (cf. 5:20) is expressed in love for enemies in explicit imitation of their heavenly Father, who raises the sun and lets the rain fall on the just and the unjust alike. This text is often under-

---

[27] This *imitatio Dei* of the just is strikingly illustrated in the aforementioned sovereign response of "the blameless man" in 18:20-25, who ends up having to stem the ferocity of the avenging Logos/Sophia with a *logos*.

stood as an expression of universalism. Love for enemies is then a kind of indiscriminate generosity imitative of a largely disengaged, if benign, deity. Such love is cool.

If we are permitted to look at the Matthean wisdom text through the eyes of pseudo-Solomon, then we might see the following. To raise the sun over the just and the unjust alike, to make the rain fall on the just and the unjust alike, is a deliberate act of love on the part of God. It is intended for the specific purpose of transforming enemies into friends—more, into divine sons and daughters. Sun and rain are not the phenomena of an autonomous and predictable creation, but deliberate and specific acts with which the impious are pursued with love. Only so can they be seen as acts of love.

Just as philanthropy in Wisdom of Solomon is to be exercised in imitation of God, so in Matthew, God's sovereign generosity and perfection[28] are to be imitated by those who call God their father (cf. Wis. 2:16 and Matt. 5:45). Pseudo-Solomon thus alerts us to see in Jesus' demand in Matthew to love enemies a call to sovereignty and rulership for the servants and children of God.[29] Love of enemies requires the regal freedom of those who could do otherwise, justifiably. True, pseudo-Solomon names only *philanthropia* and *philopsychia* (11:26), not *agapechthria* ("love of enemies"), if I am allowed a neologism. Nonetheless, when philanthropy is exercised toward the enemies of God and those of his servants, then we have at least an implicit form of love of enemies.

LOVE FOR ENEMIES AS ENGAGEMENT IN CREATION

The hermeneutical questions are significant and troubling. First, the myth of the Divine Warrior presupposes a cosmology

---

[28] Cf. *teleios* (τέλειος) in Matt. 5:48 and the "perfect power" (*dynamis teleiotes*, δύναμις τελειότης) expressed in mercy in Wis. 12:17.

[29] Hans Windisch cleverly refers to the attribution of divine sonship to peacemakers and lovers of enemies in Matthew 5 as "die Apotheose der Menge," in "Friedensbringer—Gottessohne," *Zeitschrift für die neutestamentliche Wissenschaft* 24 (1925): 240.

quite different from a modern mechanistic or immanentist one. It is a cosmology in which creation and the cosmos as a whole are at the immediate behest of a sovereign and engaged deity. Second, such a cosmology affects the realm of ethics. The paradigmatic figure of the victimized "servant of the Lord" or "child of God" must be able to count on divine intervention (chaps. 2–5) and on creation serving those divine intentions. Furthermore, since such a sovereign God manipulates creation for both blessing and woe, a just judge must be able to exercise legitimately some sovereignty over circumstances as well. Philanthropy—especially its radical expression in love for enemies—presupposes the freedom and sovereignty of the sons and daughters of God to "manipulate" circumstances and behavior in a way that emulates the freedom of the Divine Warrior and judge over creation.

Such an ethic has little, if anything, in common with a stoic notion of philanthropy as tolerance and acquiescence, or for that matter with the clemency exercised by the strong toward the weak.[30] It also has little in common with a view of the just one as a powerless sufferer. It is thus also in considerable tension with non-retaliation as eschatologically motivated deferral of gratification. And it is much too dualistic for an anthropologically optimistic pacifism.

Rather, philanthropy and love of enemies are subsumed under the exercise of sovereign power in a strategy of transformation of real evil oppressors,[31] which, if unsuccessful, might give way

---

[30] See the important discussion by Luise Schottroff, "Non-Violence and the Love of One's Enemies," in *Essays on the Love Command* (Philadelphia: Fortress, 1978), 18–20.

[31] So also Schottroff, "Non-Violence," 14. She locates love for enemies sociologically in the particular strategy of the weak toward the strong. See also Walter Wink, *Engaging the Powers: Discernment and Resistance in a World of Domination* (Minneapolis: Fortress, 1992). My reading of Wisdom of Solomon—and via that lens, Matthew 5—suggests that love for enemies as the practice of mercy is to be no less the strategy of the strong toward the strong, even if "strength" and "power" manifest themselves in radically different fashion.

to punitive warfare. Philanthropy is premised on the imitation of a God who, out of mercy and the desire to see repentance, exercises power in such a way as to permit humankind to see the sun in the morning and the rain in the afternoon. It is the imitation of a God who could do otherwise, who has done otherwise, and who, barring the repentance of the impious, *will* do otherwise again.

Thus philanthropy, as also love for enemies, must always find expression in specific sovereign and free acts of mercy intended to lead to the specific result of repentance, the transformation of enmity into friendship, and of enemies into friends. In the end, just as God expresses divine sovereignty and love in the gracious sustaining of creation, so love for enemies and *philanthropia* generally will be the most consistent and persistent dispositions of the sons and daughters of God as they exercise their regal responsibilities in private *and* public life. To restate the challenge "Solomon" puts to his readers: mercy and love of enemies is the public policy of sons and daughters of God charged with the care of the world. It is precisely to such perfect mercy (to combine Matt. 5:40 and Luke 6:36) that Jesus calls would-be sons and daughters of God.

9

Reimaging Power
Toward a Theology of Nonviolence

RAY C. GINGERICH

INTRODUCTION

My studies in the late 1960s with Millard Lind helped me gain my first genuine appreciation for the Hebrew Scriptures. Three particular aspects of this appreciation come to mind: (1) the significance of the prophet in the Judeo-Christian faith; (2) the intricate linkage of the Old Covenant with the New Covenant (specifically the historical and social rootedness of the Jesus story within the community and tradition that preceded); and (3) the phenomenon of Yahweh as one who does not will his people to engage in violence, but claims the right to vengeance and violence for himself. Lind had completed his dissertation on a theology of warfare in the Old Testament by this time and was at work revising it into *Yahweh Is a Warrior*. He often tried out his thoughts on his students.

Precisely the themes that I so much appreciated from Lind were also the ones that then, and in the years since, created troubling questions for me. Lind's anti-dispensationalist stance, emphasizing the continuity between the Old Testament and the New, made it more difficult to dismiss the accounts of violence in the Old Testament as "no longer applying to God's children" or as irrelevant to the followers of Jesus. The graduated, phased-in "progressive revelation," a perspective promoted by Guy F. Hershberger and, to a lesser degree, by C. K. Lehman (both at least a half generation before Lind),[1] were attempts to soften the problem, but provided me little help. John Howard Yoder's culturally sensitive theology focused more on "obedience" to God in a specific ancient cultural context than on not killing. Yoder seemed to imply that certain kinds of human violence could constitute a form of faithful Yahweh-worship. However, it seems to me that such a theology obscures the theological question of a "warrior God" by creating a cultural gulf and placing God on the other side of it.[2]

The traditional biblical-theological framework for a pacifist understanding of Jesus as God's representative for thought and action was no longer available to me. To state the issue more succinctly, if I took seriously the nonviolent Jesus of Nazareth as normative for Christians striving to be God's redemptive children, I could no longer believe in the Warrior-Yahweh. This, even though certain writings within the Hebrew Scriptures do depict Yahweh as a warrior.[3]

---

[1] Hershberger's view of God's wrath and retributive justice is perhaps best expressed in his pioneering work on nonviolence, *The Way of the Cross in Human Relations* (Scottdale, Pa.: Herald Press, 1958), 17–21. He drew heavily from Emil Brunner and Paul Ramsey. Although Lehman was a theologian much interested in peace issues, his assumptions regarding the nature of Scripture seemed to override the theological concerns raised in this paper regarding the violence of God or violence in the name of God. See the first of his two volumes on biblical theology, *Biblical Theology*, vol. 1: *Old Testament* (Scottdale, Pa.: Herald Press, 1971), Part 1.

[2] Yoder's classic argument on this theme is his account of Abraham sacrificing his son Isaac in *The Original Revolution* (Scottdale, Pa.: Herald Press, 1972), "If Abraham Is Our Father," 91–111.

[3] For pacifists who claim the authority of the canonized Judeo-Christian Scriptures cannot easily be dismissed, the complexity and magnitude of the problem of a violent God. John Howard Yoder did not directly address this problem in *The Politics of Jesus* (Grand Rapids: Eerdmans, 1972) or in his later published works. I cannot examine this issue here, since it needs extensive treatment in its own right. However, in *The Politics of Jesus*, Yoder suggests that God will fight nonviolently, or less violently, or even through the instrumentality of the "enemy" (cf. chapter 4, "God Will Fight for Us"). In a recent writing, "On Not Being in

Not only was such a warrior God less and less imaginable as being the God of Jesus the Messiah; I began to see the concept itself as idolatrous—as the product of warrior kings and sheiks who believed the ultimacy of power to reside in violence. In the end, to believe in a warrior God would mean that I—speaking for myself and not for Lind or others—could not believe in the ultimacy of nonviolence as a way of life. To believe in such a God while holding Jesus to be the revelation of this God would be to deny Jesus as the harbinger of a new humanity. To state it positively, if Jesus is, as Christians traditionally maintain, the fullest revelation of God available to humanity, then the very fabric of the universe itself and the God of that universe must be nonviolent.

Lind's oft-repeated reminder, "Vengeance is mine, I will repay, says the Lord," only reinforced the dilemma that I faced.[4] If we hold to a violent God, in the name of justice, as being the one to rectify all things, we deny the way of the nonviolent cross of Jesus as being the revelation of God and the harbinger of God's new humanity.[5]

Charge" (*War and Its Discontents: Pacifism and Quietism in the Abrahamic Traditions*, ed. J. Patout Burns [Washington: Georgetown University Press, 1996], 74–90), Yoder, in arguing for nonviolence on the basis of the faithfulness of letting God be in charge, or, as he was often heard to say, of not taking history into our own hands, again does not directly address the *theological* issue.

[4] Deut. 32:35; Rom. 12:19. The whole problem of the *legitimation of violence* by God through retributive justice is not directly addressed in Lind's commentary on Ezekiel (*Ezekiel*, Believers Church Bible Commentary [Scottdale, Pa: Herald Press, 1996]. He places the issue in a larger sociopolitical context of human accountability. (See esp. "The Sword of the Lord," 176–83. Note also the comments on the "two-kingdom" theory of the sixteenth-century Anabaptists, 184–85.) Perry Yoder, in his generally useful work, *Shalom: The Bible's Word for Salvation, Justice, and Peace* (Newton, Kan.: Faith & Life Press, 1986), takes a similar approach. See particularly "God's Justice Versus Human Standards," 34–36.

[5] In *The Nonviolent Coming of God* (Maryknoll, N.Y.: Orbis Books, 1992), James W. Douglass develops a particularly poignant case for iden-

The problem of a "warrior God" for pacifists is a major one.[6] In this chapter I wish to focus on only one small aspect of that much larger task, on a single phenomenon that is woven warp and woof into our peace theology—*power*—not simply violence versus nonviolence, but power in its various forms. Mennonite concerns for peace have traditionally been accompanied by refusal to deal with power issues or even denial of their relevance. This stance has become increasingly problematic. Over the past half-century, Mennonites have been directed less and less by the power of charismatic individuals and instead are increasingly dominated by institutions of power, particularly in two major areas: denominational church institutions, and a Western capitalism that is beyond the pale of either congregational or denominational control.

Power lies beneath the surface of our consciousness, shaping our assumptions about God, determining what is "Truth" for us and what constitutes the fabric of our universe. Subconscious assumptions about power are central to our worldview and are a major contributing force in how we think and how we do theology. How *do* we understand power in the structure of life? Is power, divine power, ultimate power, essentially *coercive*? Is violence—even ultimate violence—fundamental to the character of God, and consequently to the lives of those who would act in harmony with the way of God?

---

tifying the Jesus event as the appearance of the "new humanity" (cf. esp. chap. 2).

[6] Gordon D. Kaufman's more recent theology is theocentric rather than christocentric. His entire framing of the problem of God follows a path significantly different from the one taken in this essay. Nevertheless, Kaufman shares the epistemological concerns expressed in this chapter (cf. *In Face of Mystery: A Constructive Theology* [Cambridge: Harvard University Press, 1993]). Although Kaufman does not analyze power as such—the primary focus of this essay—he does note that "a God conceived in terms of the metaphor of creativity or constructive power ... will be a very different sort from a God conceived in terms of violent destructiveness" (*Theology for a Nuclear Age* [Philadelphia: Westminster, 1993], 25-26).

FOCUSING AN ALTERNATIVE APPROACH TO POWER

Congregations, denominational offices, and even some larger institutions in the business and economic sectors of our society focus on kingdom values, such as peace, justice, reconciliation, and the creation of a life-giving counter-society. Can such institutions fulfill their purpose and move toward their goals simply by being more efficient, by using their limited resources more frugally, by gaining a greater awareness of the dynamics of human conflict, or by developing communication-enhancing strategies? Is it reasonable to assume that our organizations can actualize their purposes and goals by mastering modern marketing techniques—by being totally energized, learning management and organization theory, and developing a clientele network with more people in positions of "power" at the intermediate levels? In other words, can we as individuals and within our institutions (church and nonchurch) realize our goals of building the peaceable kingdom while accepting mainstream understandings of power and allowing our organizations to be shaped accordingly?

Our failure to come to terms with the elements of sin in the form of coercion and violence woven into the fabric of our culture—particularly our institutional structures—allows us to assume that evil can be resolved without the costly process of vulnerability ("suffering and death"). On the sacral and ritual (religious and metaphysical) side, this same unexpressed set of assumptions about reality has become a widely accepted worldview that undergirds belief in a warrior God.

Over the millennia, these assumptions have allowed the church to create an unusually elaborate and sacred set of doctrines about the life and death of Jesus—a belief system that fundamentally removes reconciliation and salvation from the social arena of suffering or of conflict transformation. These constructed supernatural "provisions of God" also set aside the theological problem of the warrior God from the perspective of the condemnation of violence.

Gene Sharp has noted that "all responses to the 'how' of dealing with ... power are rooted in assumptions about the nature of power. An erroneous or inadequate view of the nature of political power [one might add economic, religious, and spiritual power as well] is unlikely to produce satisfactory and effective action for dealing with it."[7] Although the Mennonite Church claims a heritage as a "historic peace church," much of its praxis[8] (reflection and action) reflects mainstream assumptions about power. Mennonites lack the sort of theological ethics that would bring the radical peace tradition of the Hebrew prophets and Jesus to bear both ideologically and structurally upon our everyday life and into the career world of the "church scattered."

It is precisely in the church scattered—in business, economics, law, medicine, education—that we see the most influential and powerful institutional forces shaping the church and the larger society. Recognizing the near nonexistence of a practiced comprehensive ethic of nonviolence and shalom should lead us to suspect that our career institutions are shaping and legitimating our theology. And since the careers have been adapted to the mainstream society, the ensuing theology is one that legitimates and even sanctions mainstream understandings of power.

Power is essential to the *being* of any organization and people—individually and collectively. "All political institutions," notes Hannah Arendt—and we might add *all* institutions and people, since institutions and people are *ipso facto* political—"are manifestations and materializations of power."[9] Thus, what we need is an informed praxis, an alternative understanding of *power* that will weave together into a single robust fabric the totality of our faith and action.

---

[6] Gene Sharp, *The Politics of Nonviolent Action: Part I, Power and Struggle* (Boston: Porter Sargent Publishers, 1973), 8.

[7] This term is borrowed from Paulo Freire, *Pedagogy of the Oppressed* (New York: Seabury, 1970), and will be further developed below in the section, "The Praxis of Nonviolent Power."

[8] Hannah Arendt, *On Violence* (New York: Harcourt, Brace & World, 1969), 41.

In making the current case for an "alternative approach to power," I draw on two concepts developed by Hannah Arendt: *action* and *power*. In Arendt's thought, these concepts are not merely compatible, but complementary. *Action* lays the groundwork for her later development of *power*. I am not attempting to redefine or reconstruct Arendt's thought so as to integrate it into the framework of a larger *system* of government, such as democracy.[10] Rather, my current interest lies in developing trajectories of an alternative form of power applicable to the church, a prophetic counter-society—an interest that I owe in part to Millard Lind. We wonder whether and how these trajectories can be developed into bridges (of power) for commerce with the larger society in the process of being the New in the midst of the Old. This is a topic to be developed outside the confines of this essay.

Power that achieves merely a standoff between two death-dealing forces will not advance the cause of social transformation. Power that seeks to create control of intragroup relations or encourages the collapse of order in the intergroup relations, will not be useful in building a society of justice and peace, either. Such

---

[9] Cf. Jeffrey C. Isaac, *Arendt, Camus, and Modern Rebellion* (New Haven: Yale University Press, 1992) who relies heavily on Arendt's *On Revolution* (New York: Viking Press, 1965), written after her work *The Human Condition* (Chicago: University of Chicago Press, 1958) and before *On Violence*. It is clear that Arendt's thought is supportive of grassroots democratic movements. It is far less clear that her understanding of *power* allows itself to be extrapolated into a grand *system* of governance comparable to systems currently existing, even those called *democratic* (cf. Jeffrey C. Isaac, "Oasis in the Desert: Hannah Arendt on Democratic Politics," *American Political Review* 88 [1994]: 1, 156–58).

Isaac does not include Arendt's work *On Violence* in either his article-length treatment of Arendt's politics (1994) or his book-length treatment of Arendt and Camus (1992). This suggests that Isaac does not view the political and philosophical implications of Arendt's later writings to be consistent with her earlier ones. In my view it makes Isaac's analysis of Arendt's understanding of power, violence, and nonviolence problematic.

power destroys its very raison d'être.[11] Likewise, power that sacrifices justice to peace-as-the-absence-of-war cannot finally be of help in pursuing purposes of justice, whether *within* the community or *between* racial, ethnic, religious, and economic communities.

In addressing institutional, social, and cultural relationships, we must not forget our relationship to the environment. Traditional theology of the past millennia has viewed the natural environment in terms of hierarchy and dominion. The result is that major parts of the world have been violently ravished. Power that harms the harmony and balance of the environment and the universe[12] cannot be legitimated.

Hence the question: *What kind of power?*

What might a paradigm of power look like that moves us toward life-giving purposes and goals? It would have to be an alternative to power as perceived and practiced in mainstream politics and society — one that is in keeping with peacebuilding, social justice, and a sustaining ecology *realistically* (not simply as a dream or ideal).

---

[11] Reinhold Niebuhr, *Moral Man and Immoral Society* (New York: Charles Scribner's Sons, 1930, 1960). Reinhold Niebuhr, who referred to himself as a "political realist," warned against the practice of nonviolence as a national strategy. He stands in history as America's greatest theological apologist for the Cold War between 1946 and 1990.

[12] Robert T. O'Gorman, J. R. Newbrough, and Paul R. Dokecki, "Communiogenesis in the Context of a Catholic Parish: Community Generation and Transformative Change," Jan. 1994, 4, typescript; forthcoming in a volume on "transformative community change." The connectedness of human society not merely to the environment but to our universe and the cosmos is an arena that has become a frequent focus in social scientific theory over the past two decades. But the application of these studies for an understanding of community networking is only now beginning to be made explicit. For an excellent representative piece of this type, see another unpublished essay by the above authors, O'Gorman (Loyola University, Chicago) and Dokecki and Newbrough (Peabody College of Vanderbilt University), on "Communiogenesis: Society at Peril," 1994, typescript.

I will sketch several components of such a paradigm of power that could be embodied by the institutions and people of the church (even for the whole society). Then I will highlight these categories by comparing the power of a "domination-freeing order" with the power of the "domination-sustaining system."[13] The final section moves toward praxis or embodiment of power under the alternative paradigm.

CONSTRUCTING AN ALTERNATIVE PARADIGM OF POWER

Power as Pluriform

The first dimension of this alternative paradigm is that this *power* cannot be monolithic. This power must not inherently or explicitly evoke a counterforce because it is perceived as competitive, threatening, or predatory. Those who encounter such power will not perceive it as being lodged in a single source, whether the head of a government or institution, a bullying father, a vengeful deity, or a warrior god. It is nonhierarchical power.[14] To borrow terms from the feminist thinker Marilyn French, it is *power-to* and *power-with*, rather than *power-over*.[15]

According to Gene Sharp, such power must emerge out of the broadest realities of everyday life—one's own people, one's culture, the perceived order that creates and sustains life itself. At some level it must be shared by all of the parties involved. Such an

---

[13] Walter Wink, *Engaging the Powers: Discernment and Resistance in a World of Domination* (Minneapolis: Fortress, 1992), 13-15.

[14] A fuller, systematic theological treatment of power will call for a rethinking of the traditional conceptualizations of monotheism. Regina M. Schwartz in *The Curse of Cain: The Violent Legacy of Monotheism* (Chicago: University of Chicago Press, 1997) represents an initial effort to address this problem.

[15] Marilyn French, *Power Beyond: On Women, Men, and Morals* (New York: Summit Books, 1985), 505–12. See also Nancy C. M. Hartsock, *Money, Sex, and Power: Toward a Feminist Historical Materialism* (Baltimore: Johns Hopkins University Press, 1983). Of particular relevance is chap. 9, "An Alternative Tradition: Women on Power."

understanding of power lies at the heart of what Sharp calls "people-power."[16]

French pushes one step further. Since the whole of Western culture is permeated with patriarchy, which she equates with hierarchy, we must beware of any facile assumptions that "people power" or "power-to" will emerge out of *our own* culture and people. People-power is a domination-*freeing* power that engages in noncoercive communication.[17] The more nearly it emerges from a "domination-free order," the more likely it will spawn the creation of a domination-freeing society.[18]

We must therefore examine more carefully the sociopolitical sources of our theology. We would not anticipate fresh water to be drawn from a brackish well (cf. James 3:11); why should we expect a consistent peace theology, including a nonviolent understanding of God and of power, to come from a theological tradition that does not follow the nonviolent way of Deutero-Isaiah and Jesus?[19]

Power as a Means-End Unity

The second dimension of this new paradigm of power is that such power does not create a means-end dichotomy. Rather, such power participates *already* in the goal toward which it moves. *Praxis* – the dialectic between reflection and action, being and doing – is an exercise of this power. It is what Hannah Arendt

---

[16] Sharp, *Nonviolent Action*, 8–12.

[17] Some would argue that communication itself is noncoercive, that to claim to communicate through coercion is to demonstrate one's lack of ability to communicate, and that the concept of "noncoercive communication" is therefore a redundancy.

[18] Wink, *Engaging the Powers*, 109–37.

[19] How we live determines in great measure the "reality" we perceive and the thoughts we are capable of formulating systematically. This axiom, for pedagogical reasons, underlies James McClendon's claim that ethics should be seen as *prior* to doctrine and philosophy. For both epistemological and pedagogical reasons, ethics is pivotal to liberation theologians. See James Wm. McClendon Jr., *Systematic Theology: Ethics* (Nashville: Abingdon, 1986), 41–45; Freire, *Pedagogy*.

defines as *human action.* "The end of human action," she notes, "as distinct from the end products of fabrication, can never be reliably predicted."

When she further observes that "the means used to achieve political goals are more often than not of greater relevance to the future world than the intended goals,"[20] she speaks directly to the situation I have in mind. Power on behalf of peace and justice must, therefore, be of the same quality as the goal it seeks to achieve. Human action must not be merely instrumental in arriving at some future goal. Rather, it must proleptically offer a concrete realization of the future in the here and now.

The power we seek is human *action*—sometimes costly, but always of a life-giving quality that transcends the violence and oppression of the status quo. It must transform its subjects into symbols of the society we envision for tomorrow. Transcendence that is grounded in the action of everyday sociopolitical events contrasts markedly with the transcendence that has its roots in *ideology*, whether that ideology is doctrinaire, managerial, or religious in nature. French calls the latter, ideologically driven transcendence,

> the dream underlying the drive to power: ... the accomplishment by humans of a godlike invulnerability, impregnability, ... the ability to affect others without being affected ourselves. Dominators crave an unimpeded ability to transform political and social structures, or even human nature itself.[21]

In a similar vein, Robin Teske approaches the issue of power from the perspective of the Gaia Hypothesis, which emphasizes "the instability of all reality" as it is now perceived. Teske points to the fundamental flaw in much of our linear thinking and our

---

[20] Arendt, *On Violence*, 4.
[21] French, *Power Beyond*, 510.

tremendous preoccupation with measurable outcomes.[22] The religious parallel to the "secular" drive to quantify is today's demand for absolutes, commonly expressed through rigidity of doctrine and more subtly through the sacralization of a nation (whether Islamic, Christian, or Jewish). The latter occurs whenever a nation is equated with the people of God or claims God's unqualified blessing.[23]

The more clearly we recognize the unpredictability of our future, and the more keenly aware we are of the connectedness of our future with the present, the greater will be our courage to be and to act today as we would have all people and societies live tomorrow. From such power emerges hope based not on a dream or a wish but on social reality, however partial and fragile that reality may be.

Oppressive vs. Life-Giving Power

A third dimension of an alternative paradigm for power is that such power seeks to break the spiral of domination, oppression, and violence.[24] "Violence can destroy power; but it is utterly incapable of creating it."[25] The old dictum that violence begets violence (cf. the writings of sociologist Jacques Ellul) is misleading. It too readily allows us to presume that violence begins nowhere or only from within the hearts of frustrated individuals. Conventional wisdom focuses too exclusively on the overt dimensions of violence. It fails to recognize the link between overt violence and more covert societal injustices, or with the reality that without jus-

---

[22] Robin Teske, "Power: An Interdisciplinary Approach," in *Reconceiving Reality: Women and International Law*, ed. Dorinda Dallmeyer (Washington, D.C.: The American Society of International Law, 1993), 244-45.

[23] For a sober and enlightening discussion of this phenomenon within the larger context of the Christian tradition and ecology, see Rosemary Radford Ruether, *Gaia and God: An Ecofeminist Theology of Earth Healing* (San Francisco: HarperCollins, 1994).

[24] Wink, *Engaging the Powers*, 139-51.

[25] Arendt, *On Violence*, 56.

tice there will forever be violence, experienced in the struggle for sufficiency in material things, for dignity, for participation in one's own destiny, and for social equity and solidarity.

The dictum, as Niall O'Brien has observed, would better read, "Injustice begets violence, and that violence begets counter-violence."[26] This is the message of several of the world's great models of justice and nonviolence, such as Martin Luther King Jr., Gandhi, Tolstoy, and Jesus. Echoing this theme, Arendt says, "Power and violence are opposites; where one rules absolutely, the other is absent." This statement, though categorical, is nonetheless ambiguous. Arendt further states, "Violence appears where power is in jeopardy, but left to its own course it ends in power's disappearance."[27]

It is not clear how Arendt reconciles this statement with statements about power she has made elsewhere (as in *On Revolution*). Are we to assume Arendt understands that power, and not merely violence, at least to some degree, can be nonhierarchically institutionalized?[28] Once established, organizations and institutions take on a life of their own.[29] Are these institutions bureaucratic,

---

[26] Fr. Niall O'Brien, a Colombian Irish priest and missioner to the Philippines prior to and again following the overthrow of Fernando Marcos, accompanied the sugar workers in their desperate plight on the Island of Negros. He was slowly converted from a priest of the sacrament to a revolutionary priest of nonviolence and suffering. He cries out against the violence of passivity (ideological transcendence of privileged elites) and the violence of government, both in its policies of repression and its practices of oppression. See especially *Island of Tears, Island of Hope: Living the Gospel in a Revolutionary Situation* (Maryknoll, N.Y.: Orbis Books, 1993), 101.

[27] Arendt, *On Violence*, 56.

[28] Cf. Isaac, "Oasis in the Desert." Isaac makes this assumption without critical differentiation.

[29] Peter L. Berger and Thomas Luckmann, *The Social Construction of Reality: A Treatise on the Sociology of Knowledge* (New York: Doubleday, 1967), 47–61.

oppressive, and death-dealing? Or are they life-pushing, freeing, and empowering?[30]

If we speak of power itself as nonviolent, as Arendt does,[31] or of "the power of nonviolence,"[32] with the assumption that there is also a "power of violence," this is more than a matter of semantics. It constitutes a significant debate among philosophers and social scientists. Nevertheless, the ontological aspects of this issue need not be resolved in order to make the case for an alternative approach to power. What matters here is the recognition that the practice of such power (whether the *power of nonviolence*, or simply *power* that is itself nonviolent) is *costly*. It is substantive, genuinely death-negating. It is of the "stuff" of life itself.

Violence, injustice, and the Domination System—labels we give to the oppressing, death-dealing forces of our day—cannot be *wished* away. To break their self-perpetuating cycle requires a long, patient, arduous, and costly struggle. Such power is not an abstraction. It is expressed in solidarity with the oppressed. It absorbs hostility. It even sacrifices economically and suffers physically.

Medieval substitutionary theories of atonement read back into the Christian Scriptures constitute an ideological reductionism. Such theories reduce the essence of the historical incarnation (the epiphany of the new humanity) to a doctrinal ideology. The popularity of these theories, coupled with their sacralization, is witness to humanity's penchant for salvation and immortality while ignoring its institutionalized forms of domination, oppres-

---

[30] Arendt, *On Violence*, 81, 85–86.

[31] Arendt maintains that "it is not correct to think of the opposite of violence as nonviolence. To speak of nonviolent power is actually redundant" (Arendt, *On Violence*, 56).

[32] Douglass, *The Nonviolent Coming of God*; O'Brien, *Island of Tears*; John Howard Yoder, *The Politics of Jesus* (2d ed., Grand Rapids: Eerdmans, 1994); Stanley Hauerwas, *The Peaceable Kingdom: A Primer in Christian Ethics* (Notre Dame, Ind.: University of Notre Dame Press, 1983), 111–15.

sion, and violence. Some understandings of atonement even make violence a divine necessity, strengthening the warrior-God image.

The symbol of suffering in the Christian tradition is the cross. This is a symbol less of death than of service (Luke 9:23), the giving of life. It is the symbol of power encountering the Domination System, sometimes referred to as the "Establishment." The cross is also the symbol of the death of Jesus, who countered the religious and political Domination System of his day.[33] Within this stream of thought (which also incorporates much of third-world liberation theology), the God of Jesus is not one who called for the death of Jesus, or whose nature is such that Jesus' death was *necessary* to preserve the integrity of God's character.[34] Such an interpretation is a death-dealing ideological misconstruction created by those under the reign of the Domination System.[35]

All other "power" is counterfeit and ultimately destroys life. Our current society, however, operates predominantly in the realm of the domination-sustaining system.[36] Hence, for people claiming

---

[33] On that day the representatives of the dominating political system (the Romans) and of the dominating religious system (scribes and Pharisees) collaborated to see how they might put Jesus to death, thereby supposedly ending the threatening challenge from the alternative forms of power that Jesus presented.

[34] Two recent writings supportive of the theological orientation I am reflecting are *Keeping Salvation Ethical: Mennonite and Amish Atonement Theology in the Late Nineteenth Century,* Studies in Anabaptist and Mennonite History, no. 35, by J. Denny Weaver (Scottdale, Pa.: Herald Press, 1997); and *Understanding the Atonement for the Mission of the Church,* by John Driver (Scottdale, Pa.: Herald Press, 1986).

[35] Walter Wink developed "Domination System" language in the third volume of his trilogy on the Powers (*Engaging the Powers,* 13–25). In his use, *domination* is a synonym for structured, institutionalized violence. It lends itself particularly well to the oppressive aspects of the political dimensions of modern life.

[36] The concept of a "fall," particularly the fallenness of human societies and cultures, is most centrally characterized by its understanding and practice of power as coercion, enabling humankind (individually and

the heritage of the Hebrew prophets and of Jesus, and committed to justice-with-peace in our own societies — to maintain this vision and communicate this social reality becomes in itself a significant, ongoing struggle.

The Personalization of Power

A fourth characteristic of power in this alternative paradigm is that such power is *personal*. It is attributed personality and intentionality, both individually and corporately. We must ever be on guard lest it become depersonalized and function as "a thing in itself" — not an easy task in an efficiency-oriented world of bureaucracy! Christians opposed to violence need to engage their fellow human beings empathetically. This is power that seeks to unite and transform rather than oppose and destroy. It creates lines of connectivity, overcomes alienation, and allows for participation at the workplace, in the political arena, and in one's individual and corporate destiny.

This understanding of power is in harmony with Gandhi's concept of *satyagraha*, which is not simply some external "truth-force" to be exercised by persons of a peace-loving disposition. Instead, it is an inseparable quality or being of individuals and society who are transforming society and are themselves being transformed in the process.[37] The parallel concept within the Christian tradition is "truth" as referred to by Jesus of Nazareth: "You will know [experience through solidarity with the marginalized] the truth, and the truth will make you free" (John 8:32).

Stanley Hauerwas's understanding of "truth" has parallels to Arendt's understanding of power. Truth for Hauerwas, like power for Arendt, is an absolute: it needs no legitimation; it is itself the end toward which it moves. "True justice never comes

---

collectively) to maintain the illusion of holding history and the universe in their control — thereby claiming to be God.

[37] Mark Juergensmeyer, *Fighting with Gandhi* (San Francisco: Harper and Row, 1984); Joan V. Bondurant, *Conquest of Violence: The Gandhian Philosophy of Conflict* (Berkeley: University of California Press, 1971).

through violence, nor can it be based on violence. It can only be based on truth, which has no need to resort to violence to secure its own existence."[38] The term that best captures this concept is "incarnation," understood as participation with the life-giving, creating power of the cosmos.

James Douglass is an anti-nuclear activist and cofounder of Ground-Zero, a community that tracked the missile-carrying "white trains" across the U.S. and provided public resistance to the launching of Trident Missile submarines in Puget Sound, Washington. Douglass refers to this new approach to power as "the nonviolent coming of God in a new humanity."[39]

Personalized power contrasts with *bureaucracy* or depersonalized power. In analyzing violent forms of force, Arendt astutely observes,

> Today we ought to add the latest and perhaps most formidable form of such domination: bureaucracy or the rule of an intricate system of bureaus in which no men, neither one nor the best, neither the few nor the many, can be held responsible, and which could be properly called rule by Nobody.... Rule by Nobody is clearly the most tyrannical of all, since there is no one left who could ever be asked to answer for what is being done.[40]

Later she adds, "The greater the bureaucratization, ... the greater ... the attraction to violence."[41]

Seldom has the impersonalized domination of bureaucratic institutionalization been better depicted than by John Steinbeck in *The Grapes of Wrath*:

> All of them were caught in something larger than themselves.... If a bank or a finance company owned the land, the owner man said, The Bank—or the Company—

---

[38] Hauerwas, *Peaceable Kingdom*, 114–15.

[39] Douglass, *Nonviolent Coming of God*, 29–59.

[40] Arendt, *On Violence*, 38-39.

[41] Arendt, *On Violence*, 81.

needs — wants — insists — must have — as though the Bank or
the Company were a monster ... which had ensnared them.
These last would take no responsibility for the banks and
companies because they were men and slaves, while their
banks were machines and masters all at the same time....

Sure, cried the tenant men, but it's our land. We measured
it and broke it up. We were born on it, and we got killed on
it, died on it....

We're sorry. It's not us. It's the monster. The bank isn't like
a man.

Yes, but the bank is only made of men.

No, you're wrong there. The bank is something else than
men.... The bank is something more than men, I tell you.
It's the monster. Men made it, but they can't control it.[42]

The quotation is offered here partially because of its date.
Intellectual theory in psychology, sociology, and political science
has shifted quantitatively since 1939. Nevertheless, Steinbeck's
analysis is as timely today as it was for the days of the Great
Depression.

The columns on the next page constitute a transition from
paradigm to *praxis* (see following section) by somewhat starkly setting the alternative forms of a "Domination-Freeing Order" alongside the forms of the "Current Domination System."

I am indebted to Walter Wink for some of the terms used
here, including "Domination System." I have adapted his "domination-free order" to speak of a domination free*ing* order. *Domination System* and *domination-freeing order* clearly denote the structural dimensions of the power with which we are dealing.[43]

---

[42] John Steinbeck, *The Grapes of Wrath* (New York: Viking Press,
1939), 42-45, as quoted by Wink, *Engaging the Powers*, 50.

[43] Wink, *Engaging the Powers*, 46–47.

210 • *Peace and Justice Shall Embrace*

Modes of Power	Power in the Current Domination System	Power in a Domination-Freeing Order
Theoretical	• Power over: power to dominate, to take life, to destroy	• Power with: to act in concert with, empowering, life-enhancing
Operational Structures	• Linear: goal-oriented, end justifies means • Conquest: to command and to be obeyed	• Dialectic, process oriented, unity of means-end • Dialogue: diplomacy, seeking common ground
Organization-al Structures	• Hierarchical: patriarch-al, bureaucratic, posi-tioned to control • Secrecy (executive ses-sions) • Extra-governmental agencies unhooked from accountability	• Horizontal: interconnect-edness, people power, par-ticipation, solidarity, posi-tioned to share • Openness, honesty • All agencies structured with multiple lines of ac-countability
Relational Patterns	• Politics of ranking, patriarchal • Domination, masculine • Impersonal, abstract • Win-lose	• Politics of fairness, dia-logue • Partnership, feminine dis-closure, cooperation • Personal, concrete • Win-win
Peace	• The absence of war, coerced tranquility • Through "work": end justifies the means; "peace through pow-er": military force, economic exploitation, and coercion	• Wholeness of society and individuals; well-being • Through "action": nonvio-lent process, no means-end justification, an end in itself (an absolute whose sphere can be expanded only by peace itself)
Justice	• Retributive: "legal," impersonal, punitive, hierarchical • Violence is maximiza-tion of power • Exclusiveness	• Restorative: sufficiency of goods; personal and ethnic dignity; participation in one's destiny • Violence signals a power failure, a breakdown of justice • Inclusiveness
The Environment	• Exploitation, control, mastery, contempt, usurpation	• Participation, harmony and balance, cooperation, respect, codependency, interconnectedness

Of course, in the world of everyday reality there are ambiguities with no sharply contrasting lines. The reader should view these columns as heuristically defining the centers of two confluent orders reflecting an emerging paradigmatic shift in the understanding of power, and not as defining their outer limits.

THE PRAXIS OF NONVIOLENT POWER

Praxis is the dialectic of reflecting, acting, and becoming.[44] Praxis, whether violent or nonviolent, whether death-dealing or life-giving, is the stuff out of which youths are reared, institutions are built, history is constructed, traditions are woven, peoplehood and values are created and passed on, and power is embodied. Taking the concept beyond its dialectic roots in Freire's thought, praxis can be defined biblically and theologically as "the way," the path or the process by which we become who we are.[45] The praxis of nonviolent power expressed individually and corporately is a core element in the epiphany of God's new creation. It is the praxis of this domination-freeing power that I will now examine.

To disclose, to empower, and to transform constitute three dimensions or movements of power in the alternative paradigm outlined above. These movements are in dialectic relationship to each other, neither independent of each other nor linearly sequential. But for purposes of analysis, I will treat them sequentially.

The "revelatory [disclosing] quality of ... action [praxis] comes to the fore when people are with each other and neither for nor against them," notes Arendt.

> Although nobody knows whom he reveals when he discloses himself in deed or word, he must be willing to risk the disclosure.... Without disclosure of the agent in the act,

---

[44] See Freire, *Pedagogy*.

[45] Hannah Arendt has developed the concept of human *action*, which has significant parallels with Freire's concept of praxis. Arendt focuses less on the individual and more on structures (*Human Condition*, chap. 5). Arendt's concept of *action* is implied in my use of the term *praxis*.

action loses its specific character and becomes one form of achievement.[46]

The negative force of those individuals and institutions bound by the Domination System begins to fade when masks are removed and the truth—whether of fact or perception—is seen clearly. Disclosure itself moves powerfully toward a domination-freeing order. Disclosure revises perceptions. Disclosure realigns people and puts them into new partnerships. But disclosure is often a gradual and cautious process. With the power of truth revealed, there is often pain, resistance, or even reentrenchment.

The power of disclosure is central to the way of the cross in Pauline perspective. Christ "disarmed the rulers and authorities [the Domination System] and made a public example of them" (Col. 2:15). Domination and violence are forms of masquerading. To unmask nonviolently, to reveal the Powers for what they are through the praxis of the cross, is actually to *disempower*, to defeat them.

The praxis of disclosure entails empowerment. To unmask, to show one's real face, is to reveal truth. To perceive truth is to be empowered. In the praxis model, the *being* of the doer is externalized *in action* within a social context. The actor gains new clarity of the self and of the relationship of the self in an "objective" social environment.[47] "In action the being of the doer is somehow intensified.... Thus, nothing [and no one] acts unless [by acting] it makes present its latent self."[48]

People become harbingers of the kingdom when "disclosing action" empowers the "other" either as an individual or as an organization of which the individual is an organic part. This development of "power-to" is a key task. "Power-to," notes French, "is achieved not by individuals but by communities or networks of

---

[46] Arendt, *Human Condition*, 180.

[47] Cf. Peter L. Berger and Thomas Luckmann, *The Social Construction of Reality: A Treatise on the Sociology of Knowledge* (New York: Doubleday, 1967), 60–61.

[48] Dante, as quoted by Arendt, *Human Condition*, 175.

supporting individuals."[49] Just as individuals do not create power, so it is never the property of an individual. "*Power is action in concert.*" Power belongs to people, not in isolation but in togetherness.[50] And it remains in existence only so long as and only to the degree that people are bonded and knit together.[51] Whoever reveals to the other who one is, closes the distance, even among those who already perceive themselves to be equals. This is to empower the other.

If we maintain distance—whether through hierarchial structures, or through professionalism, or through economics or race—we maintain control. If we remove distance, we remove barriers and empower others.

When we unmask oppression, violence, and injustice, we take away from the person or institution the "power of domination." If we free another from "domination power," we also freed ourselves from "domination power." Where secrecy is removed, there distrust and fear are removed, because the "oppressor" must now play with an open hand.

Just as individuals can become "corrupted," so institutions can lose their power and become participants in the Domination System. "Once firmly organized, an institution tends to assume an identity of its own which makes it independent of the people who have founded it or those who constitute its membership," notes Peter Blau.[52] And just as an institution that was once relatively domination-free can become a part of the current Domination System,[53] so this institution can again be transformed into the reality it was intended to be by engaging it in the alternative powers.

---

[49] French, *Power Beyond*, 505.

[50] Arendt, *On Violence*, 44, emphasis mine.

[51] Barry Wellman and Barry Leighton, "Network, Neighborhoods, and Communities: Approaches to the Study of the Community Question," *Urban Affairs Quarterly* 14 (1979): 364–65.

[52] As quoted by Wink, *Engaging the Powers*, 81.

[53] Berger and Luckmann, *Social Construction of Reality*, 89–90.

Wink avers,

> The Jesus who died at the hands of the Powers died every bit as much for the Powers as he died for the people.... Death [and the vulnerability of solidarity with the marginalized as the praxis of the cross] is not, then, merely an unmasking and exposure of the Powers for what they are, ... but an effort to transform the Powers into what they are meant to be.[54]

I do not hold the bureaucratic and institutionalized forces of violence and oppression (whether of government or economic systems) to have ontological status or to be intrinsically evil and therefore irredeemable or unable to be transformed. Nor do I believe that the legalized violence of the military, the police, or the legalized oppression of transnational capitalism can be legitimated on the basis of "maintaining peace and order" or as being "the lesser of evils." Rather, structures of violence and oppression are human constructions. Only as we begin to unmask them, seeing them as human constructs with all their destructive, dominating potential, can we work creatively toward a transformed society.[55]

How much imaginative action is required? How readily are we deceived? Marilyn French penetratingly asserts, "The structural manifestation of patriarchal values is hierarchy; and so pervasive is this form that we can hardly imagine alternative forms."[56]

Nevertheless, the action of justice-and-peace by those engaged in the praxis of the cross can become a converting catalyst in a local setting (our Nazareth). When it links a partially unmasked organization with a larger system of partially unmasked and empowered, transforming organizations, it can and will reach deeply into the roots of the Domination System (our Jerusalem and Rome), not merely dismantling them but also transforming them.[57]

---

54 *Engaging the Powers*, 82.
55 Wink, *Engaging the Powers*, 84.
56 French, *Power Beyond*, 23.
57 Wink, *Engaging the Powers*, 61.

This orientation does not suggest that the "government which governs least governs best." Nor does it imply with Hobbes that governments are necessary only because people are evil and need to be defended from each other. Governments are necessary also because people are good and need to construct creative organizations to meet each other's needs and to maintain harmony with the other fauna and the flora of planet Earth.[58]

CONCLUSION

The church is to be the harbinger of the New Society, "the holy city, the new Jerusalem, coming down out of heaven from God" (Rev. 3:12; 21:2, 10). It is to be a this-worldly embodiment of that which cannot be communicated except as it is lived out incarnationally. But this same nonviolent, life-sustaining, life-creating power is not to be limited to an elitist sectarian group. It is to constitute the fabric of our institutions and to be lived out by the whole of society — an epiphany of the Way of God and of the fabric of the universe itself.

This is the vision of the prophetic communities of Amos and of Jeremiah as held forth by Millard Lind to his students and in his writings. However, today, no less than in the pre-exilic times and in the Exile itself, the communities clinging to such a vision are fraught with the temptation of survival through passive nonengagement and inaction. Withdrawal can take place geographically or through a spirituality of the apolitical soul. Either way, it is as damaging as the myth-maintaining power of domination.

The Christian church needs to answer some questions: (1) How should we read the Old Testament — through the eyes of the kings or of the prophets? That is, where is the locus of our biblical

---

[58] This more global and cosmic vision of harmony is not "New Age," nor is this an understanding that is first emerging in our times. The sixth-century BCE prophetic voice of Deutero-Isaiah (Isaiah 40–66) shared this vision with the community of that era. Within most branches of the Judeo-Christian tradition, however, this vision has been "spiritualized" out of existence.

norms? And (2) what are the images of God that shape our under-standings of the Ultimate? Is the primal image of God that of a warrior whose ultimate power is epitomized in the "rightness" to exercise vengeance? Or is God the Servant, one whose power lies in vulnerability, and whose being is most clearly made known in self-giving nonviolence? Surrounding these issues is the question of power — our power and our corresponding *action*.

The more any church detaches itself from its sectarian moor-ings and participates in the structures of the larger society, the more imperative it becomes to its survival and its mission for it to develop images of a nonviolent God and understandings of power as nonviolent praxis. No theology and no community can hold forth the prophetic vision of the kingdom of peace and sustain it without participating in the praxis of the cross — the way of the Christ, the power of God. The community that gains its life from this power of God is univocally called to display that power in its persevering engagement with the powers of domination.

Millard C. Lind
A Biographical Sketch

PAUL KEIM

Millard C. Lind was born the fifth of seven sons in Bakersfield, California, on October 10, 1918. He grew up near Albany, Oregon, in a place called Sweet Home. He was reared in the home of his parents, Bishop N. A. and Sarah Lind, where he was introduced to the work of the church at an early age. He left there at the age of twenty to enter Hesston College, in Hesston, Kansas. In 1942 he received a B.A. degree from Goshen College, and in 1947 a B.D. degree from the Goshen College seminary. He married Miriam Sieber in 1943. In 1944 he was ordained to the ministry. The next three years he served as pastor of the Kouts Mennonite Church, in Kouts, Indiana. In 1946, he also began part-time work for the Mennonite Publishing House, in Scottdale, Pennsylvania. In 1947 he joined the editorial staff there.

Lind received a Th.D. from Pittsburgh Theological Seminary (1965). He studied in Israel and Greece with Hebrew Union College (1965), the American Schools of Oriental Research (1968–69), and the Ecumenical Institute at Tantur (1975–76). He co-led study groups to the Near East in 1973, 1975, and 1982. Lind was an associate trustee of the American Schools of Oriental Research, 1981–83, and has had a continuing interest in Middle Eastern archaeology, especially as it relates to the Bible.

Lind is professor emeritus of Old Testament at the Associated Mennonite Biblical Seminary, where he taught for many years. Several of his admiring students have gone on to complete doctoral studies in such diverse fields as biblical studies, theology, ethics, and related disciplines. Others were called to pastoral ministry, counseling, editing, or other professions. He has served as a pastor, writer of adult Sunday school Bible studies, editor of a community-family magazine, and participant in Bible conferences. He has taught missions throughout the United States and Canada, Israel and Egypt, Britain and Europe. He has written such books as *Yahweh Is a Warrior* (1980), *Monotheism, Power, Justice* (1990), and *Ezekiel* (1996), and published articles in scholarly and church magazines.

Millard Lind is an active member of the College Mennonite Church, Goshen, Indiana, and husband of writer Miriam Sieber Lind. Together they have reared seven children, one a foster son with disabilities, in whose continuing care they participate. Known as "Abba," he is grandfather to sixteen grandchildren, and great-grandfather to three great-grandchildren.

Publications by Millard Lind

COMPILED BY SARAH LIND

Articles

1945. Daily Devotional Guide. *Gospel Herald* 37:903, 999, 1015, 1047.

1945. Daily Devotional Guide. *Gospel Herald* 38:7.

1945. "Our God is Able." Radio Sermon. Valparaiso, Ind. (Kouts, Ind., unpublished, personal files).

1945. "A Mighty Fortress." Radio Sermon. Valparaiso, Ind. (Kouts, Ind., unpublished, personal files).

1945. "The Untroubled Heart." Radio Sermon. Valparaiso, Ind. (Kouts, Ind., unpublished, personal files).

1946. "A Bruised Heel." *Gospel Herald* 39:561–62.

1948. "An Important Discovery." *Gospel Herald* 41:733.

1953. "The Gates of Hell Shall Not Prevail Against the Church." In *Prophecy Conference: Report of Conference Held at Elkhart, Indiana, April 3-5, 1952*. Scottdale, Pa.: Mennonite Publishing House.

1953. Chester Lehman, H. S. Bender, Millard Lind. "The RSV: An Examination and Evaluation." *Gospel Herald* 46:433–34, 437; 484–91.

1953. Chester K. Lehman, H. S. Bender, Millard Lind. "Preliminary Report of the Special Committee on the Revised Standard Version." *Gospel Herald* 46:1–2, 21.

1954. "Bible Principles Governing Race Relations in the Church." *Gospel Herald* 47:961–62, 981.

1954. "Adventure with the Spirit." *Youth's Christian Companion* 35/48:381.

1954. "Adventures with the Bible." *Youth's Christian Companion* 35/49:389.

1954. "Adventure in Prayer." *Youth's Christian Companion* 35/50:387, 395.

1955. "Adventure in Fellowship." *Youth's Christian Companion* 36/2:15.

1955. "Adventure in Service." *Youth's Christian Companion* 36/4:29, 32.

1955. Alta Mae Erb and Millard Lind. "A Family Conference? Why Not?" *Gospel Herald* 48:346.

1956. "A Movement Literature." *Gospel Herald* 49:697–98.

1966. "The Hermeneutics of the Old Testament." *Mennonite Quarterly Review* 60:227–37.

1967. "The Nature of Particularism and Universalism." AMBS, Dean's Seminar. Unpublished paper, Mennonite Historical Library.

1969. "Israeli or Jacobi?" *Gospel Herald* 62:514–16.

1970. "The Concept of Political Power in Ancient Israel." *Annual of the Swedish Theological Institute* 7:4–24.

1971. "Paradigm of Holy War in the Old Testament." *Biblical Research* 16:1–16.

1972. Presentation at Colloquium on Peace Studies, Elkhart, Ind., June 5–8. Unpublished paper, Mennonite Historical Library.

1972. "Politics of the Spirit." *Gospel Herald* 65:169–71.

1973. "Love is Forever." *The Mennonite* 88:311

1976. "Man of Two Mountains." *AMBS Window*, Oct. 4/1:1.

1976. "Reflections on Biblical Hermeneutics." *Kingdom, Cross and Community*, eds. J. R. Burkholder, Calvin Redekop (Scottdale, Pa.: Herald Press), 91–102. Reprinted in *Essays on Biblical Interpretation*, ed. Willard Swartley (Elkhart, Ind.: Institute of Mennonite Studies, 1984), 151–64.

1978. "Is There a Biblical Case for Civil Disobedience?" *God and Caesar* 4/3:6–8.

1978. "The NIV Old Testament, a Partial Evaluation." *Gospel Herald* 71:792–93.

1978. "This Kept Us Married." *The Christian Reader*, Sept-Oct.

1979. "The RSV Revisited." *Builder*. Feb., 2.

1979. "Christian Living: Yesterday and Today." *Christian Living* 26/1:19.

1980. "The Anomaly of the Prophet." *The New Way of Jesus*, ed. William Klassen (Newton, Kans.: Faith and Life Press), 17–28.

1981. "Biblical Economics: A 'Bottom-Up' Social Order." *The Window* 8/3:1–3.

1981. "Economic Structure in the Old Testament." *Occasional Papers of the Council of Mennonite Seminaries and Institute of Mennonite Studies*, ed. Willard Swartley (Elkhart, Ind.: Institute of Mennonite Studies) 1:59–69.

1981. "The Sting of Death Is Sin." *Gospel Herald* 74:289–91.

1981. "Teaching Old Testament from a Missional Perspective." *Occasional Papers of the Council of Mennonite Seminaries and Institute of Mennonite Studies*, ed. Willard Swartley (Elkhart, Ind.: Institute of Mennonite Studies), 2:65–83.

1982. "Law in the Old Testament." *The Bible and Law, Occasional Papers of the Council of Mennonite Seminaries and Institute of Mennonite Studies*, no. 3, ed. Willard Swartley (Elkhart, Ind.: Institute of Mennonite Studies), 9–41. Also published 1983 in *Quarterly, Christian Legal Society* 4/2–3:32ff.

1982. "Refocusing Theological Education to Mission: The Old Testament and Contextualization." *Missiology: An International Review* 10:141–60.

1982. "The Rule of God: Agenda for the City." *The Covenant Quarterly*, May 40/2:3–18.

1982. "With Open Hands: Economics as if Yahweh Matters." *The Other Side*, Nov., 16–22.

1983. "Associated Mennonite Biblical Seminaries and Albright Institute." *American Schools of Oriental Research Newsletter*, May 8, 12.

1983. "Interpreting the Interpreters: Which Commentaries Can We Trust?" *The Other Side*, Aug. 19/8:26–28.

1984. "Hosea 5:8–6:6." *Interpretation* 38:398–403.

1984. "Monotheism, Power and Justice: A Study in Isaiah 40–55." *Catholic Biblical Quarterly* 46:432–46.

1984. "Paul Erb Remembered, A Versatile Person." *Gospel Herald* Memorial Issue 77:516.

1986. "Transformation of Justice, From Moses to Jesus," New Perspectives on Crime and Justice: Occasional Papers of the MCC Canada Victim Offender Ministries Program and MCC U.S. Office of Criminal Justice, Dec. 1986, issue no. 5.

1987. "Announcing the Reconciler." *Gospel Herald* 80:889–91.

1987. "Prince of Peace: Temple or Palace?" *Gospel Herald* 80:857–59.

1987. "Traditional and Not-So-Traditional Values." *Gospel Herald* 80:873–75.

1990. "The Gospel: It Doesn't Fit." *Gospel Herald* 83:177–79.

1990. "Law, Theology of." *The Mennonite Encyclopedia* (Scottdale, Pa.: Herald Press), 5:511–12.

1990. "Let the Pax Christi Rule." *Gospel Herald* 83:489–91.

1993. "But They Did Fight Wars in the Old Testament, Didn't They?" *Gospel Herald* 86/3:1–3.

1994. "Peter, Cornelius, and 'Balkanization': From No Prejudice about Food to No Prejudice Against People." *Gospel Herald* 87/6:1–3.

1996. "Statement Prepared by Millard Lind for a Vigil at St. Mary's Catholic Church, Michigan City, Ind., the Night of Tommie Smith's Execution, July 17, 1996." *College Mennonite Church Peace Ministries Center, Occasional Paper* 2:1–2.

1997. "The Shepherd Psalm." Unpublished sermon in memory of Clara Hershberger, College Mennonite Church, July 19 (personal files).

1997. "Political Implications of Isaiah 6." *Writing and Reading the Scroll of Isaiah: Studies of an Interpretive Edition*, eds. Craig C. Broyles and Craig A. Evans (Leiden: Brill). Pp. 317–338.

Forthcoming. "The Prophetic Emphasis of the Sinai Tabernacle Directive (Exodus 25:10–22)." In *Festschrift* for Waldemar Janzen upon his retirement. Ed. Gerald Gerbrandt.

Editorials

1949. "His Witnesses." *Gospel Herald* 42:1259–60.

1949. "The Use of Power." *Gospel Herald* 42:387.

1949. "An Important Find." *Gospel Herald* 42:291.

1950. "'Be Clothed … Be Fed.'" *Gospel Herald* 43:123.

1950. "Mennonite Aid, Inc." *Gospel Herald* 43:99.

1950. "Christian Fellowship." *Gospel Herald* 43:51–52.

1950. "War unto Death." *Gospel Herald* 43:27–28.

1950. "The Holy Spirit in the Life of the Early Church." *Gospel Herald* 43:3.

1952. "Modern Family Life." *Gospel Herald* 45:1075.

1952. "Corporate Worship in the New Testament Church." *Gospel Herald* 45:835.

1952. "'After This Manner.'" *Gospel Herald* 45:787.

1953. "The Worth of the Individual." *Gospel Herald* 46:339.

1953. "'Understandest Thou?'" *Gospel Herald* 46:51.

1953. "The Stewardship of Time and Talent." *Gospel Herald* 46:99.

1953. "His Witnesses." *Gospel Herald* 46:459.

1953. "Exhortation to Prayer." *Gospel Herald* 46:363.

1954. "Something Old and Something New." *Christian Living* 1/1:3.

1954. "What's a Man?" *Christian Living* 1/2:3.

1954. "What's a Community?" *Christian Living* 1/3:3.

1954. "Sign of the Fish." *Christian Living* 1/4:3.

1954. "Christianity Backstage." *Christian Living* 1/6:3.

1954. "Source in the Mountains." *Christian Living* 1/7:3.

1954. "Can Advertising Be Christian?" *Christian Living* 1/8:3.

1954. "What About Our Luxuries?" *Christian Living* 1/9:3.

1954. "The Christian Community and Missions." *Christian Living* 1/10:3.

1954. "National Book Week." *Christian Living* 1/11:3.

1954. "What's Wrong with Father." *Christian Living* 1/12:3.

1955. "Go Tell." *Gospel Herald* 48:243.

1955. "Some Negatives for 1955." *Christian Living* 2/1:3.

1955. "Two Isms Which Oppose Nonconformity." *Christian Living* 2/2:3.

1955. "Our Summer Vacation, 1955." *Christian Living* 2/3:3.

1955. "You'll See Him Again." *Christian Living* 2/4:3.

1955. "We Observe Family Week." *Christian Living* 2/5:3.

1955. "What About That Guilt Complex?" *Christian Living* 2/7:3.

1955. "After Seventeen Years." *Christian Living* 2/8:3.

1955. "The Child in the Midst." *Christian Living* 2/9:3.

1955. "Lesson in Simplicity." *Christian Living* 2/10:3.

1955. "Do You Know?" *Christian Living* 2/11:3.

1955. "Reliving the Incarnation." *Christian Living* 2/12:3.

1956. "Why Preach the Gospel?" *Christian Living* 3/2:3.

1956. "A Lay Ministry." *Christian Living* 3/3:3.

1956. "Simplicity." *Christian Living* 3/6:3.

1956. "Not Too Indigenous." *Christian Living* 3/7:3.

1956. "Tomorrow Is Today." *Christian Living* 3/8:3.

1956. "What Purpose Education?" *Christian Living* 3/9:3.

1956. "Property and Community." *Christian Living* 3/10:3.

1956. "The Squeeze." *Christian Living* 3/12:2.

1957. "'The Good That I Would.'" *Christian Living* 4/1:2.

1957. "Those Sixty Versions." *Christian Living* 4/2:2.

1957. "Specialization and Plain Christianity." *Christian Living* 4/3:2.

1957. "Good Morning." *Christian Living* 4/4:2.

1957. "The Indispensable Emotion." *Christian Living* 4/5:2.

1957. "Life as Usual?" *Christian Living* 4/6:2.

1957. "Dedication of Babies." *Christian Living* 4/7:2.

1957. "Gospel of Forgiveness." *Christian Living* 4/8:2.

1957. "Crossing the Barrier." *Christian Living* 4/9:2.

1957. "Flight into Reality." *Christian Living* 4/10:2.

1957. "Literacy for What?" *Christian Living* 4/11:2.

1957. "The New Ice Age." *Christian Living* 4/12:2.

1958. "The Real and the Ideal." *Christian Living* 5/1:2.

1958. "What Is Christianity?" *Christian Living* 5/2:2.

1958. "The People in the Other Rooms." *Christian Living* 5/3:2.

1958. "The Gospel We Preach." *Christian Living* 5/4:2.

1958. "Teach Us to Pray." *Christian Living* 5/5:2.

1958. "The Cross and Christian Marriage." *Christian Living* 5/6:2.

1958. "People or Shade." *Christian Living* 5/7:2.

1958. "Freedom and Education." *Christian Living* 5/9:2.

1958. "Explanations that Don't Explain." *Christian Living* 5/10:2.

1958. "The Miracle of Christmas." *Christian Living* 5/12:2, 39.

1959. "Walk in the Spirit." *Gospel Herald* 52:99.

1959. "The Spirit and the Church." *Gospel Herald* 52:459.

1959. "Priesthood of Believers." *Gospel Herald* 52:603.

1959. "On Cooperation." *Gospel Herald* 52:3.

1959. "The Greatest Heresy." *Gospel Herald* 52:723.

1959. "The Great Commission." *Gospel Herald* 52:339–40.

1959. "Fellowship Is Given." *Gospel Herald* 52:171.

1959. "The Buck Stops Here." *Christian Living* 6/1:2.

1959. "Is It Worth a Quarrel?" *Christian Living* 6/3:2.

1959. "J. B." *Christian Living* 6/4:2.

1959. "Education for the Crisis." *Christian Living* 6/9:2, 39.

1959. "Alternation." *Christian Living* 6/10:2.

1959. "New Thoughts on Old Themes." *Christian Living* 6/11:2.

1959. "Transforming the Day." *Christian Living* 6/12:2.

Curriculum Writing

1947–1950. *Advanced Sunday School Quarterly.* Scottdale, Pa.: Mennonite Publishing House, 41–44/1.

1950–1955. *Herald Adult Bible Studies.* Scottdale: Mennonite Publishing House, 44/4–49/3.

1956–1957. *Herald Adult Bible Studies.* Scottdale: Mennonite Publishing House, 50/2–51/2.

1958. *Herald Adult Bible Studies.* Scottdale: Mennonite Publishing House, 52/1.

1960. *Herald Adult Bible Studies.* Scottdale: Mennonite Publishing House, 54/2–4.

1963. *Herald Adult Bible Studies.* Scottdale: Mennonite Publishing House, 57/3.

1966. *Herald Adult Bible Studies.* Scottdale: Mennonite Publishing House, 60/4.

1967. *Adult Bible Studies.* Scottdale: Mennonite Publishing House, 61/4.

1968. *Adult Bible Studies.* Scottdale: Mennonite Publishing House, 62/3.

1974. *Adult Bible Studies.* Scottdale: Mennonite Publishing House, 69/1.

Books

1950. *Answer to War.* Scottdale, Pa.: Herald Press.

1952. *Requesta a la Guerra.* Trans. Alfredo J. Bradford. Scottdale, Pa.: Herald Press; Corrientes 728, Buenos Aires: La Aurora.

1953. Chester Lehman, Millard C. Lind, Harold Bender. *The Revised Standard Version: An Examination and Evaluation.* Scottdale, Pa.: Herald Press.

1957. *Answer to War* (Japanese trans.). Mennonite Central Committee in Japan and Japan Mennonite Mission.

1973. Biblical Foundations for Christian Worship. Scottdale, Pa.: Herald Press.

1980. *Yahweh Is a Warrior*. Scottdale, Pa.: Herald Press.

1990. *Monotheism, Power and Justice: Collected Old Testament Essays*. Elkhart, Ind.: Institute of Mennonite Studies. Text-Reader series, no. 3.

1996. *Ezekiel*. Believers Church Bible Commentary. Scottdale: Herald Press.

Theses

1942. "Study of Twenty-Eight Households of Clinton Frame Mennonite Church in Clinton Township, Elkhart, Ind." B.A. paper, Sociology major. Mennonite Historical Library, Goshen, Ind.

1955. "The Old Testament Background of the New Testament Word *ekklesia*." Th.M. thesis. Pittsburgh Theological Seminary, Pittsburgh, Pa.

1963. "The Theology of Warfare in the Old Testament." Th.D. dissertation. Library, Pittsburgh Theological Seminary, Pittsburgh, Pa.

Book Reviews

1962. John Bright, *History of Israel*. In *Gospel Herald* 55:19–20.

1965. James Smart, *The Old Testament Dialogue with Modern Man*. In *Gospel Herald* 58:393.

1966. Martin Noth, *The Old Testament World*. In *Christian Century*. Sept. 1, 1028.

1971. *The New Westminster Dictionary of the Bible*. In *Christian Century*. July 6, 867.

1976. Frank Epp, *The Palestinians*. In *Mennonite Reporter* 6/23:8.

1980. Peter Craigie, *The Problem of War in the Old Testament*. In *Sojourners* 9/12:31–34.

1980. Jose Miranda, *Marx and the Bible*. In *Mission Focus* 8/3:52–56.

1980. L. John Topel, *The Way to Peace*. In *Mission Focus* 8/1:29–31.

1982. Walter Brueggemann, *Genesis: A Bible Commentary for Teaching and Preaching*. In *Christian Century*. Nov. 4, 1208.

1982. Elmer Martens, *God's Design: A Focus on Old Testament Theology*. In *Festival Quarterly* Aug./Sept./Oct.:24.

1985. Norman Gottwald, ed., *The Bible and Liberation: Political and Social Hermeneutics*. In *Mission Focus* 13:13.

1986. Claus Westermann, *Genesis 12–36: A Commentary*. In *Christian Century* 103/30:891.

1986. Norbert Lohfink, ed., *Gewalt und Gewaltlösigkeit im Alten Testament*. In *Essays on War and Peace: Bible and Early Church*. Occasional Papers, no. 8. Institute of Mennonite Studies, 73–82.

1986. Dale Patrick, *Old Testament Law*. Review essay. In *Journal of Law and Religion* 4:479–85.

1988. Ben C. Ollenburger, *Zion, City of the Great King: A Theological Symbol of the Jerusalem Cult*. In *AMBS Bulletin*. Feb. 12–13.

1989. Philip B. Harner, *Grace and Law in Second Isaiah: "I am the Lord."* In *Journal of Biblical Literature* 108:697–98.

1990. Jonathan J. Bonk, *The World at War, the Church at Peace: A Biblical Perspective*. In *Mennonite Quarterly Review* 64:86–87.

1991. Sa-Moon Kang, *Divine War in the Old Testament and the Ancient Near East*. In *Catholic Biblical Quarterly* 53:288–90.

1992. Gisela Kittel, *Der Name über alle Namen*. In *Catholic Biblical Quarterly* 54:326–27.

1992. Gordon Matties, *Ezekiel 18 and the Rhetoric of Moral Discourse*. In *Direction* 21/1:100–2.

1993. Gerhard van Rad, *Holy War in Ancient Israel*. Trans. and ed. Marva J. Dawn. In *Hebrew Studies* 34:219–20.

1993. Van der Woude, ed., *In Quest of the Past*. In *Catholic Biblical Quarterly* 55:206–7.

1993. Horst Preuss, *Theologie des Alten Testaments*, vol. 1. In *Catholic Biblical Quarterly* 55:348–50.

1994. Norbert Lohfink, *Die Väter*. In *Catholic Biblical Quarterly* 56:115–16.

1994. Horst Preuss, *Theologie des Alten Testaments*, vol. 2. In *Catholic Biblical Quarterly* 56:776–77.

1995. Joachim Becker, *Grundzüge*. In *Catholic Biblical Quarterly* 57:542–43.

1995. Edgar W. Conrad, *Fear Not Warrior*. Unpublished, personal files.

1996. John W. Miller, *Origins of the* Bible: *Rethinking Canon History*. In *Mennonite Quarterly Review* 70:248–49.

Forthcoming. John N. Oswald, *The Book of Isaiah*. In *Journal of Biblical Literature*.

Forthcoming. Gregory A. Boyd, *God at War: The Bible and Spiritual Conflict*. In *Catholic Biblical Quarterly*.

Scripture Index

GENESIS
1.1–11 26
12:1-3 171
18 82
19:6 130
21:30 131
26:15 131
26:18 131
26:19 131
26:21 131
37 123

EXODUS
1:8 165
7:24 131
12:8 155
12:46 155
13:3 123
13:14 123
15 .... 56, 175, 181
16:12 155
20:2 123
20:17 171
22:28 170
23:6-8 74
29:32 155

LEVITICUS
7:18 155
19:13-18 172

NUMBERS
14:11 155

DEUTERONOMY
5:6 123
5:21 172
6:12 123
7:8 123
8:9 162
12:20 155
12:31 160
18:18 59
18:21-22 56
24:14 152
28:29 152
28:33 152
32 .... 175, 181
32:35 194
33:1-2 181

JUDGES
7 .... 23, 26
8:22-23 26
9:8-15 27

1 SAMUEL
8:5-22 27
13:6 131
14:11 131
19:7 164

25:33 123
29:8 164

2 SAMUEL
10:2 153
22:9-16 181

1 KINGS
5:27ff. 121
11:28 121
21 69
21:17-24 52
21:23-24 54

2 KINGS
8:28 160
9:3 54
9:6-10 54
9:20 57
9:36 54
9–10 .... 51, 53, 54, 55
10:6 54
10:10 54
10:17 54
10:30 .... 53, 54
12:10 131
24 116
25 .... 123, 124
25:3 143
25:4 132

2 CHRONICLES
16:14 131
22:5 160
25:23 133
36:6 123

EZRA
1:1 160
8:15-20 119

JOB
5:2 155
24 169
24:16 131
30:6 131
35:9 152

PSALMS
18 175
18:8-15 181
22 .... 96, 97
22:7-8 101
22:1 101
23:4 153
25:9 77
27:2 156
37:24 160
46 37
48 37
71:21 153
76 37
77:16-18 181
86:17 153
103:6 151
105:18 123
107:14 122
119:101 123
119:82 153
137 119
137:9 124
144:14 132
146:7-8 124
149 123

PROVERBS
6:10 154
6:16 150
6:34 155
10:18 154

12:9 51
13:23 169
14:30 .... 154, 155
14:31 169
15:16 154
15:16,17 51
16:8 .... 51, 154
17:1 154
17:12 51
18:23 169
24:33 154
27:4 155
28:15 169
29:9 154
30:21-23 172

ECCLESIASTES
1–3 154
1:1 146
1:1-2 147
1:2–6:9 148
1:2 .... 147, 148
1:8 156
1:11 165
1:12–2:26 .... 161, 169
1:12-15 153
1:13 157
1:18 156
2:12-17 153
2:13 157
2:14-21 156
2:18-23 153
2:21 154
2:22-23 156
2:24 153
2:24-26 149
2:25 160
2:26 157
3 .... 149, 156
3:1-8 149
3:1-15 149

3:1-22 .... 149, 152
3:9-15 149
3:10 157
3:12 153
3:16 156
3:16-22 149
3:17 149
3:22 .... 149, 153, 160
4 ..... 145, 146, 147, 149, 150, 154,
   161, 165–166, 167, 169, 170
4:1-3 .... 149, 150, 151, 154, 158,
   159, 164, 165, 168
4:1-12 .... 149, 150
4:1 .... 150, 155, 156, 167
4:2 150
4:3 .... 150, 158
4:4-5 156
4:4-6 .... 151, 154, 164, 165, 168
4:4-8 158
4:4 .... 150, 154, 155, 167
4:5 .... 154, 155, 168
4:6 ...... 150, 155, 156, 158, 166, 167
4:7-8 .... 151, 156–158, 164, 165
4:7 .... 150, 156
4:8 ...... 150, 157, 158, 162, 167, 168
4:9-12 .... 151, 157, 164, 166, 168
4:9 .... 150, 158, 159
4:10-11 167
4:10 .... 150, 159
4:11 159
4:13 .... 161, 163, 165, 172
4:13-16 ...... 149, 150, 151, 159–165,
   166, 168, 169, 173
4:14 .... 150, 160, 162, 163
4:15 .... 150, 161, 162, 164
4:16 .... 150, 161, 162, 164
5:8-12 169
5:1-17 16
5:8 163
5:9-11 157

5:10-12 156
5:11 154
5:12-16 157
5:13 .... 151, 157
5:18 151
6:2 171
6:3-9 156
6:4 160
6:5 154
6:6 158
6:8 156
6:10–12:8 148
7:7 147
7:15 156
7:27 146
8:1-5 169
8:12 160
8:12-13 169
8:14 156
8:16 .... 157, 160
9–12 158–159
9:1-3 156
9:4 153
9:6 155
9:10 152
9:11 156
9:13-15 170
9:13-18 169
9:14-16 165
9:15 165
9:15-16 .... 162, 165
9:16 170
9:17 154
10:5-7 172
10:16 158
10:16-20 169
11:6 150
11:9 169
12:8-14 147
12:8 .... 147, 148

12:9-10 148
12:9-11 167
12:9-14 146
12:14 169

SONG OF SOLOMON
5:4 131

ISAIAH
1:12-17 90
1:27 77
2:1-4 81
5:8 171
5:20 74
6:5 158
8:1-4 42
11 36
11:8 131
11:13 155
19:22 73
20 43
28:2 181
28:15 179
29:3-10 181
30:13 132
30:15 154
31 81
31:4-5 87
37:32 154
37:33-35 87
40:1 153
42:1-4 .... 97, 165
42:7 124
42:22 131
43:6 123
43:23-24 90
45:14 .... 123, 124
49:1-6 .... 97, 165
49:13 153
49:26 156

50:4-9 165
50:4-11 97
51:3 153
51:12 153
52:2 122
52:9 153
52:13–53:12 .... 97, 98, 165, 179
58:2 90
58:6-10 90
59 181
59:15-20 180
59:19 180
61:1 124
66:15-16 181

JEREMIAH
1:13-15 133
2:34 131
6 81
6:18-21 90
7:1-12 87
7:3 90
7:4 87
7:5 90
7:7 90
7:8-11 89
7:11 92
9:1-15 91
9:16 91
9:23-24 87
9:24 .... 77, 82, 91
11:14 91
13:1-11 42
13:12-14 42
15:1 91
16:1-13 42
19:1-15 42
20:1-18 96
20:7 101
20:7-10 100

20:9 94
20:10 100
20:14-18 100
22:13-16 82
22:15-16 91
22:24-30 37
25:11 41
26:8-11 87
27 94
27:3-11 38
27:8 38
27:9 92
27:10 38
27:11 38
27:12-15 38
27:14 92
27:16 92
27:16-17 39
27–28 .... 37, 38, 92
28 116
28:2-4 40
28:10 93
28:11 40
28:13 93
28:13-14 42
28:15-16 42
28:17 42
29:5-7 105
31:13 153
32 42
32:1-5 102
32:2 123
32:15 103
32:28 103
34:13 123
36:5 87
37:2 143
37:15 104
38:4 98
38:6 123

39:7 123
40:1 123
47:1 123
49:16 160
50:33 151
51:34-35 122
52:6 143
52:24 143
52:28 116

LAMENTATIONS
1:1 143
1:3 144
1:11 143
1:16 153
1:18 144
2:8 144
2:12 143
2:21 .... 143, 144
3:7 123
3:7-9 143
4:4 143
4:9-10 143
5:9 144

EZEKIEL
3:22-27 143
3:27 43
4 43
4:1-3 143
4:2-3 132
4:14 155
5 43
5:1-17 143
8:7 129
8:7-8 .... 129, 132
8:7-12 129
8:8 129
8–11 .... 129, 140

12 143
12:1-16 133
12:13 133
14:14 80
17 81
21 144
26:9 132
32:7-8 176
33:30-33 119
34:16 77
40–48 142

DANIEL
1–6 126
5 165
6 165
11:9 160

HOSEA
1:4 .... 52, 53, 55
1:4-5 .... 51, 52–53
1:6 53
1:9 53
2:19 77
5:1-2 90
5:6 90
6:1 73
6:5 .... 59, 60
6:6 90
7:3 59
7:7 59
8:4 59
8:13 90
9:15 59
10:12 82
12:6 82
12:14 59
13:9-11 59
14:9 63

AMOS
1–2 .... 69, 76, 81
2:6 .... 69, 72, 81
2:7 70
3:2 70
3:9 152
4:1 171
4:3 132
4:4-5 90
4:6-11 72
5 81
5:6-7 73
5:10 74
5:14-15 74
5:21-24 75
6:1 67
6:4-7 71
6:6 76
6:12 75
7:8 72
8:3 67
9:2 131
9:7-12 76
9:11-15 .... 73, 77

NAHUM
1:13 122
2:13 (Hebrew) 131
3:10 123

MICAH
2:1-3 171
6:4 123
6:6-8 90

HABAKKUK
3 .... 175, 181

ZEPHANIAH
1:14-18 176

ZECHARIAH
1:17 153
9 94
9:10 96
9:11 123
9:12 124
14:12 131

TOBIT
2:7 131
8:9 131

WISDOM OF SOLOMON
1:1 178
1:14 182
2 181
2:6-9 184
2:10 186
2:11 .... 179, 184, 187
2:12-16 187
2:12-20 179
2:13 179
2:16 .... 180, 186, 189
2:18 .... 180, 186
2:19-20 181
2:21–3:4 181
2:24 182
2–5 .... 179, 183, 190
3:2-4 180
3:5 183
3:13 181
3:14-15 181
4:7-9 182
5 182
5:1 .... 182, 186
5:2 182
5:3 182
5:3-13 184
5:6 182
5:6-14 181

5:8 182
5:13 182
5:15-16 .... 183, 186
5:15-23 .... 179, 181
5:17 180
5:17-23 185
5:20 180
5:21 180
5:22-23 180
6:1 187
6:1-2 178
7:15–8:1 178
7:17-22 .... 182, 183
10:1–11:10 178–179
10–19 180
11:11-14 182
11:15-20 181
11:20 .... 178, 182, 183
11:21-23 184
11:23 184
11:24 184
11:25 183
11:26 .... 184, 187, 189
12:2 184
12:8-10 184
12:10 184
12:11 184
12:13 185
12:16 .... 179, 184
12:17 .... 184, 185, 188, 189
12:18 185
12:19 .... 186, 187
12:19-20 187
12:19-22 .... 187, 188
12:20 184
12:22 187
12:26-27 185
12:27 182
16:16-29 181
16:23 183

16:24 .... 178, 181
17:20-21 181
18:2 182
18:14-20 179
18:20-25 .... 179, 188
19:6 180
19:6-21 180
19:20 183

SIRACH
13:13 164
39:16-35 176
39:31 176

MATTHEW
5   .... 189, 190
5:20 188
5:40 191
5:45 .... 177, 188, 189
6:1-18 87
6:7-8 88
9:13 90
12:1-8 90
12:7 90
12:9-14 90
21   96
21:1-17 92
21:12 92
21:12-13 44
21:13 92
23:23 90
23:37 99
24:29 176
26:47-50 100
26:69-75 100
27:32-56 96
27:41-43 100
27:46 101
28:1-10 102

LUKE
6:6-11 43
6:36 191
9:23 206
13:10-17 43
14:1-6 43
19:45-48 44
21:25-26 176

JOHN
3:3 180
4:1-38 44
4:27 44
8:32 207
11:25 107

11:47-50 99

ROMANS
12:19 194
13:3 170

JAMES
3:11 201

REVELATION
3:12 215
8–9 176
19:11-21 79
21:2 215
21:10 215

Author Index

Ackroyd, Peter R. 128, 113, 114
Adams, R. M. 121, 122
Ahlström, Gösta 117, 118
Albrektson, Bertil 175
Albright, William F. 118
Allain, A. 138
Allen, Leslie C. 128
Andersen, Francis I. 58, 59
Arendt, Hannah 197, 198, 201,
    202, 203, 204, 205, 208, 211,
    212, 213
Avila, Rafael 90
Barré, Michael L. 161
Barrett, C. K. 44
Barth, Karl 24
Barton, George A. ... 145, 146, 149,
    157, 159
Barton, John 70, 112
Bauman, Clarence 22
Bender, Harold 29
Berger, Peter 204, 212, 213
Berkovits, Eliezer 78
Berquist, Jon 115
Berrigan, Daniel 102
Bhabha, Homi 109, 110
Bhartiya, V. 139
Blau, Peter 213
Blenkinsopp, Joseph 128, 133
Block, Daniel 128
Boers, Arthur Paul 15

Bondurant, Joan 207
Borkan, J. 138
Bownes, I. 139
Brailey, K. 138
Brenneman, James E. 14
Bright, John 27, 41, 93, 113
Bromiley, Geoffrey W. 118
Broome, E. C. 126
Broshi, Magen 118
Brownlee, William H. 128
Brueggemann, Walter 50, 69,
    94, 178
Brunner, Emil 193
Buber, Martin 96
Bulhan, Hussein 141, 142
Burkholder, J. R. 60
Burns, J. Patout 194
Callahan, Daniel 101
Calvin, John 21
Camus, Albert 198
Carlier, I. 138
Carter, Charles 118
Childs, Brevard 127
Classen, C. 140
Clements, Ronald E. 71, 128
Coggins, Richard 128
Collins, John J. 176, 178, 182
Conybeare, F. C. 130
Coote, Robert C. 67, 68, 69, 73
Crenshaw, James L. 146, 152

Cross, Frank Moore 175
Crüsemann, Frank 22
Cullmann, Oscar 98
Dallmeyer, Dorinda 203
Dandamaev, Muhammad A. . 120
Davidson, J. 139
Davies, Peter R. 114, 115
Davis, Ellen Francis 128
Dawn, Marva J. 175
Dever, W. G. 115
DeWaard, Jan 72, 75
Dijkstra, Meindert 128
Dinkler, Erich 176
Dixon, P. 139
Dokecki, Paul R. 199
Donner, Herbert 113
Douglass, James W. 101, 194,
205, 208
Driver, John 206
Duguid, Iain M. 128, 132
Dunn, James D. G. 78
Duran, Bonnie 142
Duran, Eduardo 142
Eichrodt, Walther 109, 126
Eller, Vernard 31
Ellul, Jacques 31, 57, 203
Enz, Jacob 108
Errera, P. 138
Fanon, Frantz 141, 142
Farmer, Kathleen A. 146, 148
Finkelstein, J. J. 163
Foa, E. 139
Fohrer, Georg 127, 128
Foster, Raymond 114
Fox, Michael V. 146, 147, 149,
151, 153, 156, 160, 161
Frankfurt, Henri 17, 18, 19
Fredericks, Daniel C. 146, 148
Freedman, David Noel 58, 59,
117, 163

Freire, Paulo 197, 201, 211
French, Marilyn 200, 201, 202,
212, 213, 214
Fulco, William 120
Fullerton, C. 139
Gammie, John G. 178
Georgi, Dieter 176, 177, 179,
182, 186
Gersons, B. 138
Gibson, J. C. L. 164
Gilbert, M. 176
Gingerich, Ray 15
Gordis, Robert .. 149, 150, 157, 161
Gorst-Unsworth, Caroline 125
Gottwald, Norman K. 23, 67,
112, 113, 175
Grabbe, Lester 112
Grant, George 66
Greenberg, Moshe 127, 128,
129, 163
Grimsrud, Ted 14, 66, 79
Halperin, David 108, 126, 127,
129, 130, 131, 133, 134, 144
Hanson, Paul D. 175
Harris, Nigel 111
Hartsock, Nancy C. M. 200
Hasel, Gerhard F. 73
Hauerwas, Stanley ... 66, 205, 207,
208
Hayes, John H. 37, 113, 116
Heidel, Alexander 17, 18
Herion, Gary 163
Hershberger, Guy F. 192, 193
Heschel, Abraham J. 90, 101
Hiebert, Theodore 175
Hill, Joe 30
Hillerman, Tony 83, 85
Hobbes, Thomas 215
Holladay, William 87, 88, 91,
97, 100

Horst, Samuel 21
Huebner, Harry 66
Isaac, Jeffrey C. 198, 204
Jacobsen, Thorkild 17, 19
Jameson, Frederick 51, 56
Jastrow, Marcus 162
Jeremias, Joachim 179
Jobling, David 98
Johnson, Raymond E. 157, 159
Jordan, Clarence 89, 102, 104
Juergensmeyer, Mark 207
Kao, Tzu-Cheg 139
Kaufman, Gordon D. 195
Kaufmann, Yehezekel 58
Keller, Ludwig 29
Kierkegaard, Soren 32
King, Philip 117
Klein, Ralph 113, 114
Klostermann, A. 126
Knibb, Michael 128
Koopman, C. 140
Kovacs, Brian W. 97
Kraus, C. Norman 66
Kugel, James L. 166
Kuhrt, Amelie .. 116, 121, 124, 125
Lang, Bernhard 128
Langdon, Stephen 120
LaSor, William S. 118, 133
Lebacqz, Karen 64, 66
Lee, Dallas 89
Leeming, David Adams 19
Lehman, C. K. 192, 193
Leichty, Daniel 14, 31, 33
Leighton, Barry 213
Liddell, Henry George 187
Lind, Millard 11-16, 17, 19, 21,
    22, 28, 29, 33, 34, 37, 43, 45, 50,
    51, 56, 59, 60, 65, 66, 68, 78, 79,
    80, 82, 94, 108, 145, 174, 175,
    192, 193, 194, 198, 215

Lind, Miriam 108
Lind, Sarah 16
Loader, J. A. 149
Lohfink, Norbert 155
Lu, F. 141
Luckenbill, D. D. 124
Luckmann, Thomas   204, 212, 213
Lukoff, D. 141
Lust, Johan 128
May, Herbert G. 53
Mays, James Luther 68, 70, 72,
    74, 76, 80
McClendon, James 201
Miller, Douglas B. 15, 147, 153,
    167
Miller, J. Maxwell 37, 113, 116
Miller, Marlin 31
Miller, Patrick D. 175
Miranda, José Porfirio 81, 90
Modood, Tariq 110
Moltmann, Jürgen 29
Morris, A. 138
Murphy, Nancey 66
Murphy, Roland 152, 162
Murray, John B. 137, 139
Nation, Mark 66
Neely, Alan 90
Newbrough, J. R. 199
Nicholson, Ernest W. 96
Nickelsburg, George W. E. ... 177,
    179, 186
Niditch, Susan 128
Niebuhr, Reinhold 199
Noth, Martin 115, 119
Nozick, Robert 64, 66
O'Brien, Niall 204, 205
O'Gorman, E. 139
O'Gorman, Robert T. 199
Occhiogrosso, Julia 105
Oded, Bustenay 115, 116, 119

Ogden, Graham 149, 150, 161, 166
Ollenburger, Ben 37
Overholt, Thomas W. 86
Palmer, Parker 16
Patterson, Orlando 120
Paul, Shalom M. 70, 71, 72, 74, 75, 76
Perdue, Leo G. 97, 167, 176, 178, 186
Phillips, Anthony 128
Podechard, E. 161
Pritchard, James B. 19, 163
Rad, Gerhard von 93, 97, 175
Raitt, Thomas 113, 114
Ramsey, Paul 193
Rawls, John 33, 64, 66
Redekop, Calvin W. 60
Redford, Donald B. 123
Reese, James M. 176, 179
Rehling, G. 139
Reis, S. 138
Robinson, H. Wheeler 104
Ross, Rupert 83
Rousseau, Jean-Jacques 30
Royko, Mike 89
Rudman, Dominic 149, 150, 159, 161, 164
Ruether, Rosemary Radford .. 203
Rutschman, Richard 106
Saggs, H. W. F. 124
Sanders, James A. 61
Sayers, A. 139
Schaberg, Jane 179
Schoors, Antoon 158
Schottroff, Luise 190
Schroeder, David 66
Schuller, Robert 95
Schwartz, Regina 200
Scott, James 112

Scott, R. B. Y. 152
Scott, Robert 187
Seow, C. L. 146, 148, 152, 154, 155, 156, 158, 160, 161, 166
Shaffer, A. 158
Sharp, Gene 196, 200, 201
Shay, Jonathan 140
Shiwach, R. 139
Shvartzman, P. 138
Smalley, William 72, 75
Smith-Christopher, Daniel L.
.... 15, 111, 112
Sobrino, Jon 89, 92
Speiser, E. A. 163
Spiegal, D. 140
Stalker, D. M. G. 93
Stalker, Peter 109
Stassen, Glen H. 66
Steinbeck, John 208, 209
Stern, Ephraim 117
Stock, George 130
Stone, Michael E. 176
Stringfellow, William 88, 107
Suggs, M. Jack 179
Sutker, P. 138
Swartley, Willard M. 66
Tadmor, H. 175
Taubes, Jacab 176
Teske, Robin 202, 203
Thompson, Thomas L. 114, 115
Tolstoy, Leo 204
Toombs, Lawerence E. 175
Torrey, C. C. 112
Turner, R. 141
Uddo, M. 138
Ursano, R. 139
Van der Toorn, Karel 163
Van Goudoever, J. 128
Van Leeuwen, Raymond C. ... 172
Van Seters, John 115

Weaver, J. Denny 14, 206

Weinberg, S. S. 117

Weinfeld, Moshe 120, 121, 175

Weissbach 120

Wellhausen, Julius 112

Wellman, Barry 213

Werbner, Pnina 110

Whitelam, Keith 163

Whybray, R. N. 145, 149, 152, 153, 156, 160

Wilkie, J. M. 114, 122

Wilson, John P. 137, 138

Wilson, Robert P. 91

Windisch, Hans 189

Wink, Walter 44, 49, 190, 200, 201, 203, 206, 209, 213, 214

Winston, David 177

Wiseman, Donald 116

Wolff, Hans Walter 52, 53, 57, 60, 70, 95

Wolterstorff, Nicholas 81

Wright, Addison 148, 161, 169

Wright, George Ernest 175

Yoder Neufeld, Tom 15, 174, 179, 180, 186

Yoder, John Howard ... 22, 29, 32, 105, 106, 193, 194, 205

Yoder, Perry B. 66, 81, 194

Zehr, Howard 66, 77, 80, 81

Zimmerli, Walther 127, 128, 133

Subject Index

Abraham 45, 46, 47, 171, 193
Action 198, 202, 213
Ahab 52, 53, 54, 55, 69
Amos 67-77, 171, 215
Anabaptists 28, 30, 33
Anarchism 31
Anti-kingship tradition 22-29, 60
Atonement 205, 206
Baal 52, 54
Belshazzar 165
Bender, Harold 29
Biblical politics 13, 17, 21-28
Bureacratization 208
Calvin, John 21
Christian Peacemaker Teams
   (CPT) 34-36, 44-45, 46, 48
Christian political theology 31
Cleansing of the temple 44, 46,
   47, 92, 93
Community 158, 159, 165, 168,
   172, 170, 171
Conquest of Canaan 57
Contentment 156
Covenant 68, 69, 71, 72, 76, 78
Creation 77, 78-79, 175, 177,
   179-185, 188, 190
Critical biblical study methods
   .... 13, 50, 51, 56
Cross 206
Cyrus 80

David 153
Deutero-Isaiah 96, 97, 122, 165,
   201, 215
Disclosure 212
Divine warfare 177, 179, 180,
   185
Divine Warrior (warrior-God)
   .... 174-176, 180-182, 185, 187,
   189, 193-196, 206, 216
Domination 200-203, 205, 206,
   209, 210, 212-216
Egyptian politics 18-19, 20-21,
   178, 180, 182
Elijah 51, 52, 54, 55, 56, 57, 58,
   59, 60, 61, 63
Elisha 51, 54, 55, 56, 57, 58, 59,
   60, 61, 63
Enemies 174
Enoch 178
Environment 199, 210
Ethics 190, 197
Evil 79-80, 187, 188, 196, 214,
   215
Exile 37-43, 55, 92, 109,
   111-126, 215
Exodus 178, 180, 183, 188
Ezekiel 43-46, 80, 108-144, 194
False prophets 95, 101
False religion 89, 94
Falwell, Jerry 105

247

Fanon, Frantz 141, 142

Fundamentalism 24–25

Futile work 157, 158, 165, 167

Gaia Hypothesis 202

Gandhi 30, 204, 207

Globalization 111

Gomer 52, 53

Haiti 34–36, 46–48

Hananiah 39–40, 41, 42, 93, 94

Healings 43

Hebel ("vapor", "vanity") 147, 148, 150, 153, 157, 159, 165

Hermeneutics 49–51, 56, 59, 61, 62

Hosea 51–63, 73, 97

Hussein, Saddam 53

Ideology 202

Idolatry 180

Image of God 79

Imitation of God 188, 189, 191

Individualism 146, 171

Injustice 67–73, 76, 81, 91, 167, 169, 203, 213

Institutions 195, 196, 197, 200, 204, 213, 214, 215

Isaac 193

Isaiah 42, 44, 46, 73, 87, 97, 133, 145, 179, 183, 186

Jehoiachin 37

Jehu ... 52, 53 54, 55, 57, 58, 59, 60, 62, 63

Jeremiah 37–42, 44, 45, 46, 47, 86–106, 116, 215

Jeroboam II 55, 67

Jesus 43–44,46, 47, 48, 79, 86–107, 192, 193, 194, 196 201, 204, 206, 207, 212, 214

Jezebel 52, 54

Jezreel 52, 53, 55

Job 80, 176

Joseph 123, 162, 164

Josiah 88

Jubilee 12

Judgment 71, 72

Justice 33, 64–85, 90–91, 163, 165, 183, 193, 196, 198, 199, 202, 204, 207, 210

King, Martin Luther, Jr. ... 30, 204

Kingdom (reign) of God ... 36, 39, 44, 46, 47, 95, 196, 211, 212, 215

Lamentations 112, 119, 143

Land 68

Latino Youth 106

Law 12, 70

Liberation 39, 106

Lies 86

Love ... 174, 175, 177, 183, 187–191

Love and justice 82–84

Love of enemies 189–191

Machiavelli 172

Marcos, Fernando 204

Marxist thought 29, 30, 31

Materialism 146

Matthew 86, 189

Mennonites 13, 195, 197, 216

Mercy 184, 185, 188

Mesopotamian politics 19–21

Mission 45

Moses 22, 59

Naboth 52, 54, 69

Navajo justice 83–85

Nebuchadnezzar 37, 38, 39, 41, 47, 92, 114, 116, 120, 121, 132, 144, 165

Negotiating texts 49–51, 55, 59, 61, 62

Nehemiah 133

Noah 80

Nonviolence, pacifism 29, 31, 33, 36, 45, 62, 66, 79, 93, 192,

193, 194, 195, 197, 198, 201, 204, 205, 211, 216
Northern Kingdom (Israel) 67, 99
Nuclear threat 95
Old Testament prophets ... 12–13, 21, 23, 28–29, 34, 43, 44, 49, 51, 60, 171, 192, 207
Old Testament theology 49–50, 62
Omri 52
Oppressed people 174
Oppression 146, 151, 152, 153, 159, 161, 163, 165, 168, 169, 171, 173, 181, 183, 203, 205, 213, 214
Oppressors 188, 190
Patriarchy 201
Paul 170
Personal power 207
Postexilic Judaism 115
Posttraumatic stress disorder 135–144
Power 146, 169, 170, 174, 177, 181, 184, 185, 187–189, 194, 195–216
Praxis 201, 209, 211, 212, 216
Qohelet 145–173, 183
Rahab 80
Reagan, Ronald 94, 104
Reconciliation 83
Redemption 73, 77, 79
Refugees 109–110, 111
Repentance 185
Resurrection 102–107
Retributive justice 124
Romero, Oscar 54
Rousseau, Jean-Jacques 30
Ruth 80
Salvation 173

Samuel 27
Satyagraha 207
Saul 27
Sennacherib 88
Servant of the Lord ... 98, 101, 186, 190
Servant-discipleship 29
Shalom (peace) . 197, 198, 202, 210
Slavery 119–124
Solomon (pseudo) .. 177, 178, 180, 182, 183, 184, 186, 189, 191
Solomon 69, 121, 145, 169
Southern Kingdom (Judah) 37, 42, 87, 95, 118
Sovereignty of God 149
Spirituality 33, 91
State-sponsored terrorism 124–126
Suffering 96–101, 171, 183, 196, 205, 206
Suffering servant 173
Sword 133–134
Symbolic actions 46
Temple 87, 89, 94
Tolstoy, Leo 204
Truth 30
Unity of the Bible 12, 25–26
Violence 50, 55, 57, 60, 62, 193, 194, 195, 196, 198, 202, 203, 204, 205, 206, 207, 208, 211, 212, 213, 214
Warfare 132–134
Wellhausen, Julius 112
Wisdom (Sophia) 163, 167, 168, 170, 172, 178, 182, 183, 186, 188
Wisdom of Solomon 174–191
Yahweh's concern for the vulnerable 81–82
Yahweh's word 60

The Editors

Ted Grimsrud teaches theology and peace studies at Eastern Mennonite University, Harrisonburg, Virginia. Prior to joining the EMU faculty, he served for ten years as a Mennonite pastor in Oregon, Arizona, and South Dakota.

Grimsrud holds an M.A. in Peace Studies from Associated Mennonite Biblical Seminary and a Ph.D. in Christian Ethics from the Graduate Theological Union. He is author of *Triumph of the Lamb: A Self-Study Guide to the Book of Revelation* (Herald Press, 1987).

He lives in Harrisonburg with his wife, Kathleen Temple, and teenage son Johan Grimsrud. He is a member of Shalom Mennonite Church.

Loren L. Johns is associate professor of religion at Bluffton College, Bluffton, Ohio, where he teaches biblical studies. Before joining the faculty at Bluffton, he served for eight years as a pastor at Blough Mennonite Church in Hollsopple, Pennsylvania, and for several years as an overseer in the Allegheny Mennonite Conference. He also served four years as theology book editor at Herald Press, Scottdale, Pennsylvania.

Johns holds an M.Div. from Associated Mennonite Biblical Seminary and a Ph.D. in Biblical Studies from Princeton Theological Seminary. He is coeditor of *Hillel and Jesus: Comparisons of Two Major Religious Leaders,* and author of several scholarly articles.

He lives in Bluffton with his wife, Rachel Johns. They have two daughters, Kendra and Jessica, and are members at First Mennonite Church, Bluffton, Ohio.